CONNECTI
THE DATA

Data Integration Techniques
for Building an
Operational Data Store (ODS)

first edition

ANGELO R BOBAK

Published by:
Technics Publications, LLC
966 Woodmere Drive
Westfield, NJ 07090 U.S.A.
www.technicspub.com
908-543-3050

Edited by Carol Lehn
Cover design by Mark Brye

This book is printed on acid-free paper.

ISBN, print ed. 978-1-9355042-2-1

First Printing 2012
Library of Congress Control Number: 2012937800

Contents

CHAPTER 1
Introduction and Roadmap

In today's modern business environment, corporate entities are constantly merging or splitting, internal divisions are sold to different companies, and new business lines are created in order to meet the challenges of difficult economic times. Business data integration is a complex problem that must be solved when organizations change or enhance their internal structures. New IT departments must be merged with old ones, and transactional, operational, and master data must be integrated in order to be managed efficiently, if the business is expected to grow and be profitable.

The goal of this book is to present a simple yet thorough resource that describes the challenges of business data integration and the solutions to these challenges. It will show you how the application of a technique called "schema integration" addresses these challenges.

Schema integration is both a theory and process that was pioneered by experts in the field of data management. We will apply the techniques of two of these pioneers, M. Tamer Ozsu and Patrick Valduriez in the design of an Operational Data Store (ODS) for a small business.

M. Tamer Ozsu and Patrick Valduriez also discussed distributed database architectures and related topics such as distributed transaction processing and federated database architectures in their books and papers.

For our discussions, we will utilize four small example databases: a SQL Server® 2008 database, a series of Microsoft® Excel® spreadsheets, a Microsoft Access® 2007 database and a MySQL® database all running on the popular Windows operating systems. These tools are for example purposes; Windows 7® would also work just as well as any operating system, and other database platforms like Access 2011, Oracle®, and Sybase® could also be used as the database software. The techniques described are also applicable to databases running on UNIX® or LINUX® platforms.

The examples will be simple, but have enough complexity to identify and resolve the key issues and challenges that surface when integrating data from multiple source operational databases.

This book is both theoretical (mildly) and practical. It is mildly theoretical in that it instructs and guides the reader through design steps based on the theory. It is practical in that it also presents a case study of a classic business data integration problem, the creation of an Operational Data Store (ODS).

One last item, the MySQL schema will be presented but the reader is assigned the task of performing the schema integration into the final ODS model as an exercise. This will be a good way for you to test out the theory and techniques that you learned in the discussions.

What exactly is an ODS?

An Operational Data Store (ODS) is a key component in data integration and data warehouse (DW) architectures. Its role is two-fold: to integrate data from operational systems so as to provide a single view of the enterprise data for operational reports; and for delivery to data warehouse platforms, enabling production of advanced Business Intelligence (BI) solutions.

As mentioned earlier, the design of the data model for an ODS is based on a schema integration technique pioneered by experts and academics in the field. This technique derives a unified data model based on the integration of all source database schemas that will feed the ODS. There are several flavors of schema integration. The technique that we will use is called binary schema integration which we will discuss in Chapter 3.

We will discuss not only how to use schema integration, but also show how solid data modeling techniques — logical modeling, physical database reverse engineering, and physical database modeling are used to create the ODS.

A Guided Tour of the Book

The book is composed of three sections:

- Foundational Concepts
- Preparation and Design
- Physical Implementation.

Below is a description of each section. It is suggested that you read each chapter in sequence if you are new to the concept of data integration and ODS architecture. For the more experienced reader, you may skip chapters that contain topics you are familiar with.

SECTION I – FOUNDATION CONCEPTS

Here you will get the necessary foundational concepts and learn about the theory of schema integration pioneered by Ozsu, Valduriez, and others. Chapters included are:

- **Chapter 1 – Introduction and Roadmap**. This chapter is an introduction for the reader. It highlights the contents of each chapter, introduces technical modeling terms, and presents a high level architecture for our case study. If you haven't guessed it, you are reading this chapter now!
- **Chapter 2 – What is an Operational Data Store?** This chapter provides some basic foundational concepts of the ODS: what it is, how it is used, and its role in a data warehouse architecture and data integration project. It also identifies some of the challenges faced when designing this data integration model.
- **Chapter 3 – What is Schema Integration?** This chapter introduces the process of schema integration. It identifies the three types of data conflicts that have to be resolved to integrate physical database schema, specifically naming, data type, and data structure conflicts. Additionally, it shows how to generate specifications for the ETL (Extraction, Transformation, and Load) processes that are used in the data conflicts resolution steps.
- **Chapter 4 – The Role of the ODS within DW Architectures.** The purpose of this chapter is to delve into greater detail on the role of the ODS within a data warehouse and operational reporting architecture. It describes the component layers of the ODS, together with the denormalized tables and view architecture required to support operational reporting and also data preparation for delivery to downstream data warehouses and data marts.

SECTION II – PREPARATION AND DESIGN

In this section, we will introduce our case study, a small, fictitious international coffee product distribution company that has acquired some small, independent coffee roasters and coffee equipment vendors. Each of the independent roasters uses a variety of data storage tools, including Microsoft Excel spreadsheets, Access databases, MySQL database, and SQL Server databases.

This fictitious company has four locations: London England, Paris France, Munich Germany, and Torino Italy. The database technologies used for each location are:

London – Microsoft Excel Spreadsheets
Paris – MySQL database
Munich – Microsoft SQL Server 2008
Torino – Microsoft Access.

We will reverse engineer each of the data sources so as to create a set of data dictionary reports that will provide us with the meta data we need to apply the schema integration process. The section concludes with the actual design of the integrated ODS model.

Chapters included are:

- **Chapter 5 – Reverse Engineering the four Source Schema**. This chapter introduces the case study that is the focus of the book. It describes a small, fictitious European international coffee roasting company that is about to create an ODS in order to integrate its various databases and data sources that support the order, sales, and product inventory business processes. As stated earlier, four data sources in the form of Excel spreadsheets, a Microsoft Access database, a MySQL database and a Microsoft SQL Server database will be used as the source systems. This chapter will develop the functional requirements and technical specifications for the ODS solution. We will discuss how to reverse engineer each of these different data repository platforms so we can apply schema integration techniques to create our ODS. We will also describe how to prepare the logical and physical data models for the operational data sources.
- **Chapter 6 – Designing the Interim Schema.** Having generated the necessary physical models and data dictionaries in Chapter 6, we now apply schema integration techniques to merge the models of the MS Access database and the model for the Excel spreadsheet into one model. This will be our first interim model, which will be merged with the SQL Server physical model. We leave the integration of the MySQL database with the ODS to the reader as an exercise.
- **Chapter 7 – Preparing the ETL Specifications**. In this chapter we create the ETL specifications required to resolve the data conflicts identified in Chapter 6. The specifications will be a set of spreadsheets that describe the ETL logic and a set of data flow, process hierarchy and process dependency diagrams that will be used to create the ETL processes required to stage, transform, enrich and load the data into the ODS.
- **Chapter 8 – Designing the Physical ODS Database Model.** In this chapter we will translate the final interim schema into a physical database model and also present the final DDL statements used to create the ODS. We will only address the tables included in the second integrated schema. The design of the third level of the ODS is left to the reader as an exercise.

SECTION III – PHYSICAL IMPLEMENTATION

In this section of the book, we will deal with the physical aspects of our case study. We will present some scripts to populate each of the source databases and spreadsheets. Recall that one of the outputs of the schema integration process that was discussed is a set of reports that define the logic for processes that resolve data conflicts that occur when merging or integrating data. We will use these reports to create ETL specifications for processes that load, transform, and merge data.

Chapters included are:

- **Chapter 9 – Designing Our ETL processes with SSIS**. In this chapter we develop the necessary diagrams and specifications for our ETL processes using Microsoft's SQL Server ETL tool called SSIS (SQL Server Integration Services). The example will be a bit more complex as I include the steps to load the MySQL integrated tables into the third integrated schema. The intent of the chapter is to show you how a complex solution would look like if implemented with this tool.
- **Chapter 10 – Data Quality Profiling**. In this chapter we utilized SSIS once again to show the reader how data profiling, data cleansing and data quality statistics are an important part of the ODS. We will show you how to collect statistics for data profiling such as counting column NULL values, maximum/minimum values, patterns and other statistics. We will show you how to collect these statistics into relational tables so that you can create simple web reports for data stewards to use.

Introducing our Case Study Architecture

Let's conclude our overview by presenting a high level architecture depicting the flow of data from our legacy operational data sources into the ODS. This is shown in Figure 1.1.

Notice that the data is pulled from the source systems with an instance of an ETL Server running two sets of processes. The ETL tool stages the data and then merges it into the three integrated databases on the ODS. The data is then fed to a profiling ETL process so that various data quality statistics reports can be generated. These are presented to a web server, so that data stewards can view them on a report server.

The diagram also shows how another ETL process is used to extract data and feed it to a small data mart composed of one fact table and several dimensions so that we can generate an order cube with any of the popular OLAP (Online Analytical Processing) tools available on the market. These tools are used to create multi-dimensional structures called cubes which are similar to spreadsheet pivot tables.

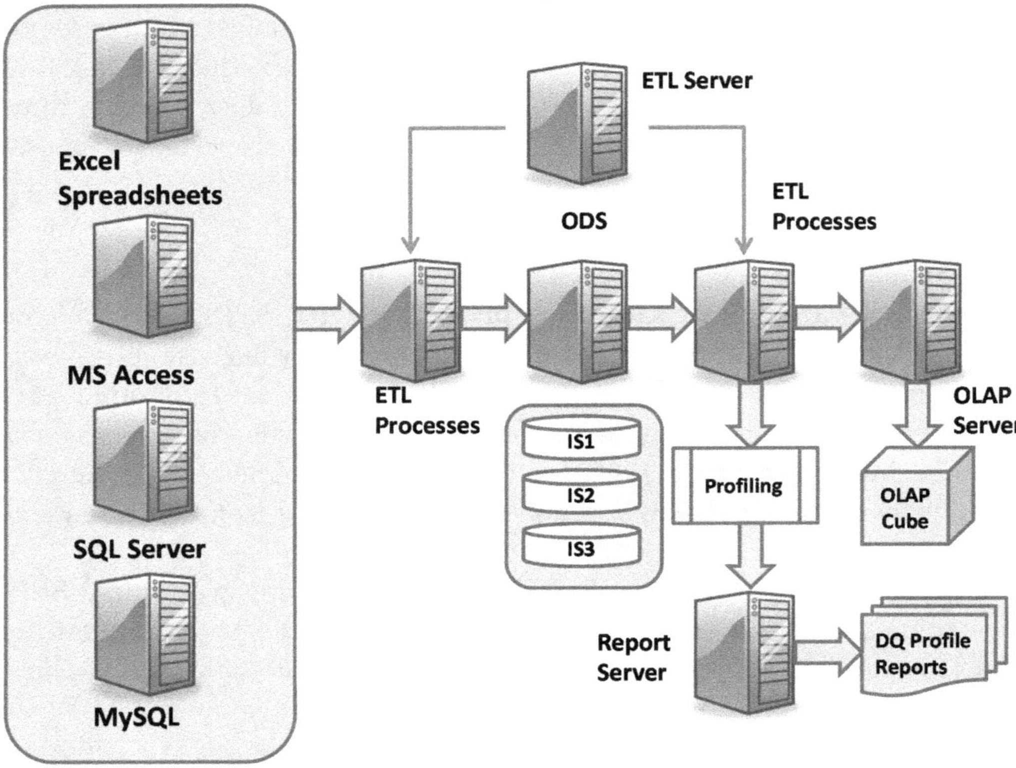

Figure 1.1 - The Café Magnifico Data Architecture

This architecture can be implemented with various vendor solutions such as Microsoft's SQL Server, Oracle or DB2®. ETL tools include Microsoft SQL Server SSIS® (SQL Server Integration Services), Informatica®, Data Flux® and a host of other vendors and tools.

Summary

So what did we cover in this chapter? We discussed the goal of the book and the approach we will take to design and build an ODS. We also discussed the definition of an ODS and some basic concepts that we will need as we progress through the design and implementation of the ODS.

Lastly, we identified the target architecture for the ODS that we will design.

After reading this book, you will have the knowledge to design and build a small ODS.

So are you ready? We are about to embark on an exciting journey! Let's grab a cup of coffee (or espresso) and get started.

In this chapter, we will discuss some basic foundational concepts of the ODS - what it is, how it is used, and its role in a data warehouse architecture. Specifically, we will address the various layers of the architecture:

- The Interface Layer
- The Data Staging Layer
- The Data Profiling Layer
- The Data Cleansing Layer
- The Data Integration Layer
- The Export Layer.

We will delve into not only the architecture, but also into some simple examples of the various main processing components that stage, profile, cleanse, and deliver the data.

In subsequent chapters, we will expand on the logic, code, and models to build a small ODS and data warehouse architecture that address all of the key challenges that arise when attempting to integrate data from heterogeneous operational platforms. Figure 2.1 depicts these layers and the flow of the data between the layers.

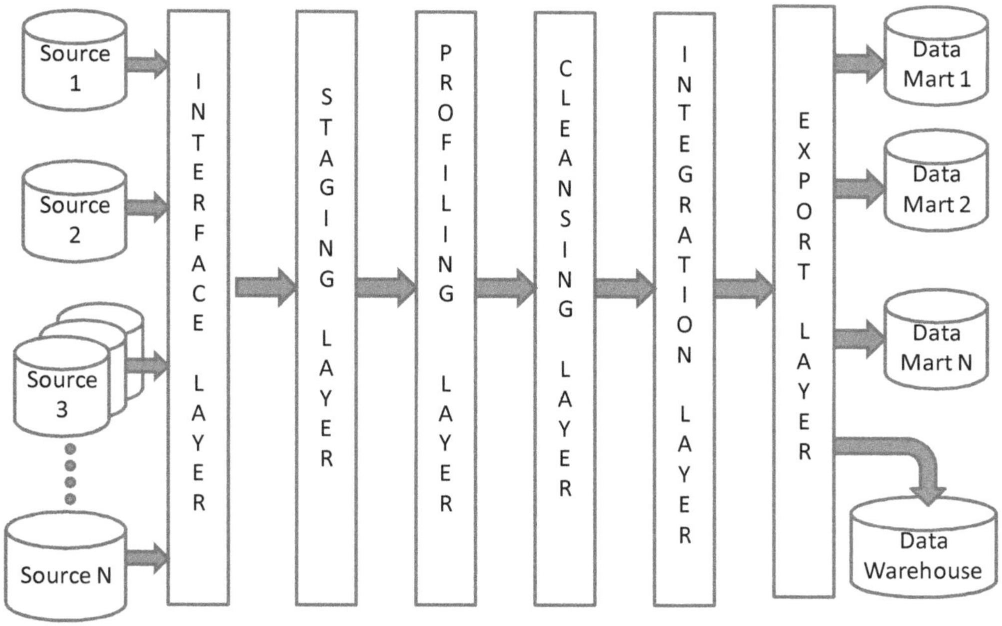

Figure 2.1 - A Layered ODS Architecture

We will also discuss some of the challenges faced when designing this model and how schema integration is used to solve these challenges.

The High Level Operational Data Store Architecture

Figure 2.2 shows a typical high level data warehouse architecture with the ODS as the target. It is a layered architecture, each layer performing a specific function to deliver data to its ultimate reporting and OLAP consumers.

(A word about notation, the cylinders in this diagram and subsequent diagrams represent data stores such as databases, spreadsheets and flat files. Rectangles represent major processes or systems such as ETL applications. Lastly, arrows represent the flow of data.)

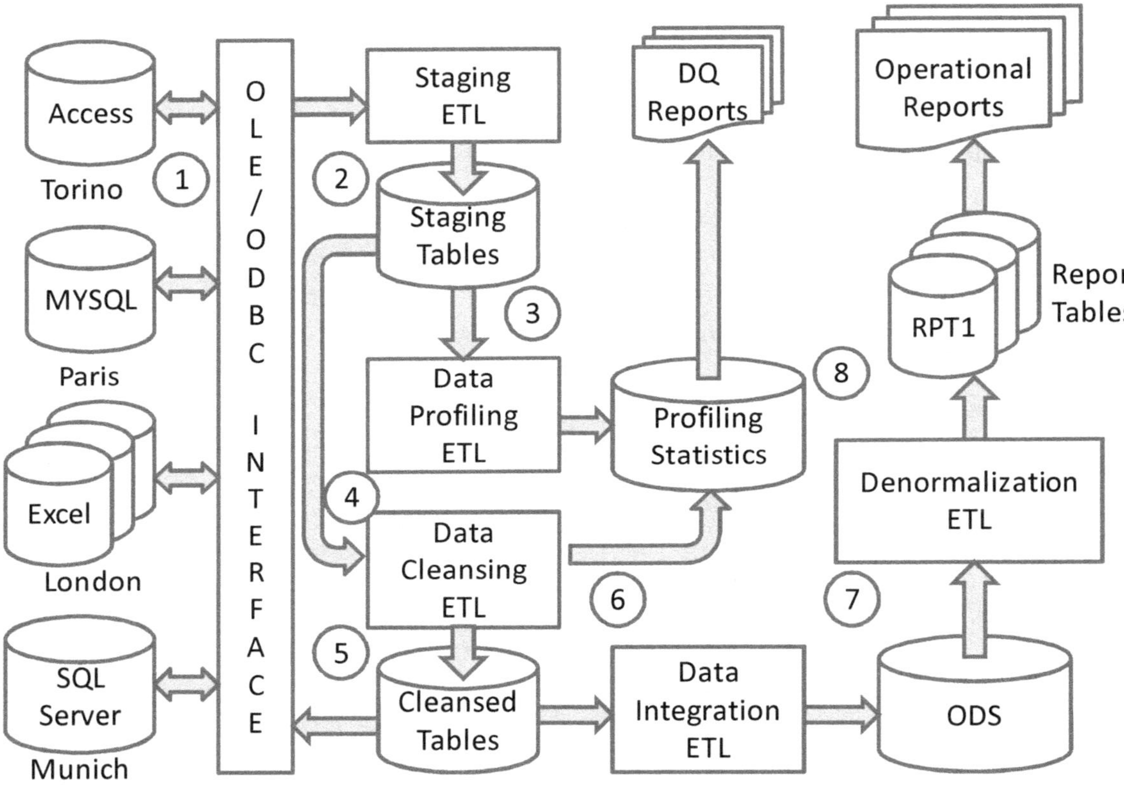

Figure 2.2 - ODS and Data Warehouse High Level Architecture

Let's examine each critical step in the architecture, after which we will discuss them in more detail. We will use this blueprint as the basic ODS architecture we will build for the Café Magnifico ODS and DW platform discussed in this book.

Beginning with Step 1, we see the source systems that will feed data into our ODS architecture. These sources can be relational databases, spreadsheets, flat files, web services, Microsoft SharePoint® Web sites, XML documents, or any other type of known repository for transactional data. In our case, we will be using a MS Access database, a MYSQL database, MS Excel spreadsheets (with several tabs), and a SQL Server 2008 database as our source systems.

Standard industry interfaces based on popular data connectivity protocols for exchanging data between heterogeneous databases and data sources include:

- OLEDB (Object Linking and Embedding Database)
- ODBC (Object Data Base Connectivity)
- FTP (File Transfer Protocol)

These and other protocols can be used, in addition to real time replication data delivery interfaces. Of particular interest are the real time data replication interfaces that allow delivery of real time data from a source transactional database to a target database. ODS architects are interested in transactional replication because it allows any data warehouse to be kept up to date with accurate data for reporting and OLAP analysis in near or real time.

Referring back to our diagram, we see a component in Step 2 called Staging ETL. This scheduled process controls the extraction of transactional data from source systems and loads it into one or more staging tables. These tables are highly denormalized, with their layout dependent on their source(s). The mapping could be one-to-one or one-to-many. That is, the staging table schema could be identical to the source schema, or it could be the product of joining two or more tables. It could also mimic the layout of a tab in an Excel spreadsheet or the layout of a flat file. (This is one example we will be examining.)

As the data is loaded into the staging tables, control information such as load timestamps or checksums of the data values, may be added. Checksums are values computed from an algorithm that looks at the data content of each column or field and computes a unique value. These values can then be used to determine if new data is being loaded. If the checksum computed on yesterday's row is the same as today's new row, then the data is identical and there is no need to reload it into the ODS.

Step 3 is the data profiling ETL process. Data profiling is a term used to measure the quality of the data. For example, the data stewards who are responsible for maintaining the data derive rules that measure the ranges, domains, uniqueness, and other data quality measures such as checking for NULL values.

A sophisticated data profiling step would identify duplicate customer names or addresses. For example, one row might have IBM as the name of the customer. Another row might have I.B.M. or International Business Machines. These may be the same customer, but we also need to look at their addresses to determine if they are at the same or different locations. Different locations suggest they may be different customers, even though they have the same or similar name. As data is profiled, statistics are collected and reported in web-based reports and scorecards on a web site, so that the data stewards can monitor the quality of the data. (We will discuss this layer later in the chapter.)

Step 4 delivers the profiled data to the data cleansing ETL process. This process applies rules to correct the data that was identified as “dirty”. The rules are derived by the data stewards and translated into programming code and data cleansing package tasks by the ODS developers. Using the example above, if we find multiple instances of the same customer, each with a slightly different spelling or name, we can apply algorithms that perform fuzzy matching and translate the different variations of the names into one common name that will be stored in our ODS.

Step 5 in the diagram shows the cleansed data loaded into a set of tables that are now ready for the integration steps that will combine common data from multiple sources into one set of tables in the ODS. Optionally, Step 5 can also deliver the cleansed data back to the source so that we do not keep on profiling and cleaning the same data over and over.

Step 6 delivers the cleansed data to the data integration ETL process. This is the most important step in our processing of the source data, although the data profiling and data cleansing steps tie for a close second. It is in this step that the three types of data conflicts between common data are resolved (naming, data type, and structural conflicts).

As a reminder, in Chapter 3, we will discuss the steps involved in resolving these data conflicts. Subsequent chapters will apply the specifications that come out of the data integration steps to the development of ETL processes that combine and load the data into the ODS.

Step 7 is where we denormalize our ODS schema so it can support the generation of operational reports and the loading of data for export to data marts and data warehouses. This step includes preprocessing the data so that aggregations and other types of processing are executed during off hours, to avoid affecting the user experience during normal operational hours.

Lastly, Step 8 depicts the set of tables that support operational reports. These reports are considered critical to the operation of the business. They are used to monitor the daily activities of the business and do not contain historical data that is older than a few days, weeks, or months. There are always exceptions, of course. Typically the ODS environment will only store data that is no older than a few months as we will store historical data in our data warehouses and data marts.

In the next section, we will take a more detailed look at the staging layer. This is where all the data that will be integrated into the ODS is staged. The completed ODS will be the solution to our business data integration challenge.

The ODS Data Staging Layer

Figure 2.3 shows a more detailed view of the interface and staging layers. The key components of the interface layer are the various drivers and protocols that enable heterogeneous data sources to exchange data. The key components of the staging layer are the tables that will store the data retrieved from the operational systems. Additionally, the various processes, libraries, and protocols that enable data transfer between the operational systems and the ODS live here!

Our diagram shows four sources, a Microsoft Access database, a MySQL database, a series of Microsoft Excel spreadsheet files, and finally a SQL Server 2008 database. This does not mean we could not have Oracle, Ingress, or DB2 databases, as well (or flat files or XML files,...).

Our focus of interest begins at Step 1. Here we see four interfaces that enable data transfer from the data sources for our ODS. Note that the interfaces in the figure correspond to the types of sources we are using.

We will be using Microsoft SQL Server, which provides a series of ODBC and OLE/DB modules that are callable from SQL Server Transact SQL code via interfaces called linked servers, shown as 2 in the figure. These interfaces allow us to view external databases, regardless of whether they are relational or not, as sources for SQL DDL commands.

Other database platforms such as Oracle or DB2 utilize similar ODBC modules to load external data.

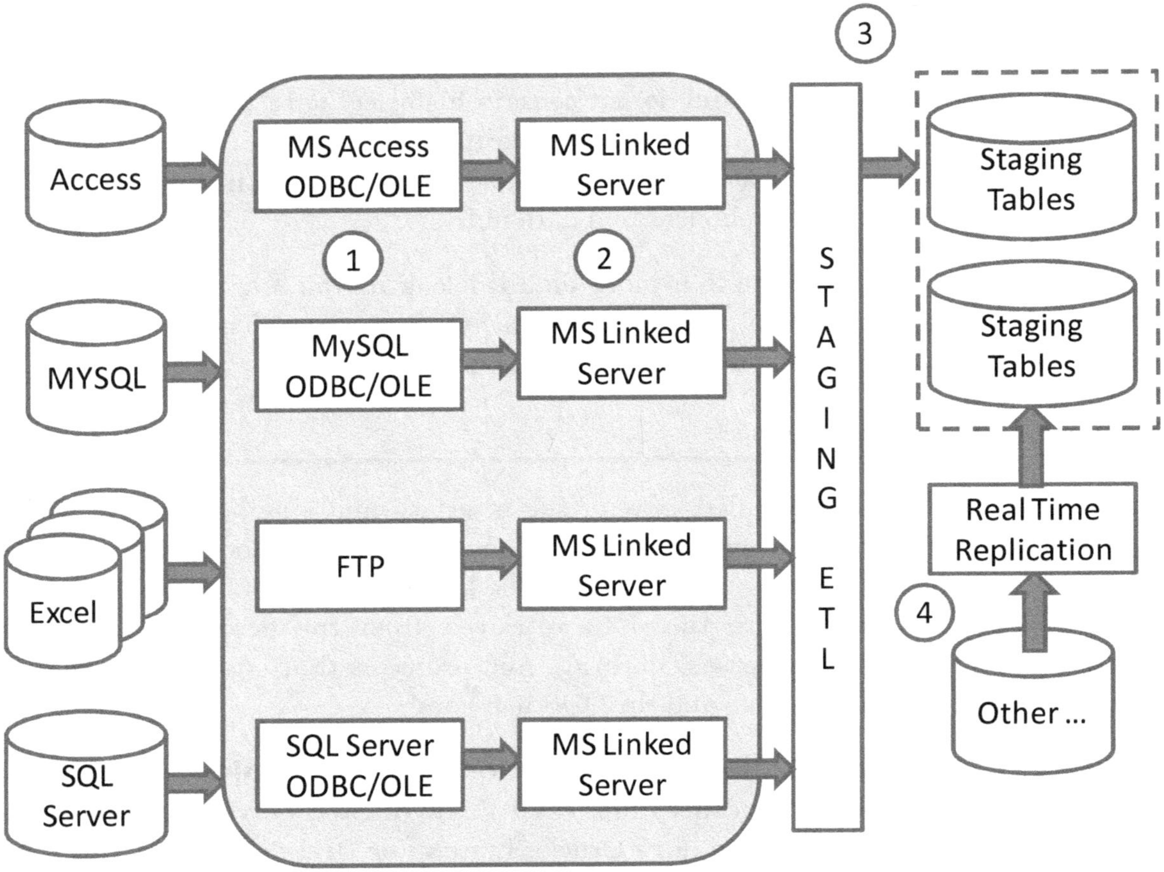

Figure 2.3 - The ODS Integration and Staging Layer

ODS Data Profiling

Data profiling consist of a set of processes that apply rules to measure the quality of the staged data that was retrieved from our operational databases. Another term for this process is "Data Assessment". For example, we might want to count the distinct values in a specific column in each row to make sure that all of the distinct values are defined in the domain definition of the data.

What do we mean by this? For example, if a column contains one of the legal state codes of the United States, we would expect 50 distinct values. If we find 52, then we know there are some illegal values.

Figure 2.4 depicts the architecture of the data profiling process flow. The numbers identify the key steps in the data profiling process.

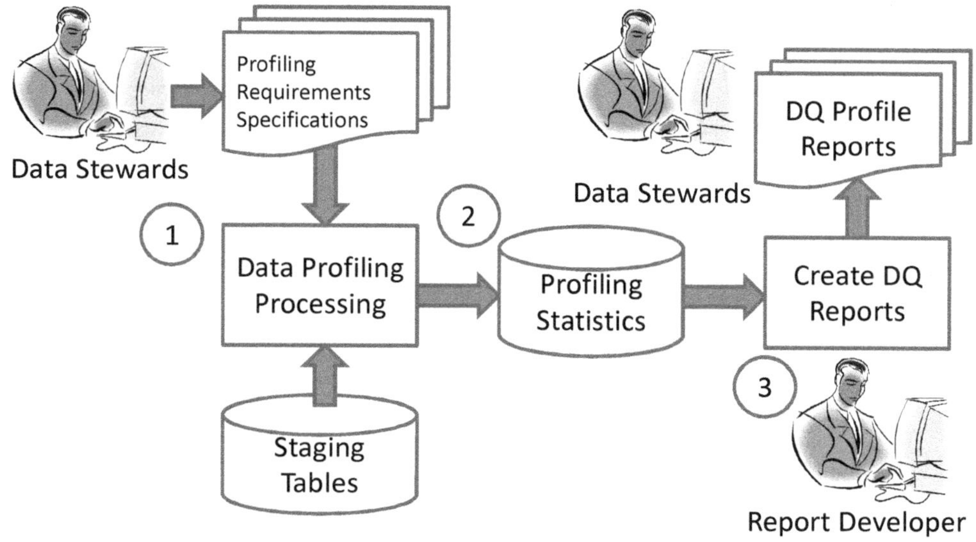

Figure 2.4 - ODS Data Profiling Layer

Beginning with Step 1, the staging tables are loaded with data from the source systems (we covered this in the interface and staging layers).

The data is ready to be profiled, so the following steps are executed:

- **Step 2** – We select logic, such as checking for NULL values or duplicates, and generate output files that contain the statistics for each of the table columns we choose to profile. These output files can be loaded into relational tables so we can keep historical profiling data.
- **Step 3** – Once the tables are loaded, a report developer creates the web site and necessary web reports that contain the profiling statistics stored in the relational tables.

In our example, the ETL processes require the addition of a couple of steps to get the results of the data profiling statistics generated into the profiling statistics table. Figure 2.5 shows the additional steps.

In Step 1, the data that is going to be profiled is extracted and fed to the profiling process.

In Step 2, output files containing profiling statistics are generated. An ETL developer processes these files so that they are loaded into relational tables.

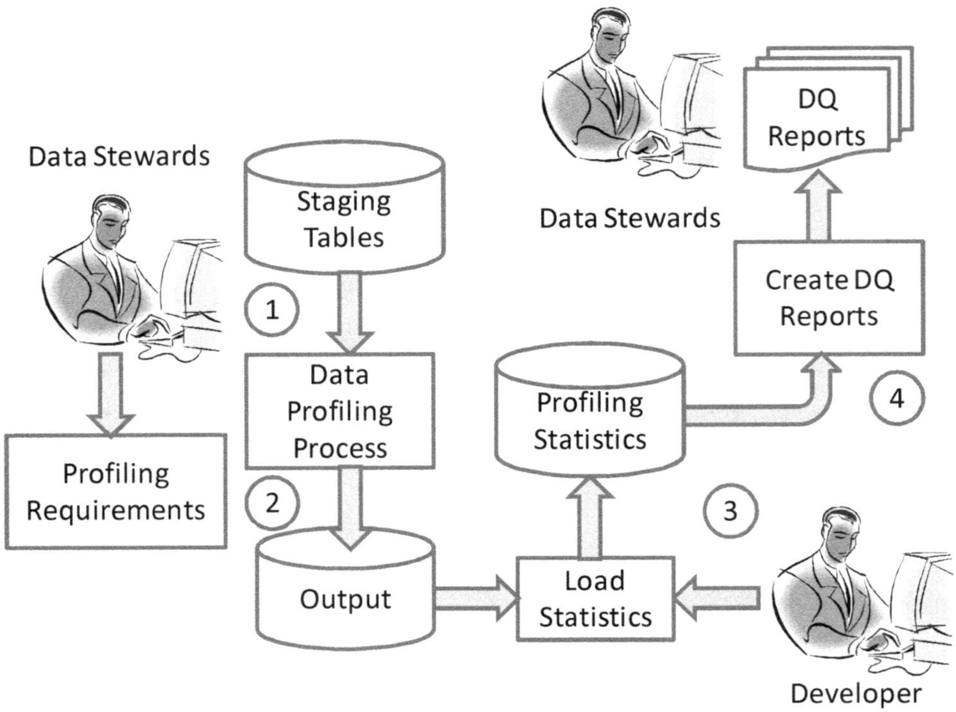

Figure 2.5 - ODS Data Profiling Layer using SSIS

ODS Data Cleansing

Whereas the data profiling layer tested the data and gave it a score, data cleansing corrects data quality issues where the profiling scores fall below acceptable ranges. Figure 2.6 shows our Data Cleansing layer architecture.

Recall from our discussion of the profiling layer how the data stewards are responsible for defining profiling rules for the data. They are also responsible for defining the data cleansing rules that correspond to the data processing rules. Let's look at a simple example using a state code profiling scenario.

Assume our profiling test on an address table determined that there are 52 unique state codes, rather than 50. Upon evaluation, we discovered that some users entered "??" and "XX" because they did not know the state codes.

Luckily, another profiling test determined that all the postal codes in the address table were legal. A simple data cleansing process to fix the problem would be:

- **Step 1** – For all illegal state codes, pull the zip (postal code) code from the row.
- **Step 2** – Check that the zip code is valid (assuming a postal code reference table is available).

- **Step 3** – If the zip code is valid, look up the correct state code in the table that maps zip codes to states (assuming there is one). There are many vendors on the internet that sell zip code databases for around $100. Typical databases are available in MS Access, Excel, and other formats. (Always check licensing requirements when implementing vendor data in a production environment with multiple users!)
- **Step 4** – If you found the missing state code, update the erroneous rows with the correct code.
- **Step 5** – If no valid zip code was found, then we must rely on the rest of the data, such as the city name, perhaps a telephone number, and also a street address, to determine the correct state code.

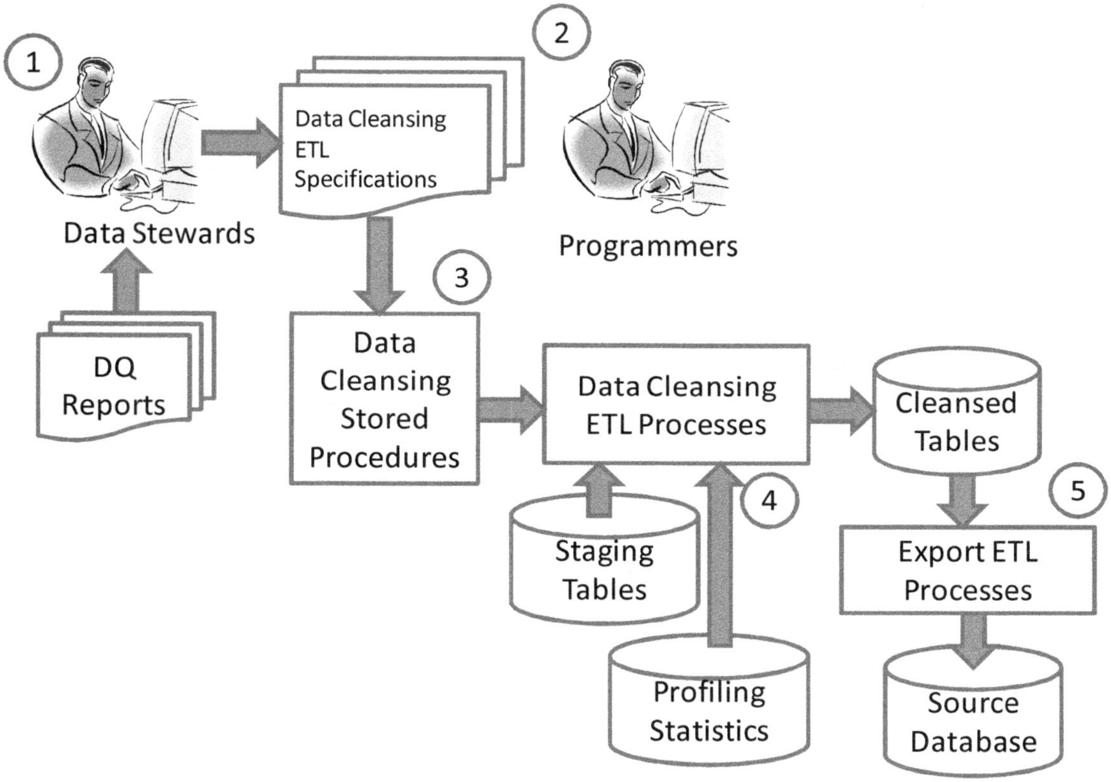

Figure 2.6 - The ODS Data Cleansing Layer

If all else fails, capture the information in some sort of log table and report so that the data steward is alerted to the data quality issues and can resolve the issue manually.

The above specification for data cleansing is prepared by our data steward and handed off to the programmer who develops the code for implementing the rule.

Stored profile statistics can also play a key role, because they can be used to automate the execution of data cleansing tasks. For example, if the statistics fall below or exceed a certain threshold, then the task is executed.

ODS Data Integration

Figure 2.7 depicts the architecture for the data integration layer of the ODS. This is where the source data from our operational systems are integrated into a common model after profiling and cleansing. Chapter 3 will be dedicated to explaining the schema integration process, which is the logic used to combine data, identify and resolve data conflicts, and derive not only the common integrated data model, but also the various ETL processes for resolving data conflicts and merging data.

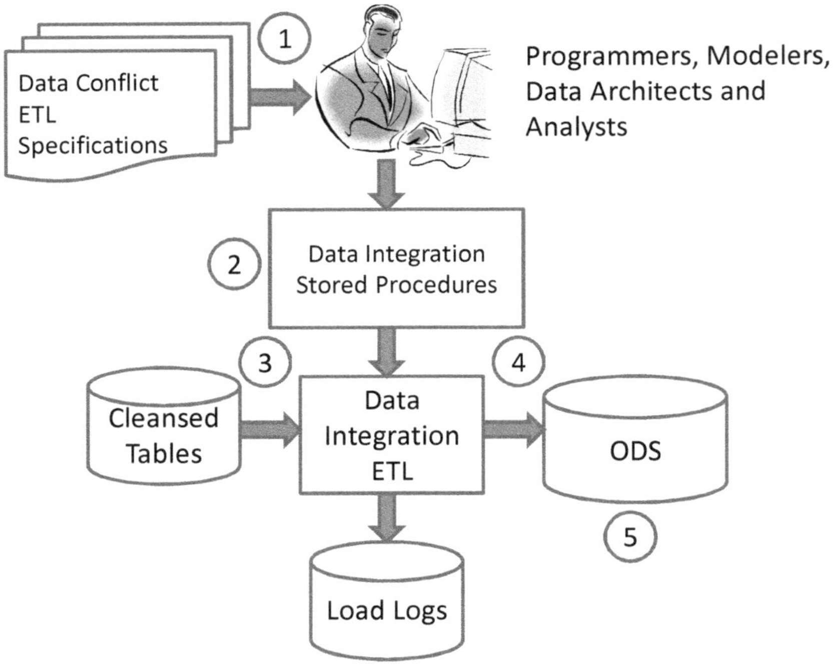

Figure 2.7 - The Data Integration Layer

As with other sections, let us start at the top. In Step 1 our data integration team (consisting of business analysts, data modelers and architects, and developers) create a set of ETL specifications for resolving data conflicts and merging common data into one set of common tables. Recall that we mentioned that data conflicts come in three flavors: naming, data type, and structural data conflicts.

There are two types of data naming conflicts: synonyms and antonyms. Synonyms are when two data objects are named the same, but have semantically different meanings. Antonyms are the opposite - data objects are named differently, but have the same semantic meaning. For example, in one database, the concept of identifying a project is solved with the column name PROJECT_ID. In a second database, it is called PROJ_NO, for project number. Now just by looking at the names we cannot figure out if this is an identifier for the project itself or if this is a column used to implement a unique surrogate key in a table. Data naming standards play a key role in solving data naming conflicts.

Expanding on the same example, let's assume that both column names are representative of the project identifier, itself. In the first source system, PROJ_ID is implemented as a CHAR(12) data type, whereas in the second system, PROJ_NO is implemented as an INTEGER.

Since both databases can hold information related to the same project, we can now see two significant issues when attempting to integrate this data - different names and different data types are used for the same data object.

The third type of data conflict is a data structure conflict. For example, one source database implemented the data object as a table with a series of attributes, while the second database has the same data object implemented as a single column in a table.

For example, expanding on our project theme one more time, the first database contains a table called PROJECT with the following schema:

Source Database 1

Column Name	Data Type	Description	NULL?	Primary Key
PROJ_ID	CHAR(12)	This is the unique identifier for the project across the company.	No	Yes
PROJ_NAME	VARCHAR(64)	This is the name of the project.	Yes	
PROJ_MGR	VARCHAR(64)	This is the first and last name of the project manager.	Yes	
PROJ_START_DATE	DATETIME	This is the start date of the project.	Yes	
PROJ_END_DATE	DATETIME	This is the projected end date of the project.	Yes	
PROJ_BUDGET	MONEY	This is the allocated budget for the project.	Yes	

Table 2.1 - PROJECT Table

There's nothing out of the ordinary with this table schema, although one issue could be that only the primary key column is identified as NOT NULL. That is, a value must be entered only for the PROJECT_ID. All other columns are identified as NULL, meaning users updating this table could leave out values. This could pose a challenge when integrating data.

Let us look at the second schema from the second source database:

Source Database 2

Column Name	Data Type	Description	NULL?	Primary Key
DEPT_ID	INTEGER	This is the unique identifier for the department.	No	Yes
DEPT_MGR	VARCHAR(64)	This is the name of the department manager.	No	
PROJECT_NAME	VARCHAR(64)	This is the name of the project.	No	

Table 2.2 - DEPT_PROJECT Table

We see that this table is used to map departments to projects. The primary key is DEPT_ID and the only way of identifying a project is by the PROJECT_NAME column.

The good news is that all columns are identified as not null. Recall that both tables may store information for the same project. The bad news is that since in this table the project is identified by the column PROJECT_NAME, even a slight variation in the spelling of the name of the project from how it was spelled in the PROJ_NAME column of the first table will pose a problem.

Let's take a look at some data from both tables, starting with the PROJECT_TABLE:

PROJ_ID	PROJ_NAME	PROJ_MGR	PROJ_START_DATE	PROJ_END_DATE	PROJ_BUDGET
1	Finance Budget Database	Joe Smith	10/10/2010	5/1/2011	$50,000.00
2	Corporate Payroll Application	Mary Jones	10/10/2010	5/1/2011	$25,000.00
3	Marketing Data Warehouse	Mary Jones	10/10/2010	5/1/2011	$75,000.00
4	Inventory Database	Joe Smith	10/10/2010	5/1/2011	$40,000.00
5	Lead Tracking Web Site	Sally Brown	10/10/2010	5/1/2011	$25,000.00

Table 2.3 - PROJECT_TABLE Data

Having looked at both the schema for the tables we examine the project name column as we know this is the only common link between the two tables.

Below is the DEPT_PROJECT table:

DEPT_ID	DEPT_MGR	PROJECT_NAME
1	Nigel Forte	Budget Database
2	Vicky Kensington	Paycheck System
3	Mario Modugno	Marketing Analytics Reporting
4	Patrick McMurphy	Product Inventory
4	Patrick McMurphy	Salesperson Lead Tool

Table 2.4 - DEPT_PROJECT Data

We can see that the project names are totally different from the project names in the first table. The table is also not in second normal form, which is one of the normalization rules that a data modeler applies in order to ensure that the data model contains no redundant attributes and that the non-key attributes are all dependent on a well-formed primary key. Second normal form states that a non-key attribute cannot be dependent on only part of the primary key. (In case the primary key is composed of two or more attributes.)

Part of the integration process will be to normalize the design and to introduce processes like fuzzy name matching, which will allow us to match the project names so that we can come up with a solid model to solve this integration puzzle. Figure 2.8 contains a data model of the integration target tables.

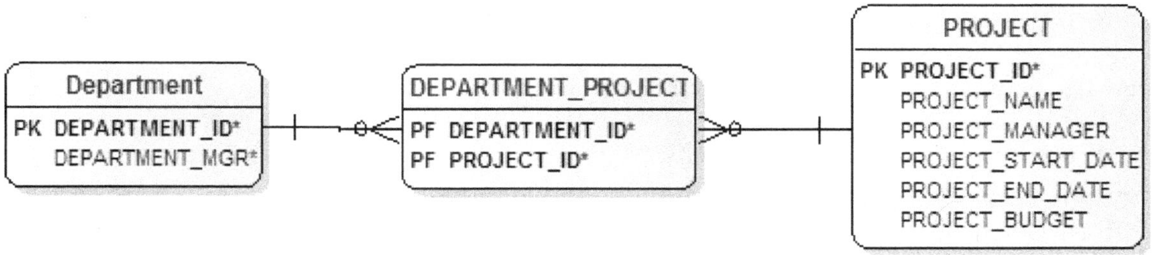

Figure 2.8 - A Normalized Schema for Our Department Project Challenge

This data model will support the following rules:

- A Department can sponsor 0, 1, or more projects.
- A Project can be sponsored by 0, 1, or more Departments.

We allow a project to exist without a sponsoring department so we can support a project in the proposal state. (Assume that when the project is approved, it will then be assigned to a department.)

We have a clean model as the target for our schema integration process, as shown in Figure 2.9. So how do we come up with a process that integrates the project information? The next figure depicts a simple process flow diagram, using ETL tools (such as Microsoft's SSIS), that could be used as a basis for the solution.

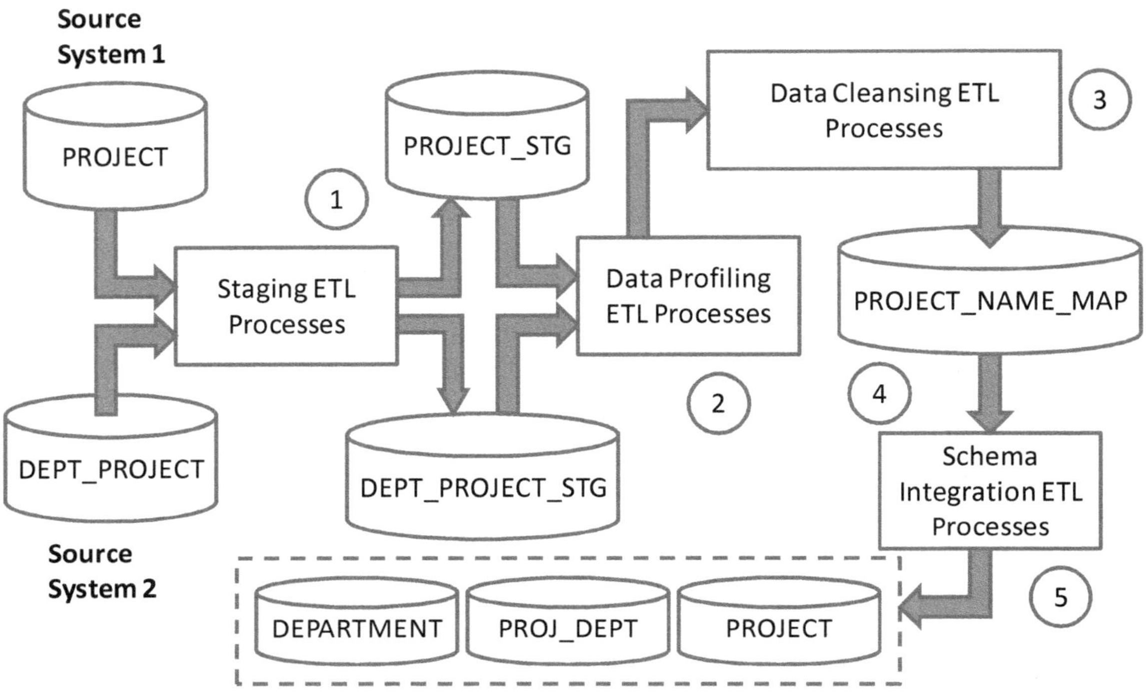

Figure 2.9 - Solving the Department Project Integration Puzzle

There are five principle steps in this scenario. Steps 1 and 2, data staging and data profiling, were covered earlier. In Step 1, we will stage the data for the PROJECT and DEP_PROJECT tables in a set of staging tables in the ODS. In Step 2, we profile the data to trap any missing or corrupt data. In Step 3, we pass the data through our cleansing ETL processes, including, for this example, applying a technique called "fuzzy matching" that attempts to match names that are similar but have different spellings. The output of this fuzzy matching process might be a temporary or intermediate table that has the following content:

KEY	SOURCE_NAME_1	SOURCE_NAME_2	MATCH_WEIGHT	TARGET NAME
1	Finance Budget Database	Budget Database	8	Finance Budget Database
2	Corporate Payroll Application	Paycheck System	3	Corporate Payroll Application
3	Marketing Data Warehouse	Marketing Analytics Reporting	5	Marketing Analytical Data Warehouse
4	Inventory Database	Product Inventory	5	Product Inventory Database
5	Lead Tracking Web Site	Salesperson Lead Tool	2.5	Lead Tracking Tool

Table 2.5 - Fuzzy Matching Output

Notice the MATCH_WEIGHT column. This assigns a numeric value to the degree that two data values are exact. The highest score of 10 would indicate a 100% match. A score of 8 would indicate that the two data values match 80%.

In Step 4, the name matching table above is fed into our integration engine, along with the metadata for the other staging tables that are involved in the integration step.

All the steps we discussed are part of the schema integration process. As stated earlier, we will discuss schema integration in detail in Chapter 3. We picked a specific example in this section of the chapter to illustrate a classic data integration problem and how it might be solved.

Making ODS Data Available to Other Systems

We now examine the last layer of our ODS architecture, the export layer. This is where we stage cleansed data for export to consuming client applications and platforms. Consuming applications examples are Customer Relationship Management (CRM) or Enterprise Resource Planning (ERP) systems that need cleansed master data or some other data to support their business processes.

Consuming platforms are typically data marts and data warehouses that need cleansed dimensional and transactional data for their OLAP (On Line Analytical Processing) cubes and analytical reports and scorecards.

Figure 2.10 shows an example of a data mart being fed from the ODS.

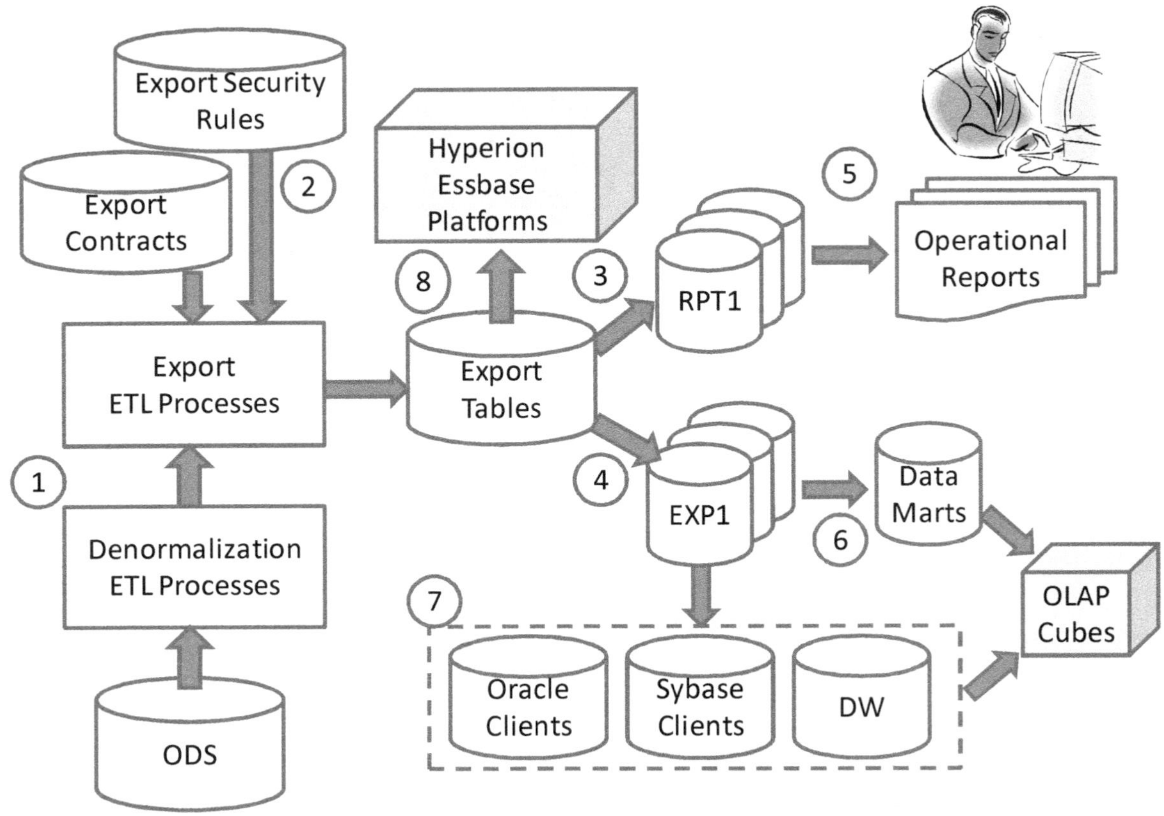

Figure 2.10 - The ODS Export Layer

The diagram above illustrates exporting data from the ODS using ETL processes as the means of getting the data from the ODS to the Export tables. However, standard ETL or other processing could also be used to move the data to the Export tables, replacing Step 1.

In Step 1 in this example, two important ETL processes come into play: The denormalization process and the export process. The denormalization process is responsible for taking the profiled and cleansed data in the ODS and applying denormalization rules, such as adding redundant columns to tables or creating derived tables that can be quickly loaded, to provide optimum performance for requesting clients.

Requestors can be anything from user reports that need ODS data on a daily basis, to downstream data marts and data warehouses that require fact and dimensional data for their OLAP cubes, scorecards, and drill down reports.

In this layer, we can also apply reformatting processes such as concatenating columns or converting data to upper or lower case. Examples of complex tasks are aggregating data, applying advanced statistical formulas, and other mathematical functions.

The denormalization package will deposit the enhanced data into export tables that can be made available to applying clients. We will normally create views on top of these tables to control the interface that the clients use to retrieve the data. This way, if we need to change the export table structures, we can change them without affecting the clients (unless the views need to change, too).

As a side bar, I like to use the following naming standards for tables in the various ODS data flow layers:

- XXXXX_STG – tables that stage source data.
- DQ_XXXXX_PROF – data quality tables used for profiling data.
- DQ_XXXXX_STAT – data quality tables used for storing profiling statistics.
- XXXXX_CLEAN – tables that store cleansed staging data.
- XXXXX_DIRTY - tables that store data that has failed profiling tests.
- XXXXX_DIM – tables that store dimensional data.
- XXXXX_FACT – tables that store fact data.
- XXXXX_REP – tables that store data used in reports (or XXXX_RPT).
- XXXXX_CUBE – tables that store data for cube loading.

Where "XXXXX" is the name of a table, like ORDER_STG, for example.

Of course your company may have its own data and naming standards. The key point is that you use some form of table and column naming standards to easily identify the role of the tables and to keep maintenance tasks as simple as possible.

Step 2 in our diagram shows two sets of tables: SECURITY_RULES and EXPORT_CONTRACTS. Security rules are a set of security constraints such as user ids, passwords, and tables that a particular client can access.

An export contract identifies what permissions a client has as far as manipulating the data in the export layer. It specifies whether the client has READ_ONLY, WRITE_ONLY, or READ_WRITE access to the tables.

As mentioned before, the client would access the tables via views unless there is a need to import data into the tables.

Figure 2.11, contains a simple data model for a Security Contract database.

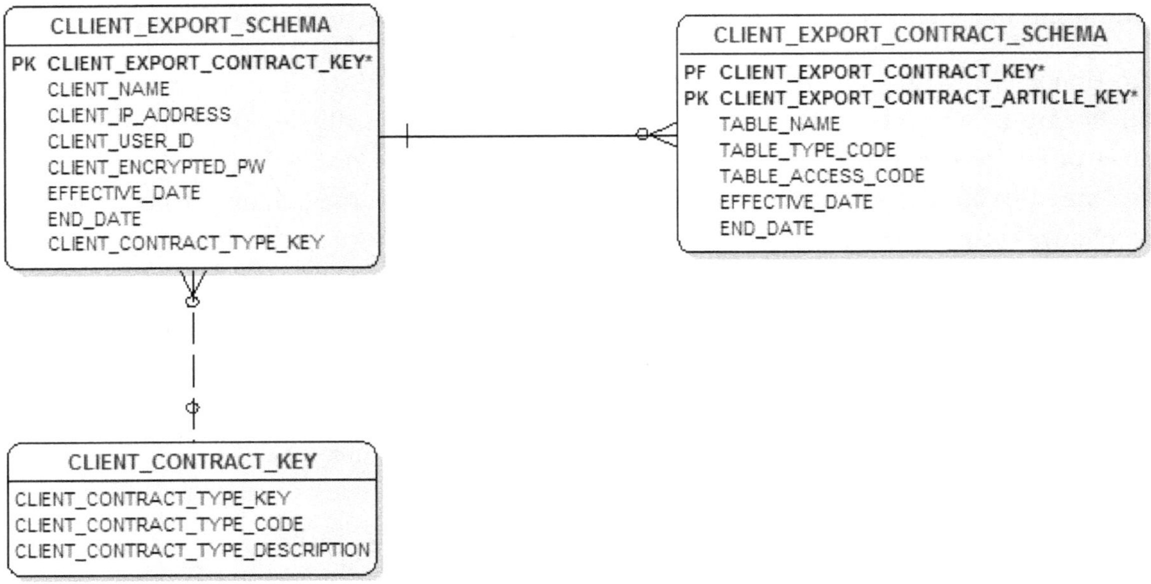

Figure 2.11 - The ODS Export Contract Data Model

Our "CLIENT_CONTRACT_TYPE" table defines the access contracts available to our clients. For our discussion, we will keep this very simple to illustrate the basic concepts of creating a database to capture the permissions we will allow our clients to have.

The type codes we could use are:

- W – a write contract only - clients can only write to the staging tables. This is used in an import or staging scenario.
- R – a read only contract - clients can only read from the export ODS database.
- B – a read and write - clients can read from the ODS export layer and write data to the staging tables.

Next, we will examine the CLIENT_EXPORT_CONTRACT_TABLE. This is where we identify the name of the client, the IP address of the requesting client, security credentials, and the begin and end dates of the contract.

Last, but not least, we have the CLIENT_EXPORT_CONTRACT_ARTICLES table, where we identify the tables and views to which a client has access.

Pretty clever, right? Adding a nice set of ASP forms on a web site will allow the ODS security administrator to control access to the ODS by updating these tables and setting the appropriate security constraints by using the available SQL Server stored procedures and queries. (Stored procedures are used in SQL Server, Sybase, Oracle and other popular database architectures.)

In addition to the SECURITY_RULES and EXPORT_CONTRACTS, Step 2 shows that the ODS data is loaded into the export tables after all the articles of the export contract have been satisfied.

Step 3 shows that tables designed specifically for reports can be loaded from the export tables. Reports can contain complex formulas, aggregation, or cross tab reports derived from millions of rows of data. Pre-joining tables and preloading the results in these tables can provide high performance response for web reporting user, who will not have to wait for hours to generate reports.

Step 4 depicts how an export from the ODS could load tables for exporting data to data marts. These could be denormalized tables with surrogate keys, defined dimensions, and aggregated facts for downstream data mart clients.

Step 5 depicts the production of reports and consumers of the data. In our architecture, they could be users who access web sites.

Step 6 depicts the multi-dimensional cubes that may be created from exported data. The cubes built in this chapter can be accessed by Microsoft Excel pivot tables for advanced and sophisticated data analysis. For our example, SQL Server Analysis services will be used to create the cubes.

Step 7 depicts how other client reporting and data warehouse solutions, implemented with other vendors like Oracle, Sybase, and MySQL can also import data from our ODS export layer.

Step 8 depicts how a specialized OLAP architecture implemented with Oracle's Essbase architecture can receive data from the ODS.

The concept of export and import contracts for heterogeneous distributed databases was introduced by several pioneers in the field. Some interesting papers and books on the topics we just discussed include:

- McLeod and Heimbigner (1985). A Federated architecture for information management. *ACM Transactions of Information Systems*, Volume 3, issue 3, 253 to 278.
- Sheth and Larson (1990). Federated Systems for Managing Distributed, Heterogeneous and Autonomous Databases. *ACM Computing Surveys*, Vol 22, No 3, 183 - 236M.

- Ozsu, T., & Valduriez, P. (2011). *Principles of Distributed Database Systems* (2nd Edition, Springer).

Summary

We based our architecture on industry standard ODS concepts, theory and processing layers introduced by Ozsu, Valduriez, Sheth and Larson, McLeod and Heimbigner, and others.

These were used to define the main critical layers and components of the ODS architecture:

- The Interface Layer
- The Data Staging Layer
- The Data Profiling Layer
- The Data Cleansing Layer
- The Data Integration Layer
- The Export Layer
- The Security Contract Model.

We also saw how to implement a small database, EXPORT_CONTRACT, that could be used to manage access to the ODS by the clients that will need the data. (These, by the way, are key components of federated architectures.)

In the next chapter, we will discuss the schema integration process. We will use this process to create the physical database design for our ODS.

In the last chapter we looked at the high level architecture of the ODS. We discussed how it is a layered architecture and that each layer has a specific role in preparing the data retrieved from operational systems so that it can be delivered to downstream clients for reporting and advanced OLAP analysis and data mining.

In this chapter we take a little detour and introduce the process of schema integration. The schema integration process identifies the three types of data conflicts that have to be resolved to integrate source system physical database schema into one global schema. Additionally, this process shows how to generate specifications for ETL that are used in the data conflict resolution steps. These specifications can be used to create the various processes that stage, profile, cleanse and integrate data so that it can be loaded in the ODS.

Note that the techniques that we will discuss in this chapter were introduced by pioneers in the field of distributed database design. Two pioneers we mentioned earlier are: M. Tamer Ozsu and Patrick Valduriez (2011) - Principles of Distributed Database Systems (2nd Edition, Springer).

So why are we interested in schema integration? We are interested in schema integration as it provides the formal steps that will allow us to design our integrated ODS physical model. It is an iterative process that allows us to combine two or more databases at a time and generate the necessary data transformations and logic to combine the data.

We will examine data integration techniques and conclude the chapter by presenting a simple process flow diagram that we can follow when we integrate selected tables from these source systems for the Café Magnifico ODS:

- A Series of Microsoft Excel Spreadsheets tabs
- A Microsoft Access Database
- A SQL Server Database
- A MySQL Database (That you will integrate as an exercise).

Binary Schema Integration – Technique 1

Binary Schema Integration, by its very name implies taking two source schemas at a time and combining them to generate one integrated schema. Figure 3.1 depicts this process.

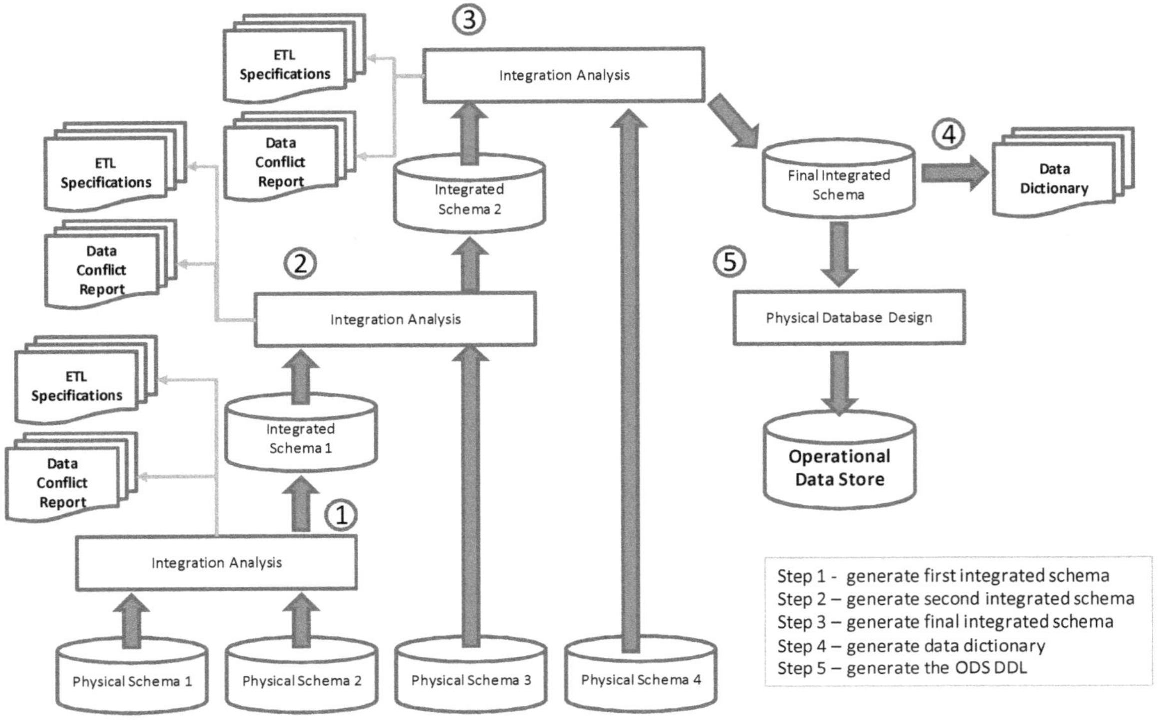

Figure 3.1 - Binary Schema Integration, Technique 1

The diagram identifies the main steps that make up the schema integration process:

- Step 1 – generate the first integrated schema
- Step 2 – generate the second integrated schema
- Step 3 – generate the final integrated schema
- Step 4 – generate the integrated schema data dictionary
- Step 5 – Generate the ODS DDL (Data Declaration Language).

For the example used in this book we will base the process on four source schema. The first two schema will be combined in order to create a first intermediate schema. This first intermediate schema will be combined with a third source database schema so as to create a second intermediate schema. Finally, the second intermediate schema will be combined with the fourth source database schema to generate the final intermediate schema which will be used to implement the ODS.

The integrated schema are platform agnostic and will serve as the blueprint for our ODS. We could create the physical ODS database with any database platform we choose.

Beginning with Step 1, we select physical Schema 1 and 2 and combine them in a step called "Integration Analysis". We will see what this step entails shortly. For now we are interested in the outputs of this process. One output is our Integrated Schema as can be seen in Figure 3.1. The integration process identifies and resolves the three types of data conflicts we discussed in Chapter 2:

- Data Naming and Semantic Conflicts
- Data Type Conflicts
- Structural Conflicts.

Additionally, outputs of this step create three sets of very important design documents and specifications:

- Data Conflict Reports
- Integration and Mapping Data Dictionaries
- ETL Specifications.

The first two documents, the Data Conflict Report and the Integration and Mapping Data Dictionary are inputs for the preparation of the third document, the ETL specifications. The ETL specifications are used to create the ETL processes that will be used to load and integrate the source data.

These specifications include:

- PHD – Process Hierarchy Diagrams
- PDF – Process Data Flow Diagrams
- PDD – Process Dependency Diagrams
- DMD – Data Mapping Diagrams
- DFC – Data Flow Charts (if necessary).

Figure 3.2 shows an example of an ETL process (implemented with Microsoft's SSIS ETL tool) that takes data from two Excel spreadsheets, loads it into two staging tables and then combines the data into one table.

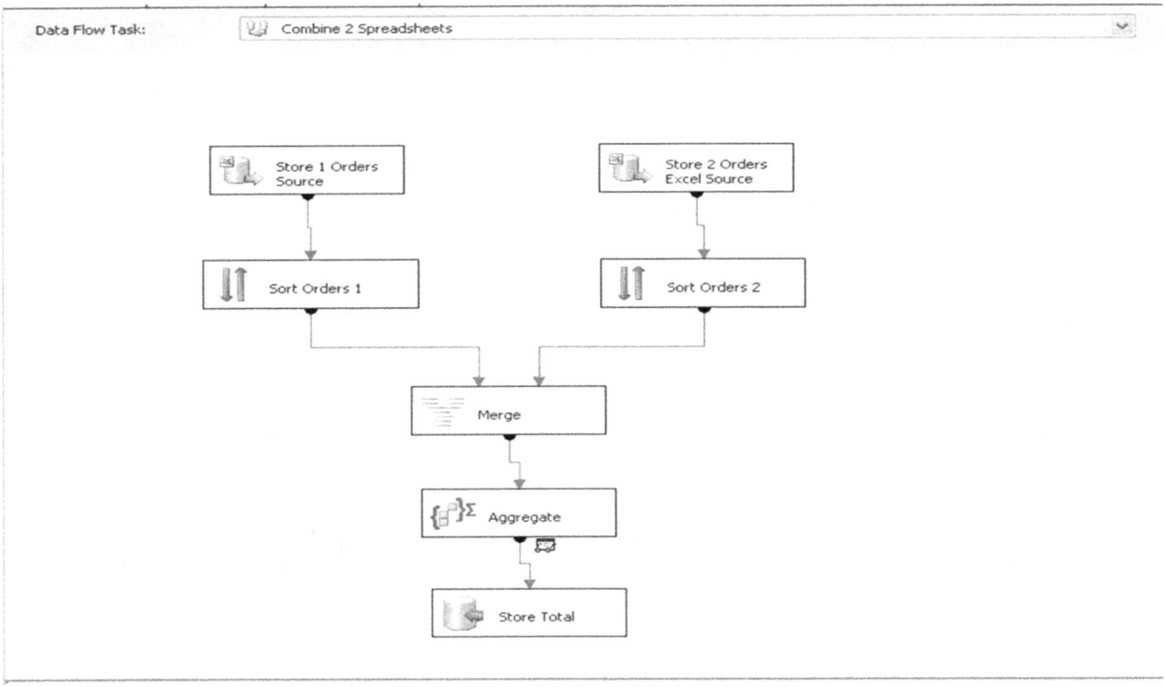

Figure 3.2 - Combining two spreadsheets with SSIS

The rows from the combined table are extracted, sorted and fed to a step that aggregates the data and feeds it to a final aggregated table.

The first two symbols with the small cylinder icons and Excel icons are the source connections to the spreadsheets. The next layer of boxes called Sort Orders 1 and 2 are tasks to sort the data being pulled from the spreadsheets. The merge task appears next. It merges the two data streams. The aggregate tasks sums up the values and the Store total box represents the target database table that the results are stored in.

All these tasks produce a series of dialog boxes when the ETL developer double clicks on. These dialog boxes allow the developer to configure the tasks.

Tables 3.1 and 3.2 contain screen shots of the two source Excel spreadsheets that are used.

As an example we use Microsoft's SSIS (SQL Server Integration Services) tool to create packages and tasks that create connections to the spreadsheets and the target database. The package will perform all the load, merge, sort and aggregation tasks (packages are like programs and tasks are like subroutines). Any other ETL tool like Informatica will work just as well.

Store	Order No	Customer	Order Date	Total Price
London	ORD100	Bentleys Gourmet Foods	12/24/2011	£100.00
London	ORD101	Bentleys Gourmet Foods	12/24/2011	£100.00
London	ORD102	Bentleys Gourmet Foods	12/24/2011	£100.00
London	ORD103	Bentleys Gourmet Foods	12/24/2011	£100.00
London	ORD104	Bentleys Gourmet Foods	12/24/2011	£100.00
Newcastle	ORD105	Newcastle Gourmet on High Street	12/24/2011	£100.00
Newcastle	ORD106	Newcastle Gourmet on High Street	12/24/2011	£100.00
Newcastle	ORD107	Newcastle Gourmet on High Street	12/24/2011	£100.00
Newcastle	ORD108	Newcastle Gourmet on High Street	12/24/2011	£100.00
Newcastle	ORD109	Newcastle Gourmet on High Street	12/24/2011	£100.00

Table 3.1 - Company Store 1 Order Spreadsheet

The second spreadsheet used appears in the table below (this has the same layout as the first spreadsheet):

Store	Order No	Customer	Order Date	Total Price
London	ORD100	Paddington Gourmet	12/24/2011	£100.00
London	ORD101	Paddington Gourmet	12/24/2011	£100.00
London	ORD102	Paddington Gourmet	12/24/2011	£100.00
London	ORD103	Paddington Gourmet	12/24/2011	£100.00
London	ORD104	Paddington Gourmet	12/24/2011	£100.00
Newcastle	ORD105	Regent Street Cappuccino	12/24/2011	£100.00
Newcastle	ORD106	Regent Street Cappuccino	12/24/2011	£100.00
Newcastle	ORD107	Regent Street Cappuccino	12/24/2011	£100.00
Newcastle	ORD108	Regent Street Cappuccino	12/24/2011	£100.00
Newcastle	ORD109	Regent Street Cappuccino	12/24/2011	£100.00

Table 3.2 - Company Store 2 Order Spreadsheet

We will discuss the main components of the package in Figure 3.2. I will assume that you are familiar with SSIS but if not, have no fear, Chapter 9 will go into some detail on how to create ETL flows with this tool.

Figure 3.3 is a screen shot of the ETL package after it executes. I added a component called a data viewer so you could see the results of extracting, sorting, merging and aggregating store sales.

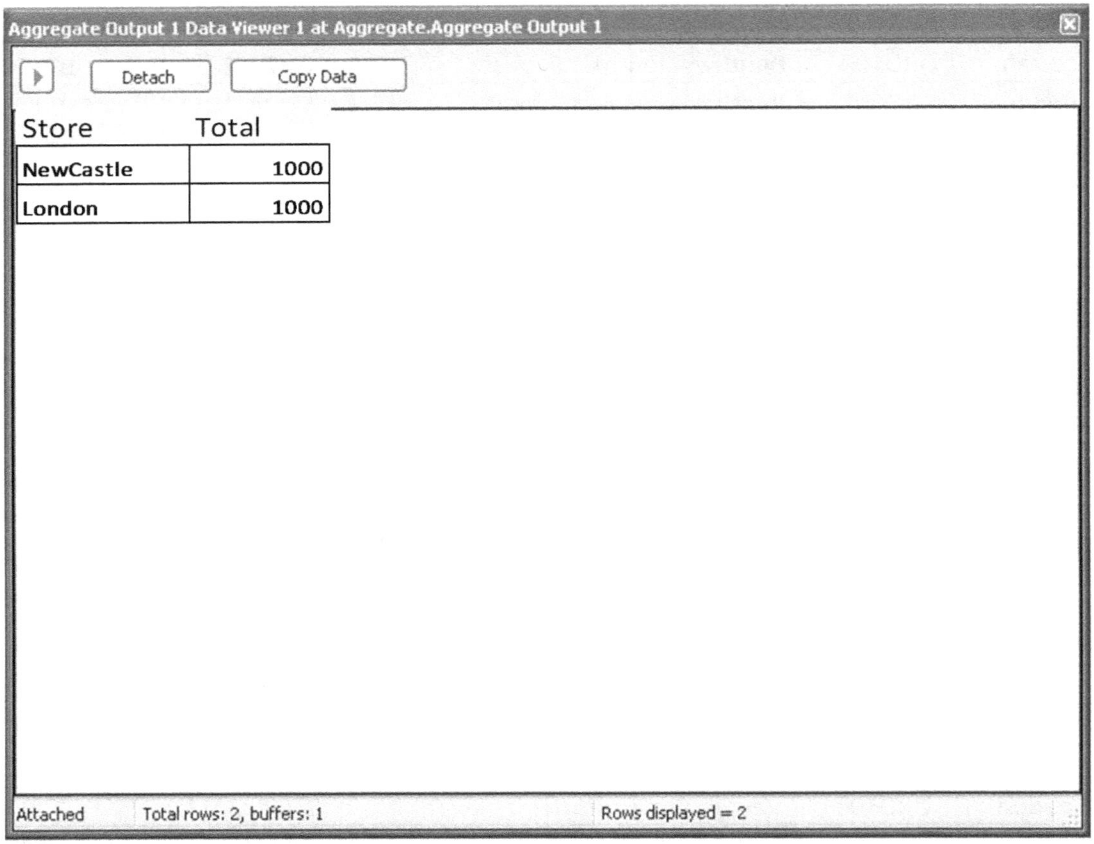

Figure 3.3 - A simple SSIS Package Data Viewer

A data viewer is a good debugging aid that can be used as you are developing your package. It allows you to view the output between critical paths of the process. I added a data viewer at the last path but I could have added one between each of the paths between the tasks if I wanted to.

Let's look at the tasks in this package:

- Company Store 1 (& 2) Orders Excel Source are actually source connections to an Excel spreadsheet that has two tabs (Store Orders 1 and Store Orders 2) that we saw earlier in the section.
- Next are two Sort tasks that take the output from each spreadsheet and sort them in preparation of the merge step (notice that the number of rows are displayed).
- Next, a merge step takes both inputs and creates a single output stream.
- Next to last we see an aggregation step that sums the rows by company so as to produce a total order amount for both stores.

- Finally we see a target destination that puts the totals into a table. Imagine that this table stores the total sales for each company's stores for each day of the year. This table could hold millions of rows (in a real production environment) and would be made available to clients in the ODS Export Layer.

A typical client could be a data mart that subscribes to this table and creates a nice order analysis cube.

Referring back to the schema integration diagram we see that the output of the first "Integration Analysis" step, namely the Integrated Schema 1 is fed into a second "Integration Analysis" step together with the schema for the second source system: "Physical Schema 3".

We go through the same steps and create a second set of ETL Specifications, Data Conflict Reports, Data Mapping Data Dictionary and a second Integrated Schema.

The second Integrated Schema, together with the schema for the third source system is fed to a third Integration Analysis step so as to produce the Final Integrated Schema. This is our design model for the physical ODS. We now perform physical database design by assigning vendor specific data types, keys, primary and foreign key constraints and other objects required to create our ODS database, tables, indexes and physical files that will support the tables.

OK, this is all great but what exactly happens in the "Integration Analysis" steps? I will tell you shortly but first we need to look at an alternate binary schema integration technique that you can add to your data integration tool kit.

Binary Schema Integration – Technique 2

The first schema integration technique we discussed in the prior section took two source schemas, integrated them so as to produce an intermediate schema and generated a set of support documents, data dictionaries and ETL specifications. The key word here is "two". This is why the inventors of this process called it Binary Schema Integration (BSI). The process continued until all source schemas were exhausted and a final integrated schema was created. Figure 3.4 shows a variation of this method.

Notice that we combine the source schema first so as to form a first layer of integrated schema. Next we take the two integrated schema and combine them, two at a time to form the next layer of integrated schema and so on, until we derive the final integrated schema.

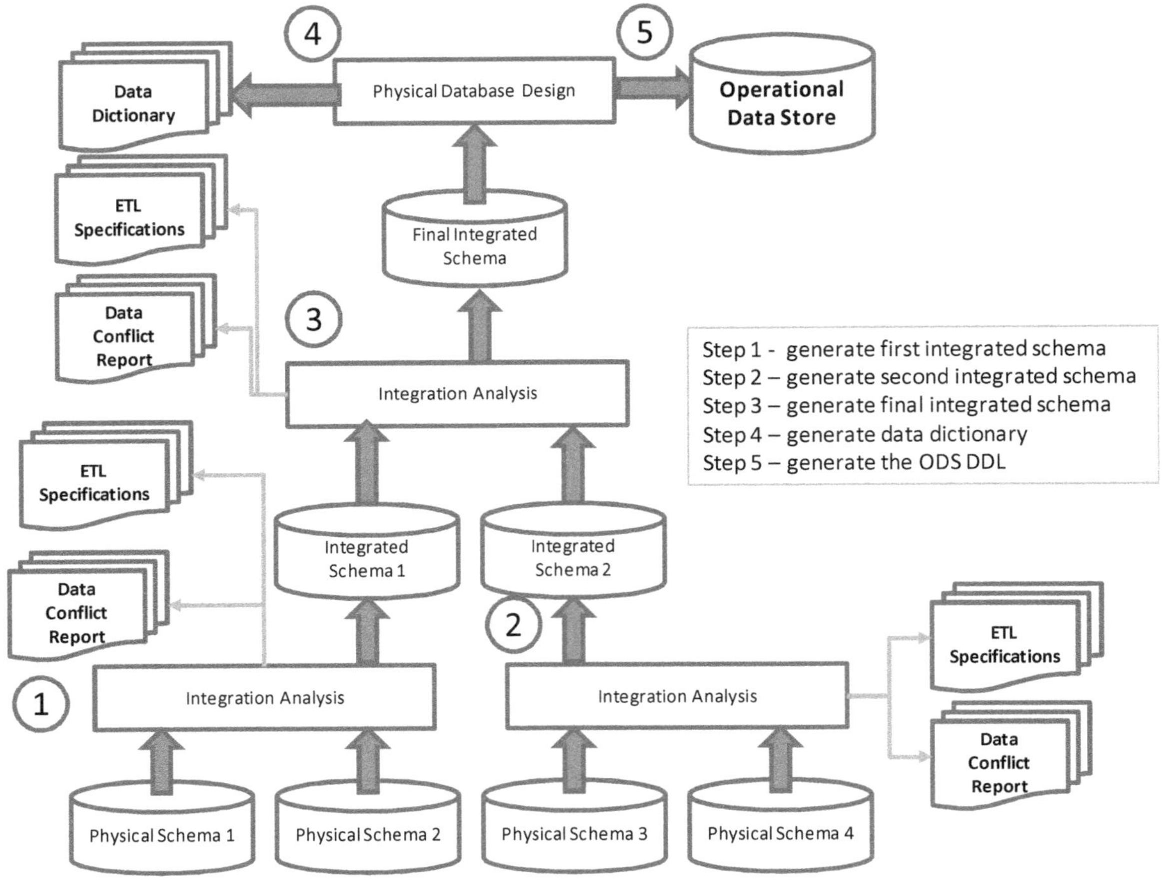

Figure 3.4 - Binary Schema Integration - Technique 2

Binary Schema Integration – Technique 3

Another integration scheme is called tertiary schema integration which takes three schemas at a time as illustrated in Figure 3.5.

This might make sense in some cases. For example we might have to integrate 100 spreadsheets that all have the same layout. For example, 100 salespersons all use the same spreadsheet layout for identifying leads and we want to load them into an ODS. Our integration Analysis step would then take all 100 spreadsheets and combine them into one integrated schema. This is illustrated in Figure 3.6.

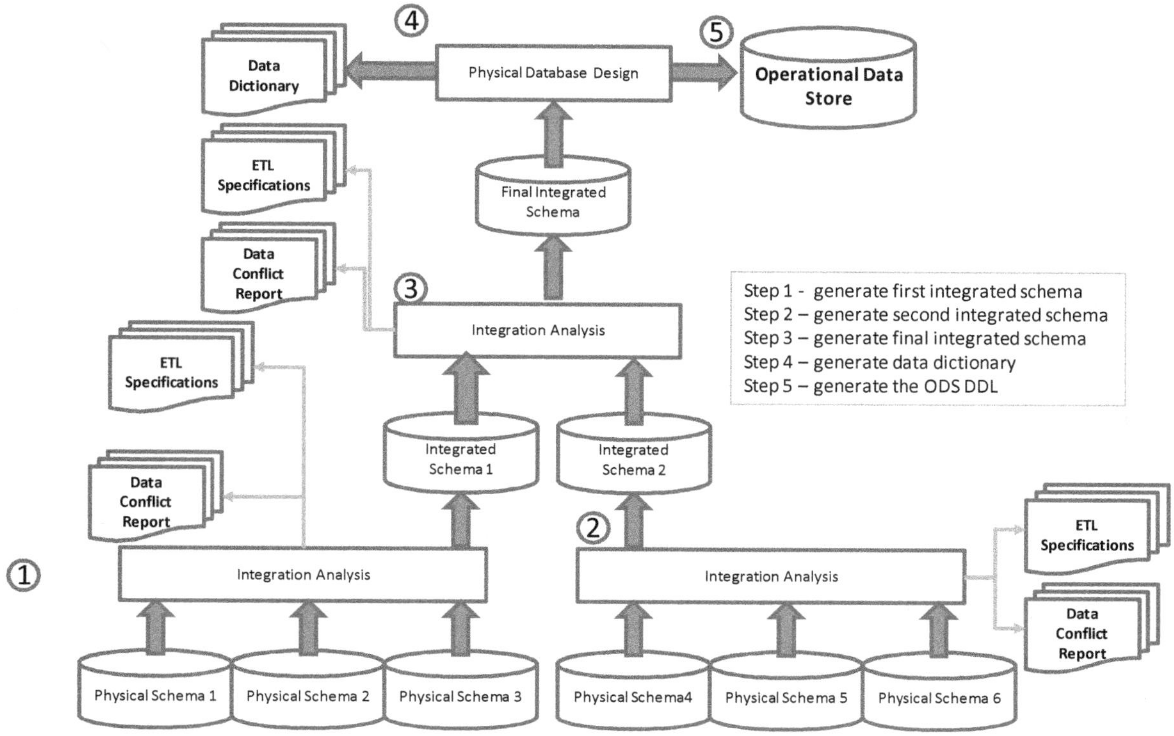

Figure 3.5 - Tertiary Schema Integration - Technique 3

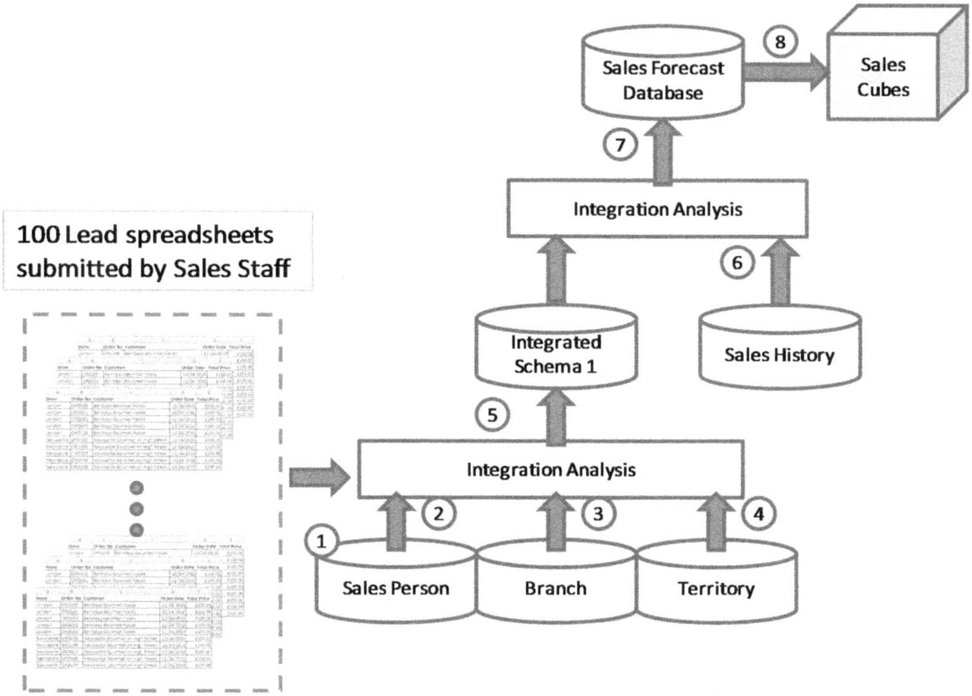

Figure 3.6 - Tertiary or N-ary Schema Integration

Now that we have examined the different types of schema integration techniques we are ready to examine the actual steps and what their inputs and outputs are.

A high level description of schema integration is the identification of common and uncommon or unique data objects in each schema. The uncommon data objects can stand on their own so we need not worry about them. It is the common objects we care about, specifically table keys, column and relationships that are common in each schema pair. This is what we will be integrating!

The flow chart in Figure 3.7 shows the steps that are followed.

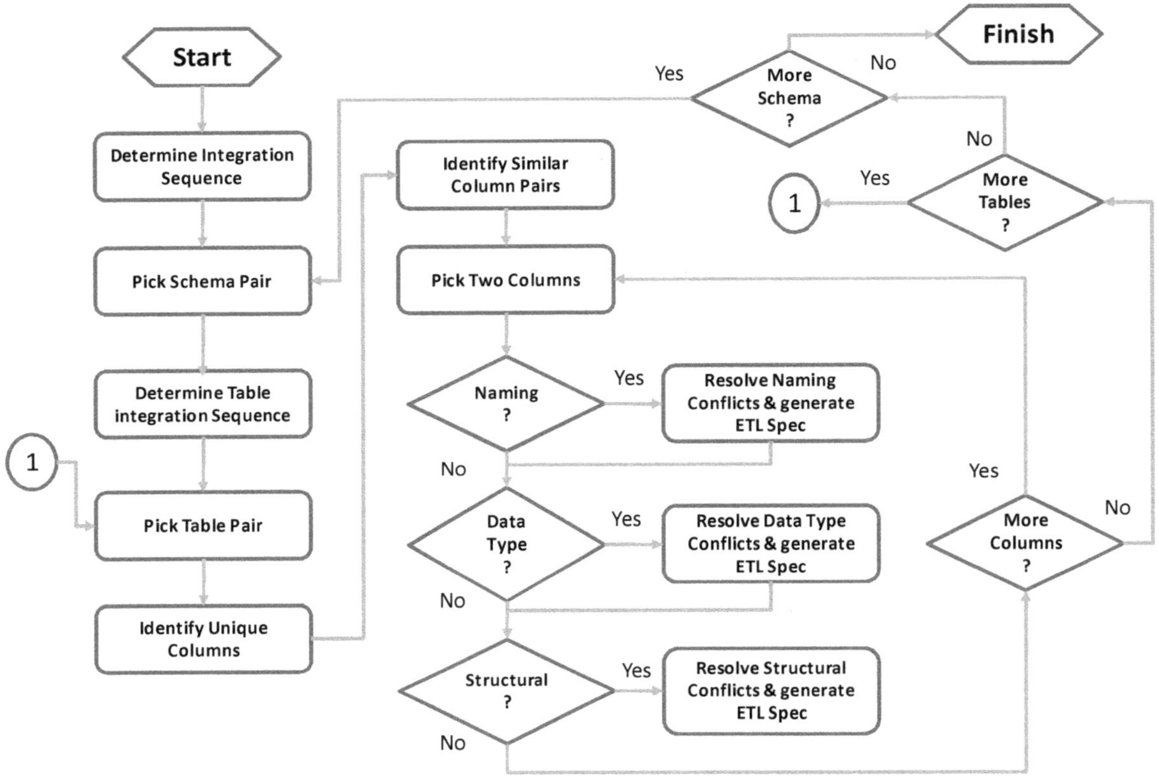

Figure 3.7 - Schema Integration Process Flow Steps

As you can see, it is an iterative process. That is, we repeat the steps until we have no more schemas to integrate.

Let's set up a schema integration scenario. Let's say we have ten schema to integrate. The flow is applied for each pair until all schema are exhausted as follows:

- **Step 1** – Compare Schema 1 & 2, output Interim Schema 1
- **Step 2** – Compare Schema 3 and Interim Schema 1, output Interim Schema 2

- **Step 3** – Compare Schema 4 and Interim Schema 2, output Interim Schema 3
- **Step 4** – Compare Schema 5 and Interim Schema 3, output Interim Schema 4
- **Step 5** – Compare Schema 6 and Interim Schema 4, output Interim Schema 5
- **Step 6** – Compare Schema 7 and Interim Schema 5, output Interim Schema 6
- **Step 7** – Compare Schema 8 and Interim Schema 6, output Interim Schema 7
- **Step 8** – Compare Schema 9 and Interim Schema 7, output Interim Schema 8
- **Step 9** – Compare Schema 10 and Interim Schema 8, output Interim Schema 9

Yes, a lot of seemingly boring steps but in scenarios like this we can assign each integration step to individual consultants or staff members (If we have the budget!).

So we can expect N – 1 (10 – 1 = 9) interim schema process steps for N schema to compare when we use this for schema integration. I leave it to the reader to analyze if the other variations of schema integration save comparison steps or use more.

Let's start with the first three steps that determine integration sequence, schema pair selection and table selection for integration:

- **Step 1** – Determining the integration sequence. This is where we determine the order of the integration of the schema based on criteria like business requirements or schema that have a high percentage of common attributes. For example, we might need to create a sales data mart because executives are demanding accurate data for sales scorecards and forecasting. In this case if we have two or three databases that contain sales data we integrate them first.
- **Step 2** – Pick schema pair. This is the first of the iterative steps. Having determined the integration sequence in Step 1, if this is the first integration sequence, we pick the first two schema. If this is a subsequent integration schema we pick the next two schema as defined by the particular version of schema integration we picked.
- **Step 3** – Now that we identified our two schemas we start by identifying tables that are common and tables that are unique. For each common pair of table we compare the two.

An example better illustrates this step:

Assume Schema 1 has the following tables: Order, Order Line Item, Customer, and Shipper.

Assume Schema 2 has Product, Part, Inventory, Order, Manufacturer, and Customer.

Right away, we see that the following tables are common in both schemas:

Order in Schema 1 is common to Order or Order Line Item in Schema 2. Customer is common in both schemas. The remainder of the tables are unique to each schema. Therefore we only need to concentrate on the three common tables: Order, Order Line Item and Customer. Pretty straight forward, do you agree?

Steps 4 & 5: now that we have picked our table pair we need to identify columns that are unique and common to both schemas. Let's look at another example. Picking the Customer tables that we discussed in Step 3, our friendly DBA has generated a data dictionary for us for the tables of interest. These can be seen in Table 3.3.

Schema 1, Customer Table A

Column	Data Type	Data Length	Description
Customer Key	Numeric	TBD	Surrogate key that maps to the customer name.
Customer Name	Character	32	The name of the customer.
Customer Description	Character	64	A description of the customer. (For example, retail chain of pastry shops.)
Customer Effective Date	Date	TBD	The date the customer started making purchases.
Credit Rating	Character	1	Customer credit rating: A = Excellent, B = Good, C = 30 days delinquent, D = 60 days delinquent, E = 90 days delinquent, F = cancel credit.
Location Identifier	Numeric	TBD	Surrogate key that maps to the customer location table for address information.
Customer Contact	Character	32	Full name for the customer contact person.
Contact Telephone Number	Character	32	Customer contact telephone number.

Schema 2, Customer Table B

Column	Data Type	Data Length	Description
Customer Identifier	Character	16	The unique identifier assigned to the customer. This is the customer id that appears on all orders, invoices, shipping documents, returns and orders.
Customer Name	Character	64	The name of the customer.
Customer Description	Character	126	A description of the customer (For example, retail chain of pastry shops).
Customer Effective Date	Date	TBD	The date the customer became our client.
Customer Country	Character	64	Country where customer is located.
CustomerState Or Province	Character	64	State or province within the customer's country.
CustomerCity	Character	64	City where customer is located.
Customer Street Address	Character	128	The street address of the customer.
Customer Postal Code	Character	16	The postal code of the customer.

Table 3.3 - First and Second Customer Table

Note: numeric and date data types are identified as TBD (To Be Decided) as we would select the data type during physical design. This is also dependent on the platform we choose.

Let's take a look at this data dictionary. First for the unique columns, we do some analysis and come out with the report shown in Table 3.4:

Schema 1 Unique Attributes

Schema	Unique Attribute	Data Type	Data Length
Credit Rating	Character	1	Customer credit rating, A = Excellent, B = Good, C = 30 days delinquent, D = 60 days delinquent, E = 90 days delinquent, F = cancel credit.
Location Identifier	Numeric	TBD	Surrogate key that maps to the customer location table for address information.
Customer Contact	Character	32	Full name for the customer contact person.
Contact Telephone Number	Character	32	Customer contact telephone number.

Schema 2 Unique Attributes

Schema	Unique Attribute	Data Type	Data Length
Customer Country	Character	64	Country where customer is located.
CustomerState Or Province	Character	64	State or province within the customer's country.
CustomerCity	Character	64	City where customer is located.
Customer Street Address	Character	128	The street address of the customer.
Customer Postal Code	Character	16	The postal code of the customer.

Table 3.4 - Unique Attributes for Schema 1 and 2

Although we know that we do not need to integrate these columns we notice that the first table has an identifier that most likely links the customer to a location table. We also notice that the second table has the location information included as several attributes.

This conflict is known as a structural conflict and we will discuss it in a later step. We flag this for later evaluation.

Next, in Step 5 we need to identify common attributes. We make a list of them and generate a report that lists the column names, their data types and their descriptions. (This report will be a valuable tool for when we need to resolve the naming and data type conflicts related to attributes.)

Here is the report we generated:

Common Attributes	Description
Customer Key	Surrogate key that maps to the customer name.
Customer Identifier	The unique identifier assigned to the customer. This is the customer id that appears on all orders, invoices, shipping documents, returns and orders.
Customer Name	The name of the customer.
Customer Name	The name of the customer.
Customer Description	A description of the customer (For example, retail chain of pastry shops).
Customer Description	A description of the customer (For example, retail chain of pastry shops).
Customer Effective Date	The date the customer became our client.
Customer Effective Date	The date the customer became our client.

Table 3.5 - Common Attribute Comparison Report

Notice I split the report into two for readability. In a real design situation we probably will have to create our own data dictionaries as none are usually available.

Let's dive in and analyze this design problem. Looking at the key attributes, we first think it is just going to be a case of slightly renaming the columns.

Upon closer inspection we see that we have a semantic conflict. Although both key attributes are used as unique keys for the customer, the first is used as a surrogate key and the second is used as a unique identifier on the various order, billing, and other types of sales documents related to processing customer orders.

Also, we see a data type conflict. The "Customer Key" is an integer while the "Customer Identifier" attribute is a 16 character string (for instance, 1234 versus CUS1234).

For now we resolve the conflict by keeping both of the columns in our new proposed integrated table (we might drop the surrogate key as this is usually used in data marts and data warehouses).

As we proceed with the design, we will implement a mapping table that links the all the old customer keys to a new customer key.

Looking at the next two pair of attributes we see that we are lucky. Both attribute pair are identical except for a minor data type conflict. "The Customer Name" attribute in the first customer table is 32 characters while in the second customer table it is 64 characters. We decide to keep the attribute that has the greater length.

Next, the "Customer Description" attribute in the first table is 64 characters while in the second table it is 128 characters.

We decide to resolve this data length by making the final data length of 128 characters so as to allow more space for detailed customer descriptions.

Before presenting you with the final schema integration report for these two columns we need to revisit the structural conflict related to identifying a customer's location.

In the first table we identified a key that pointed to a location table. In the second table the customer address information was contained in the table.

Let's examine the data dictionary for the customer location table. This data dictionary can be seen in Table 3.7.

Schema 2, Customer Table B

Column	Data Type	Data Length	Description
Location Identifier	Numeric	TBD	Surrogate key that maps to the customer location address information.
Location Key	Numeric	TBD	The unique identifier assigned to the location. A customer can have one or more locations.
Location Name	Character	64	The name of the customer location. For example: "Famous London Cakes locations".
Location Country	Character	64	Country where customer is located.
Location State Or Province	Character	64	State or province within the customer's country.
Location City	Character	64	City where customer is located.
Location Street Address	Character	128	The street address of the customer.
Location Postal Code	Character	16	The postal code of the customer.
Location Building	Character	64	The building of the location. For example, in London some addresses are in famous buildings that have a name. Example, Cromwell House.
Location Floor	Character	32	If the location is a building, the floor of the location.
Location Room Number	Character	32	The room number of the location.

Table 3.6 - Customer Location Table

This is a valuable table. Not only does it look like it contains all of the address related columns in the customer table, it also contains some additional address information like building name, floor and room number. This is very handy information for when the delivery person delivers the items ordered by the customer.

Let's generate a column comparison report to check if there are any conflicts we should resolve:

Schema	Column	Data Type	Data Length	Description
1	Customer Country	Character	64	Country where customer is located.
1	Customer State Or Province	Character	64	State or province within the customer's country.
1	Customer City	Character	64	City where customer is located.
1	Customer Street Address	Character	128	The street address of the customer.
1	Customer Postal Code	Character	16	The postal code of the customer.
2	Location Country	Character	64	Country where customer is located.
2	Location State Or Province	Character	64	State or province within the customer's country.
2	Location City	Character	64	City where customer is located.
2	Location Street Address	Character	128	The street address of the customer.
2	Location Postal Code	Character	16	The postal code of the customer.
2	Location Building	Character	64	The building of the location. For example, in London some addresses are in famous buildings that have a name. Example, Cromwell House.
2	Location Floor	Character	32	If the location is a building, the floor of the location.
2	Location Room Number	Character	32	The room number of the location.

Table 3.7 - Common Attribute Comparison Report

We are in luck. There are no data conflicts between the common columns. All data types and lengths are the same and the semantic meanings are the same. We get the added bonus of some additional location related attributes. (We may decide to use the new location table in its entirety in the final integrated schema.)

Notice how we generated the various data dictionaries during the integration process that were described earlier in the chapter. Let's generate a final report that shows the data conflicts together with their resolutions.

Table 3.8 contains the final schema integration resolution report for the customer table.

Schema	Common Attributes	Data Type	Data Length	Conflict Identifier	Conflict Type
1	Customer Key	Numeric		1	Semantic
2	Customer Identifier	Character	16	1	Semantic
1	Customer Name	Character	32	2	Data Length
2	Customer Name	Character	64	2	Data Length
1	Customer Description	Character	64	3	Data Length
2	Customer Description	Character	128	3	Data Length
2	Location Identifier	Numeric		4	Structural

Table 3.8 - Common Attribute Comparison Report

Notice how we assigned identifiers to each conflict. The resolution section contains the recommended actions for the ETL packages that will load and integrate the data from the two customer tables.

Let's take a look at some suggested resolutions:

Conflict Identifier	Resolution Identifier	Resolution Description
1	1a	Eliminate this surrogate key.
1	1b	Use this attribute as the primary key. A mapping table will be used to map new keys to old keys.
2	2a	Increase length to 64 characters.
2	2b	Use 2a.
3	3a	Increase length to 128 characters.
3	3b	Use 3a.
4	4a	Keep the key and include the Location table in the final integrated schema.

Table 3.9 - Conflict Resolution Report

Notice the enhancements we made. While going through the integration process we realized a few things:

- A customer may have multiple locations.
- A customer may have multiple contacts.

Because of these new business rules (that we verified with our customers) we decide to add some link tables: Customer Location and Customer Contact.

We could also have considered a Customer Contact Location link table as a customer contact may be reached at one or more locations.

Finally, we complete the integration specifications by creating a data model that shows the final integrated schema created with a data modeling tool called DeZign. Figure 3.8 shows the new integrated customer table, the new location table and all the necessary link tables.

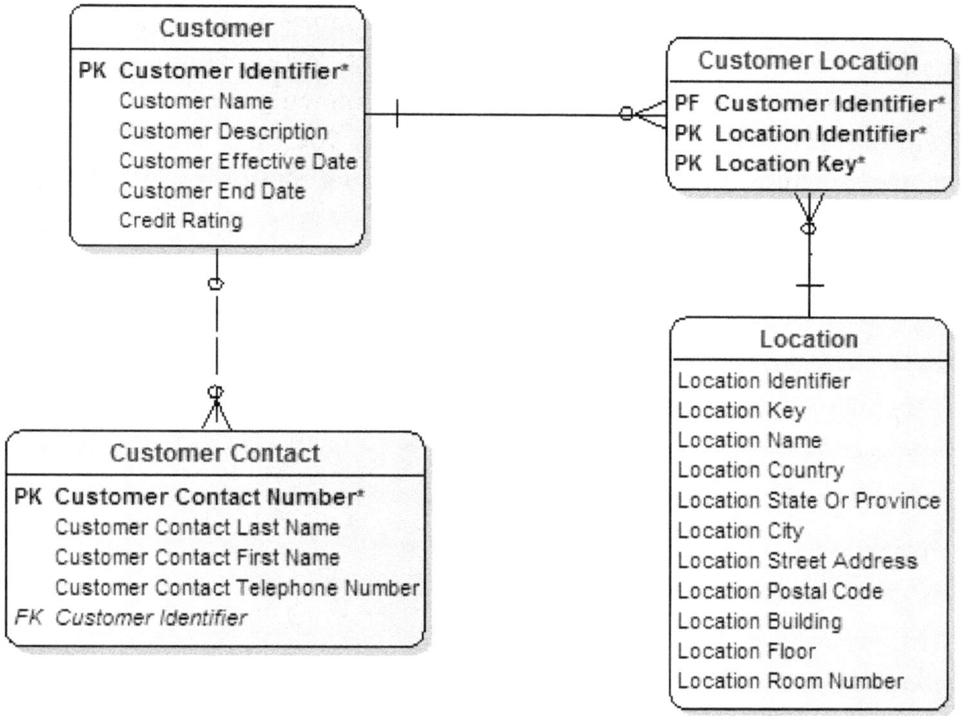

Figure 3.8 - Integrated Customer Model

The model clearly identifies the primary keys. If the figure was printed in color, you could see that they appear in red font. Foreign keys appear in green font, identifying relationships with solid lines and none identifying relationships in dashed lines.

Identifying and non-identifying relationships are terms used by the CA Erwin data modeling tool. An identifying relationship means that the primary key attributes which belong to the parent table appear in the child table primary key.

A non-identifying relationship means that the parent primary key appears as a non-key attribute in the child table and acts as a foreign key.

Summary

In this chapter we introduced the theory behind schema integration. We discussed the two types of binary schema integration and tertiary and N-ary schema integration. We also examined the actual steps involved in the schema integration process and presented a flow chart that you can use to identify steps for your project plan.

Lastly, we walked through a simple customer example and identified all the data conflicts together with the resolution for each conflict. We concluded the example with a simple set of design documents and a data model showing the solution. The example was very simple but it did illustrate the steps that you, as a data architect need to take. Next, we conclude the first section by discussing the role of the ODS in a data warehouse architecture.

CHAPTER 4
Roles of the ODS within Data Warehouse Architectures

In this chapter we will examine some of the roles that an ODS can play within the data integration scenarios. Specifically we will discuss these roles:

- As a supplier to a data warehouse architecture
- As a supplier to data marts
- As a member in a distributed architecture
- As a source for operational reporting
- As a an integrator of data for data mining
- As a member in a CMDB architecture (ITIL Configuration Management Database)
- As an enabler of data quality.

Regardless of the role, the common theme is pulling data from multiple operational sources, profiling and cleansing the data (if a data quality architecture is in place) and integrating the data into one common database. Once the data is integrated it is made available to the consumers of the data. Consumers can be data warehouses, data marts, operational reporting processes or even other systems that require cleansed and integrated data.

The data sources can be traditional operational and transactional databases or more focused databases, like databases that store availability and event information for critical components of a computer infrastructure or a power plant. For the purposes of data mining, an ODS can be used to collect scientific information, such as weather information from multiple sites or cities so as to analyze weather patterns and forecast future weather events.

Let's begin by looking at the first traditional role, that of a supplier to a data warehouse.

As a Supplier for a Data Warehouse

Data warehouse architectures are repositories of historical data, specially formatted to supply snapshots in time for analysis of the data. Analysis is performed by looking at the data in a multi-dimensional manner. That is, from multiple perspectives. Additionally, users can navigate up and down hierarchies so as to aggregate and decompose aggregated statistics all the way down to the transactional level if needed.

Figure 4.1 depicts the high level architecture for this business intelligence solution. Clearly, the ODS is at the center of the architecture and plays the role of a data integration hub.

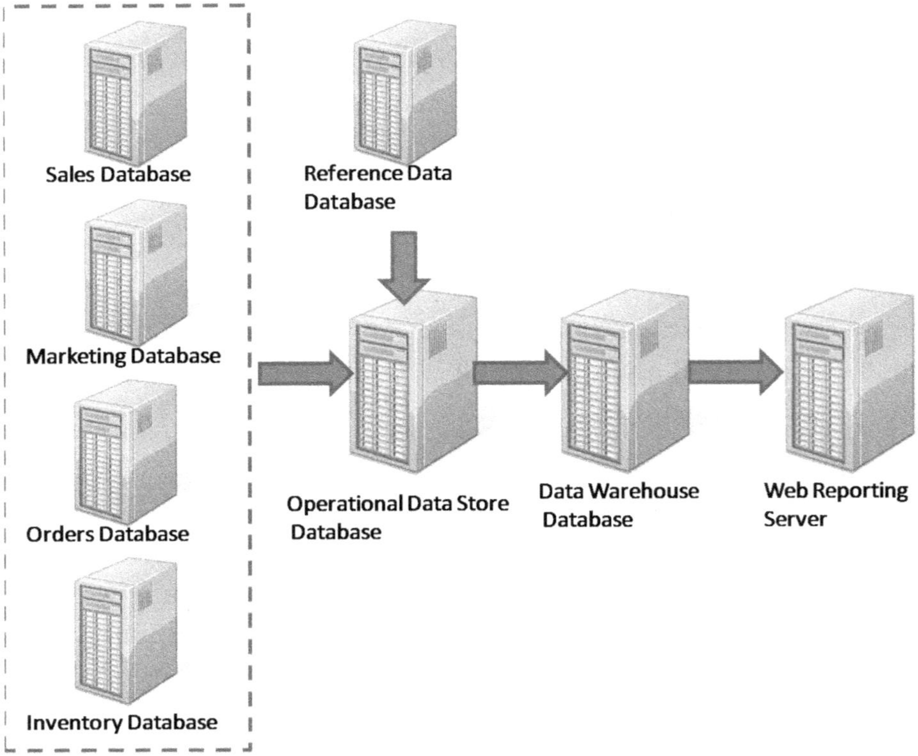

Figure 4.1 - ODS as Source for a Data Warehouse

We can see four transactional systems:

- A sales transaction database
- A marketing database (for capturing leads and sales campaign information)
- An order database
- An inventory database.

Data is pulled from these systems, profiled and cleansed in the ODS and loaded into the ODS database. The operational systems are typically relational databases with heavily normalized structures.

The ODS database is typically designed as a normalized database schema at a transaction level granularity. No history is stored in the ODS except for maybe a few months at the most for current to prior month comparisons.

As mentioned previously, the ODS consists of layers that facilitate a specific process in the ETL cycle:

- A staging layer – to pull and stage transactional data
- A profiling layer – to test the data quality of the data being collected
- A cleansing layer – to clean any data that did not pass muster in the profiling layer
- An integration layer – to integrate the data and load it into the ODS
- An export layer – to expose data in a controlled, secure manner to downstream consumers.

As a reminder, it is a good approach to divide distinct functions of the data lifecycle of the ODS into these processing and interface layers. Each layer plays an important role and can grow as the data required by consumers grows.

As a Supplier for Multiple Data Marts

Let's discuss the second role. Data marts are smaller versions of data warehouses. They have the same structures as data warehouses, namely star or snowflake models but the subject area is narrower. Figure 4.2 depicts the ODS as a supplier to four data marts, each data mart dedicated to its own subject area.

The basic functionality in this scenario is the same as that of the data warehouse architecture we discussed in the last section. Operational data is pulled, staged, profiled and cleansed. Reference data is used to clean up missing values or resolve issues like duplicate names.

The ODS then exports the data by subject area. By export we mean that it stages the data in a dedicated layer of tables and views. For example, after profiling and cleansing the sales data, it exposes it to the sales data mart. This technique adds a security layer so that only dedicated sales analysts and financial types can examine the data.

The same is performed for marketing, orders and inventory subject areas. Dedicated export layers present this data to the data marts so that cubes can be loaded, scorecards updated and dashboards refreshed so that executive managers can keep track of the company's performance.

Additional sets of control tables and processes can be used to implement "contracts" that define what a user can access and cannot access. The next role is that of a member in a distributed ODS architecture.

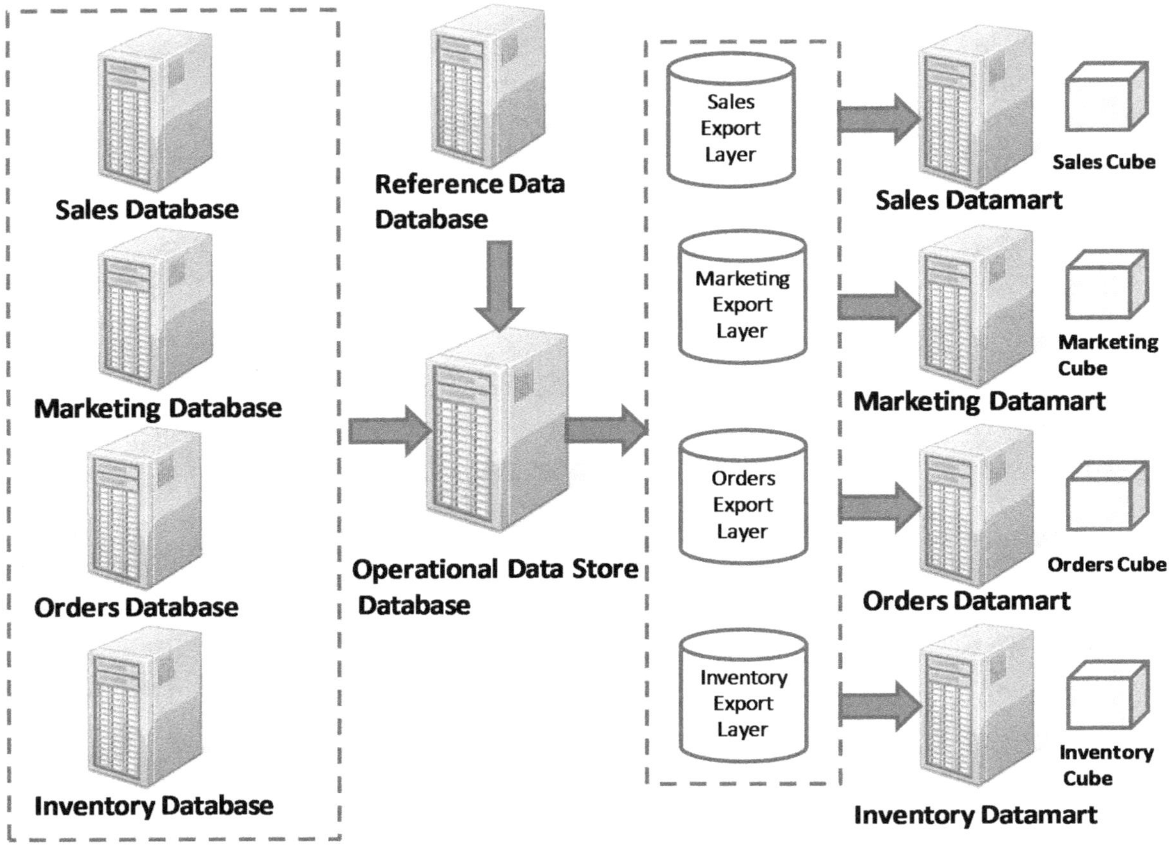

Figure 4.2 - ODS Supplying Data Marts

As a Member in a Distributed Architecture

An ODS can be part of a larger architecture. For example, Figure 4.3 depicts an international multi-ODS architecture. This is a complex architecture with multiple ODS capturing and integrating local data.

In this scenario, a series of ODS exist in Europe and in the Americas, namely the United States and Canada. Each ODS collects data from operational systems in its respective city. A regional reference database exists so as to capture customer, product and location information.

The same scenario exists for the Americas. Data from each of the city ODS are loaded into the regional Americas ODS. As each regional ODS is loaded, most likely on a daily basis, the data is replicated to the Global ODS architecture.

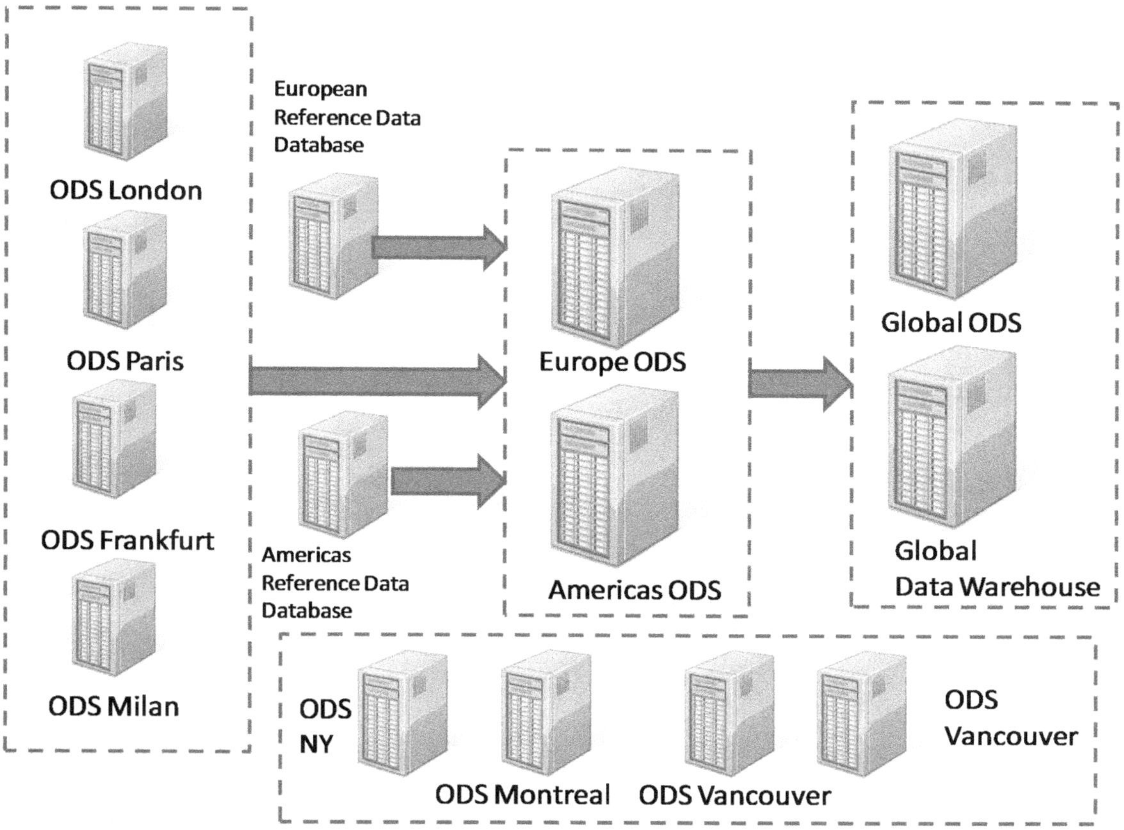

Figure 4.3 - ODS as a Member in a Distributed Architecture

The Global ODS architecture includes a global data warehouse for consolidated OLAP analysis, global scorecards and dashboards for executive management. By using replication architectures, data can be replicated globally between multiple ODS (that are part of a distributed architecture) so as to provide the different levels of data requirements and reporting.

As a Source for Operational Reporting

The next role that we discuss supports the bread and butter reporting for any organization, namely operational reporting. Operational reporting is performed on a daily basis by various levels of business users in order to monitor the daily performance of the organization.

Figure 4.4 shows how the ODS is used for this purpose.

Key reports, based on transactional data, grouped by reference data such as customer, product, location, etc., are run on a daily, weekly and monthly basis. Additionally,

CRM type reports like sales leads assist the sales team in generating new business. The marketing group also benefits from these reports so that they can tie marketing campaigns to customer groups.

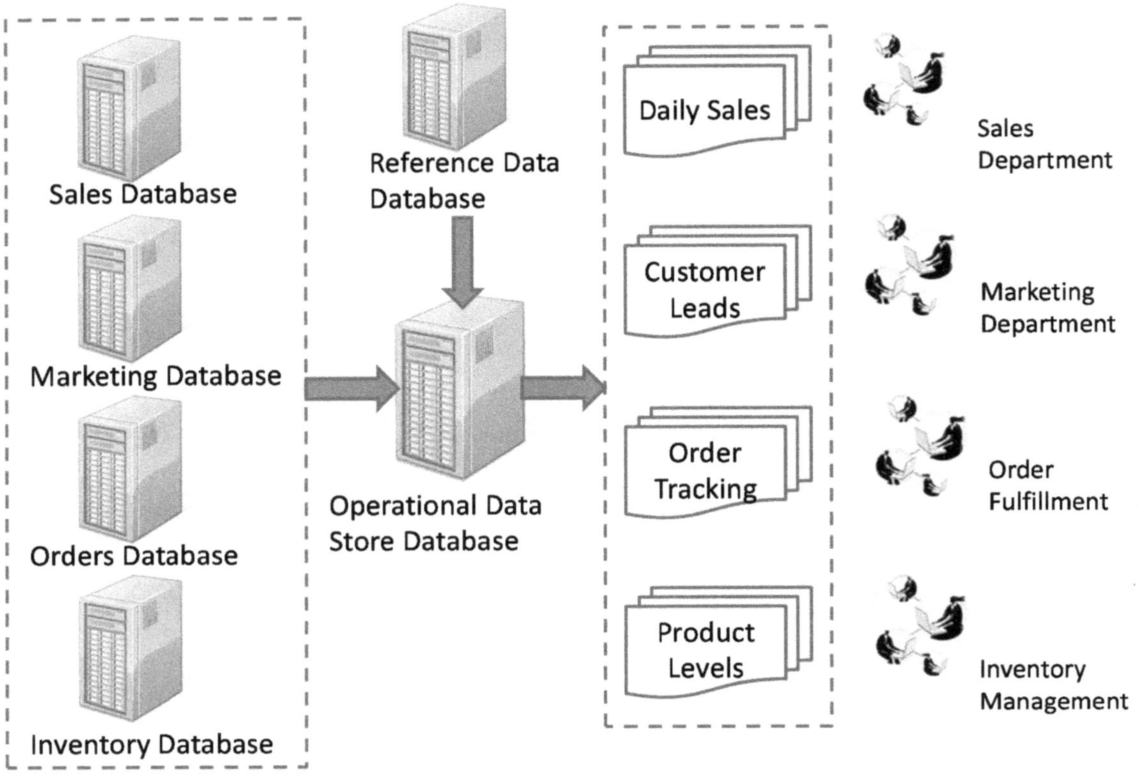

Figure 4.4 - ODS as Source for Operational Reporting

The ODS is an ideal platform to integrate all of this related sales data for the purpose of revenue generation. Sales productivity reports are also generated so as to track sales person performance and compensation.

The key to this type of role is a solid underlying data quality architecture that profiles and cleanses key data. Poor quality data will affect the bottom line.

As a Source for Data Mining Applications

Data mining is the process whereby interesting patterns of data are identified and visualized so that we can predict the future based on events of the past. Additionally, we can look at patterns so as to identify the causes of a result. For example, why do beer purchases usually appear with diaper purchases at super markets? (I didn't make this one up!)

Below we see the ODS as an integrator of sales data so that it can be presented to a knowledge worker to predict sales patterns.

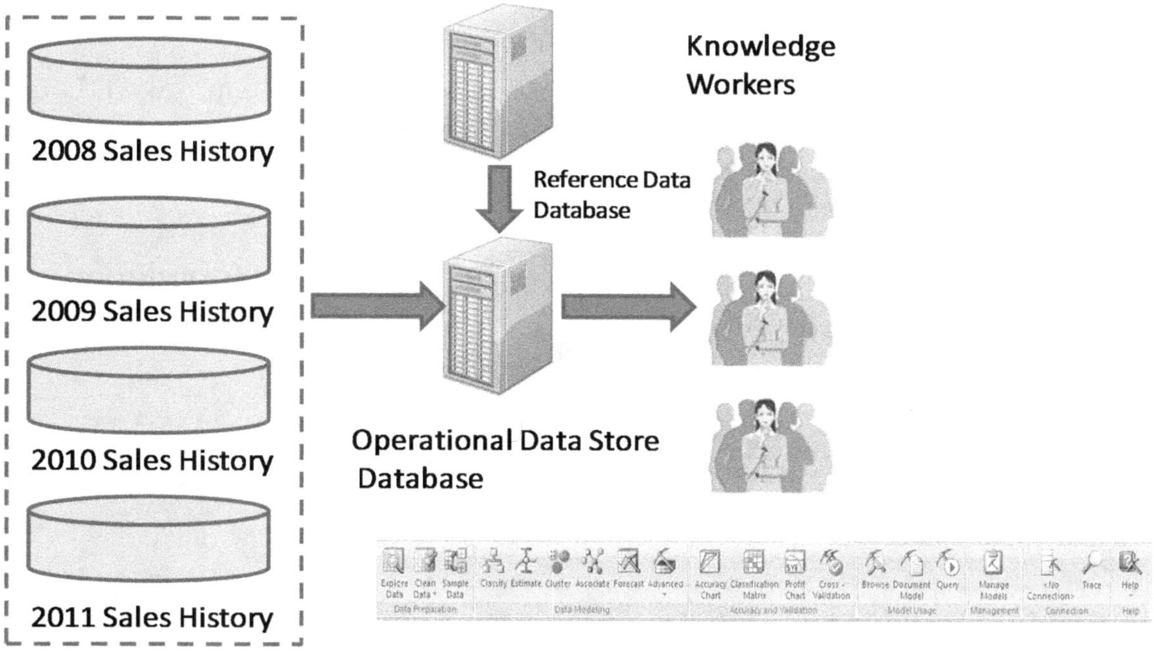

Figure 4.5 - ODS as Source for Data Mining

The knowledge worker has several tools available to him or her for this task. Shown in Figure 4.5 is an add-on to Microsoft Excel that allows one to apply several advanced artificial intelligence (AI) algorithms to explore and identify patterns. The ability to classify, cluster, associate and forecast data is a powerful tool that can be used to analyze all categories of data, from sales data to scientific data or financial markets data.

The ODS once again plays a key role. The data collection, integration and data quality processes associated with the ODS ensure that knowledge workers are delivered quality and timely data for their analysis.

As an Integrator of CMDB Data

CMDB stands for Configuration Management Database. This is an ITIL (Information Technology Infrastructure Library) compliant database that stores information related to configuration items. A configuration item is any asset in an organization that needs to be tracked and managed so as to guarantee performance and uptime (for example, servers, routers, workstations, etc.).

ITIL is a governance model that identifies the processes, models, steps and resources required to provide top service and support for IT infrastructures. Many organizations claim to be ITIL compliant and use vendor proprietary tools and CDMB databases to achieve this goal.

Figure 4.6 shows how the ODS integrates CI (Configuration Item, an ITIL term meaning an asset like a server) data from source systems for delivery to a CMDB for consumption by support technicians, managers and help desk workers.

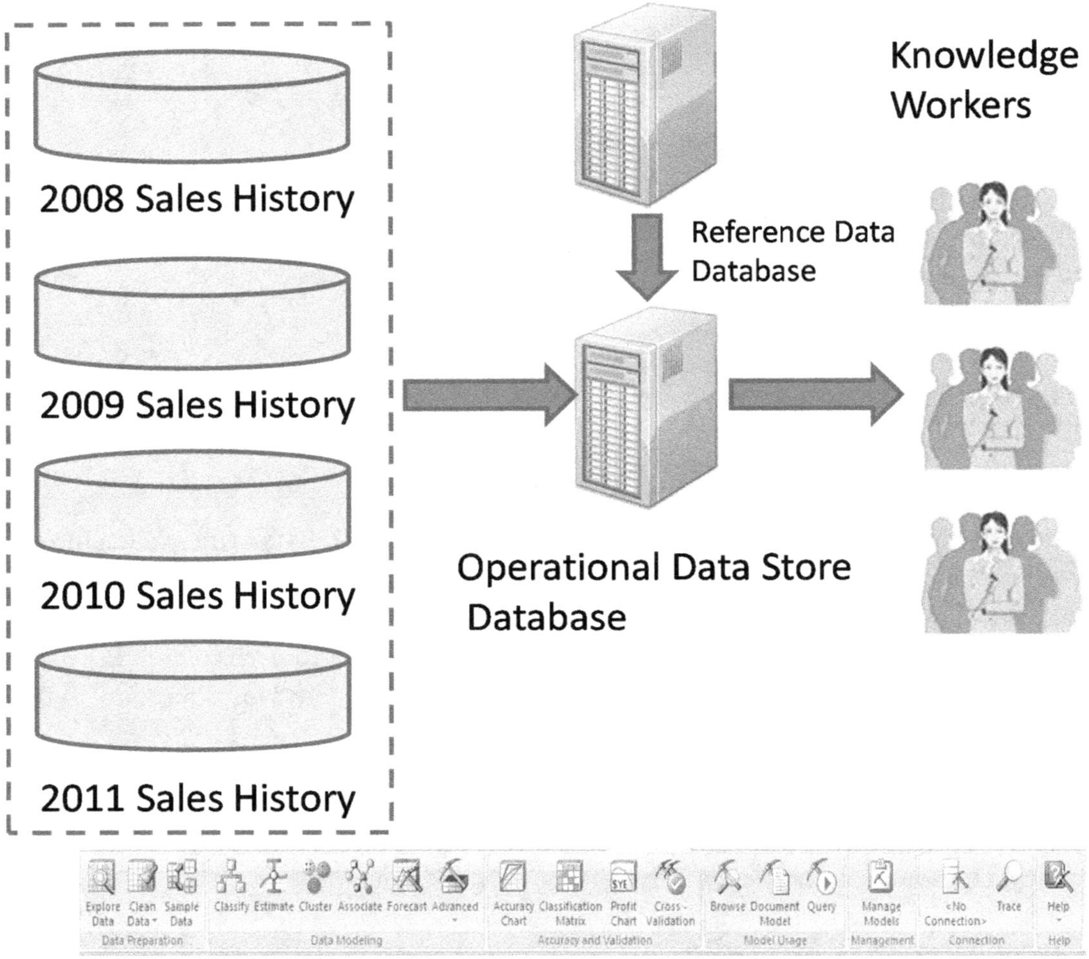

Figure 4.6 - ODS in an ITIL CMDB Architecture

One can consider the CMDB as a specialized data warehouse that stores configuration items and related reference data. A configuration item could be a server, memory in the server, CPU in the server, network information, routers, switches, racks, not to mention computer rooms, software and other items that are part of an IT infrastructure.

Configuration Items and related information are collected from the customer sites and stored in localized databases via probes, scripts and other means. The ODS plays a key part in pulling this data, cleansing it and integrating it into a common structure for consumption by the CMDB.

For example, if multiple customer databases store information for the same servers, one would want to integrate these into a common model on the ODS after the data has been profiled and cleansed. Additionally, one would want a clean source of reference data, like location data so that CIs can be associated to their location and also support staff.

At the end of this data chain are the technicians, mangers and help desk staff that use specialized tools to help them identify CIs that need servicing. They also would like to perform impact analysis if a CI goes down. For example, if a router goes down, what servers are attached to it and which users will be affected?

If one couples this ODS/CMDB architecture with a data warehouse, one can collect vital service statistics that not only measures availability and downtime of the CIs but also the response performance of support staff. This is a vital set of statistical data that allows management the capability to measure how happy customers are.

As a Data Quality Platform

Lastly we look at the ODS as a data quality platform. The ODS coupled with a reference database provides any reporting or data integration architecture with a valuable set of processes to measure and cleanse data. Figure 4.7 shows the ODS, together with a reference database and a set of data quality tables.

The Data Quality Statistics database contains a set of tables that identify the meta data related to the data objects we want to collect statistics on. Specifically, it will contain tables that identify the sources, tables and columns we want to pass through the data quality process. Additionally, we want tables that identify the processes that we want to execute against these data objects.

As an example, a data quality profile list could include the following basic processes executed against table columns:

- Check for NULLS
- Check for duplicates
- Check for maximum & minimum data ranges
- Check count of distinct values

- Check reference data against golden copies (like validating postal codes).

We would want to map these processes against the table columns so we can track and manage what tests we want to apply to the columns. The tests would then be executed against the data as it comes in and the results collected in a set of statistic tables. These tables would then feed data quality reports and scorecards available on web sites to our data stewards.

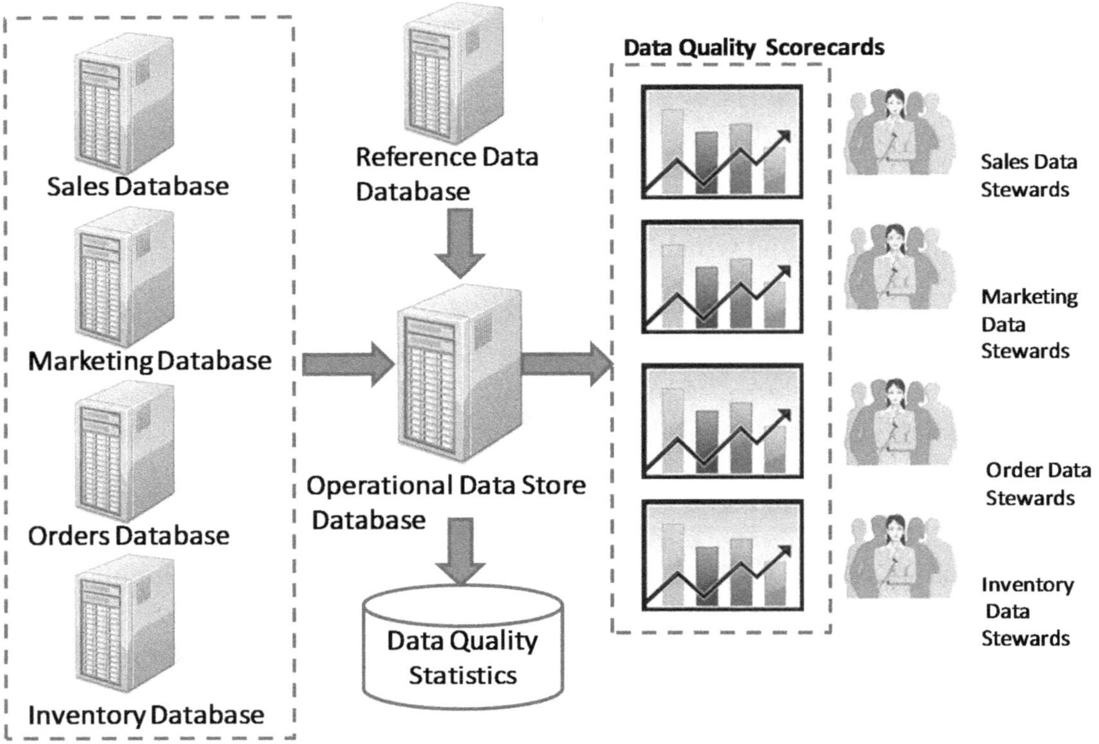

Figure 4.7 - ODS in a Data Quality Governance Scenario

Summary

We have seen in this chapter the various roles that an ODS can play, from a source of integrated data for a data mart to a platform that provides analytical data for data mining. We can agree that the integration function of the ODS is a key benefit as the downstream consumers of data need not know that one, two or more sources feed the ODS. The ODS provides one single platform of cleansed integrated data.

In this chapter we reverse engineer the various databases that will be the sources for the ODS. We will describe the steps required to reverse engineer, create data dictionaries and prepare the logical and physical data models for the operational databases.

For the sake of brevity, we will use one MS Access database, one MS Excel Spreadsheet (with several tabs), one MySQL database and one MS SQL Server 2008 R2 database as the sources.

These are simple examples so as to fit within the scope of the book. They are meant to illustrate the steps required to prepare the deliverables that will be used in the schema integration step. In an actual production project, the databases would be more complex, the models and deliverables more complicated.

Also, the designs are less than perfect. Poor design is used so as to illustrate the typical issues one finds when reverse engineering legacy databases for the purpose of data integration.

In order to generate the data models, I cheated bit and loaded a Microsoft SQL Server database using SSIS (SQL Server Integration Services) ETL tool so as to generate a default model for the London spreadsheet tabs, the Torino Access database, the MySQL database and the remaining Munich SQL Server database. From the DDL I created the physical data dictionaries. I then used the physical data dictionaries to create the logical models. (That's why they call it reverse engineering!)

Another approach would have been to manually create the models by analyzing the underlying structures and tables of the sources and creating the models. The approach I used is a good short cut, as it gives you a starting point for the creation of the source data dictionaries.

Reverse Engineering the Munich Database

As stated in the introduction above, one can generate a physical model by pulling in the source tables into the target database. Once in the database, you identify the primary and foreign key constraints so that the data modeling tool picks up the main relationships between the tables.

I created connections to the MySQL database, Excel spreadsheets, MS Access database and the SQL Server 2008 database with SSIS (SQL Server Integration Services) so as to create all the staging tables.

Figure 5.1 contains the first reverse engineered physical model that will be a source for our ODS. It is for the Munich company based on SQL Server 2008.

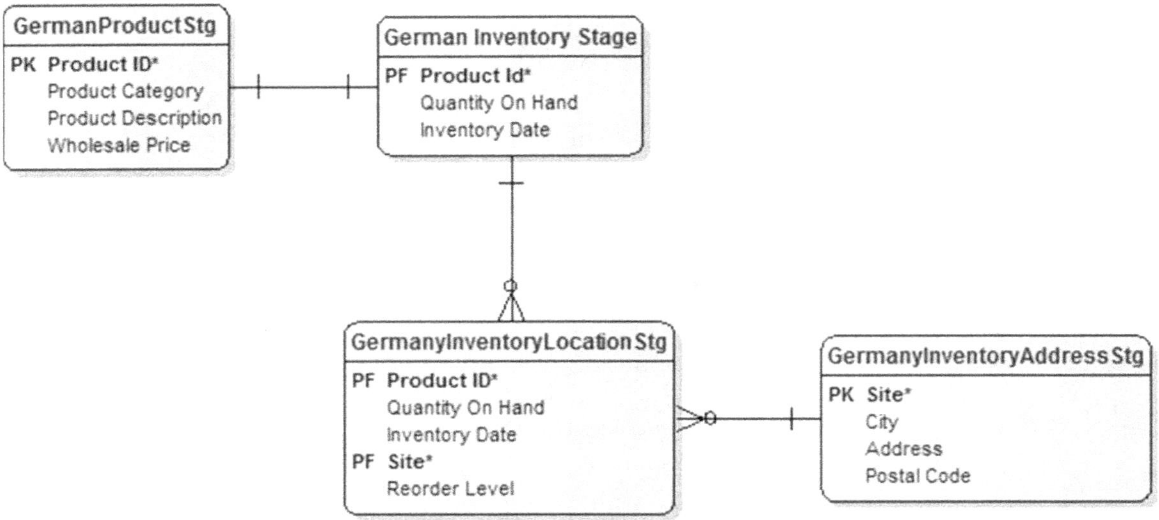

Figure 5.1 - Munich Order Database

The model has four tables and supports the following relationships:

- A product may be stored in inventory.
- An inventory has one or more inventory locations.
- A product may be stored in an inventory location.
- An inventory location has an associated address.

Now this is a simple model for an inventory subject area. Real inventory locations would have additional information related to buildings, rooms and even shelves where a product may be stored.

The data dictionaries flow for these tables. The simple standard we us for documenting our entities is based on two simple rules:

- All primary keys appear in bold underline font.
- Foreign keys appear in bold italicized font. (Foreign keys are underlined if they form part of the primary key.)

Pretty simple but it does convey the message for our purposes.

Column	Data Type	Length	Description
<u>Site</u>	Text	128	This is the unique identifier for a site name.
City	Text	128	This is the name of the city where the site is located.
Address	Text	128	This is the street address of the site.
Postal Code	Text	32	This is the postal code for the site address.
Contact	Text	128	This is the name of the contact person.

Table 5.1 - The Inventory Address Data Dictionary

As can be seen, we present the bare minimum meta data: column name, data type, length and description. The primary key which is in bold underline font is the Site name. We use generic data types as this is a logical data dictionary.

The data dictionary for the target staging table that will receive the raw source data appears below in Table 5.2:

Target Column	Target Data Type
<u>Site</u>	nvarchar(128)
City	nvarchar(128)
Address	nvarchar(128)
Postal Code	nvarchar(32)
Contact	nvarchar(128)

Table 5.2 - Inventory Address Staging Table (MunichInventoryAddressStg) Data Dictionary

Notice the large data types. As these are staging tables we retained the same data types as found in the source database. We will have an opportunity to refine them as we proceed with the schema integration steps.

Next is the simple data dictionary for the inventory table. It appears in Table 5.3:

Inventory Data Dictionary

Column	Data Type	Length	Description
<u>Product ID</u>	Text	9	The unique identifier for the product.
Quantity On Hand	Number		The number of units on hand in inventory for all sites.
Inventory Date	Date		The date that inventory was taken.

Table 5.3 - The Inventory Data Dictionary

Notice this time that our product key also plays a role of foreign key. It establishes a relationship to the product table. Recall that a product may appear in inventory.

Also keep in mind that we will use the logical data dictionaries when performing schema integration. The physical data dictionaries are for the staging tables only.

The data dictionary for the physical staging table that will store raw inventory data appears next in Table 5.4:

Target Column	Target Data Type
Product ID	nvarchar(9)
Quantity On Hand	integer
Inventory Date	datetime

Table 5.4 - The Inventory Staging Table (MunichInventoryStg) Data Dictionary

Next is our data dictionary for the Munich product table. It appears in Table 5.5 below:

Column	Data Type	Length	Description
Product ID	Text	9	A unique identifier for the product.
Product Category	Text	64	The category code for the product.
Product Description	Text	256	The name or description for the product.
Wholesale Price	Decimal	10,2	The wholesale price for the product.

Table 5.5 - The Munich Product Table Data Dictionary

This table stored basic data that describes a product such as the product category, description and wholesale price. The primary key is the Product ID column. Table 5.6 has the related data dictionary for the staging table:

Target Column	Target Data Type
Product ID	nvarchar(9)
Product Category	nvarchar(264)
Product Description	nvarchar(256)
Wholesale Price	money

Table 5.6 - The Munich Product Staging Table (MunichProductStg) Data Dictionary

Again notice the data types. These are the default data types that get generated when SSIS creates the tables. I performed one manual change in that I assigned a data type of money to the wholesale column.

Next we present the data dictionary for the Inventory Location table found in the Munich database. This appears in Table 5.7.

Column	Data Type	Length	Description
Product ID	Text	9	The unique identifier for the product.
Quantity On Hand	Number		The number of units on hand in inventory at this site.
Inventory Date	Date		The date that inventory was taken for this site.
Site	Text	11	The name of the site.
Reorder Level	Number		The level of units that indicate it is time to reorder the item.

Table 5.7 - The Munich Inventory Location Data Dictionary

Here we can see that our primary key is a composite key consisting of the Product ID and Site name columns. Additionally, both of these columns are foreign keys. The Product ID column plays the role of foreign key to the Inventory table from the Product table. The site name plays the role of foreign key from the Inventory Address table.

The data dictionary for the physical staging table that was the basis for the local data dictionary appears in Table 5.8.

Target Column	Target Data Type
Product ID	nvarchar(9)
Quantity On Hand	int
Inventory Date	datetime
Site	nvarchar(255)
Reorder Level	int

Table 5.8 - The Munich Inventory Location Staging Table (MunichInventoryLocationStg) Data Dictionary

We can agree that the models and examples presented are very simple. They do illustrate that at a minimum, when we prepare the various reverse engineering documentation we need to identify the underlying data types for the columns, the business descriptions of what the columns contain and lastly the primary and foreign key information so we can understand the relationships between tables.

Again, as a reminder we create the physical data dictionary first by creating the default staging tables and then generate the logical data dictionary and any supporting logical data models.

Reverse Engineering the London Database

We now turn our attention to the London database. Recall that the London database was implemented as a series of spreadsheet tabs using Microsoft Excel.

Figure 5.2 contains the reverse engineered model for this database.

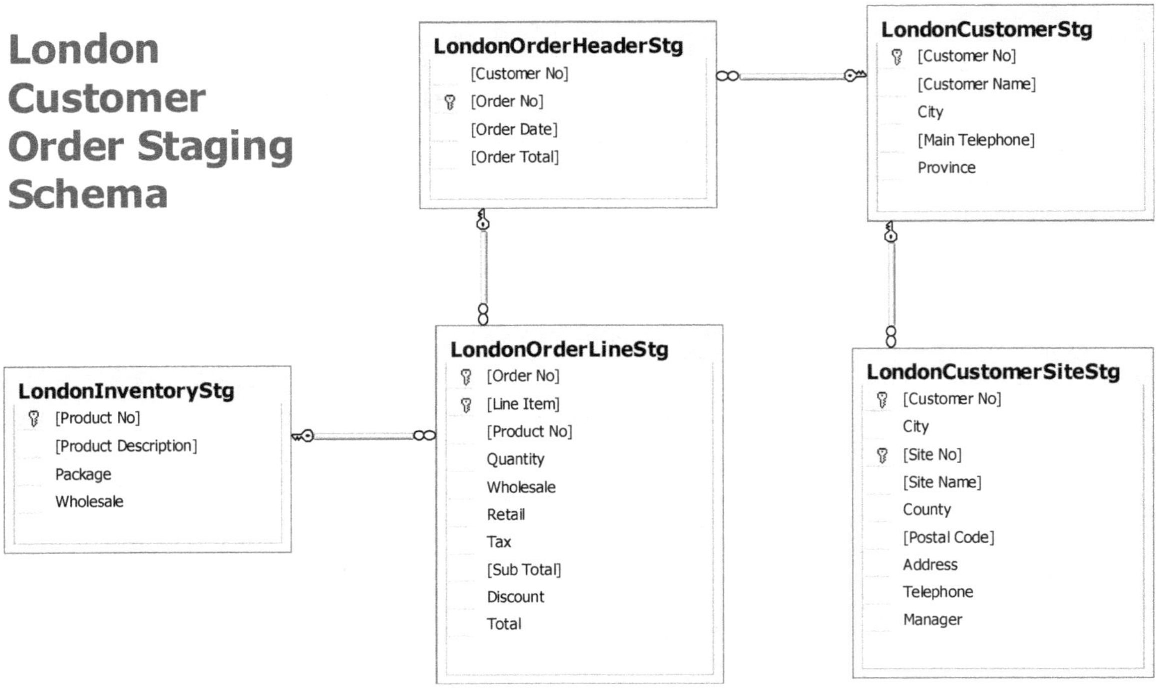

Figure 5.2 - The London Customer Order Data Model

Figure 5.2 presents the physical data model for the London Customer Order Data Model. Notice some columns have square brackets around the names. When SQL Server generates the table definitions, if a column name has a space it adds brackets around the name so that no errors occur when creating the table or using the column in a query.

The model is a bit more complex this time with five tables and more composite keys. It supports the following relationship rules:

- An order can contain one or more associated order lines (LondonOrderHeaderStg and LondonOrderLineStg tables).
- An order line can identify an inventory product (LondonOrderLineStg, LondonInventoryStg tables).
- A single product can appear on one or more order lines (LondonOrderLineStg, LondonInventoryStg tables).
- A customer can place one or more orders (LondonCustomerStg, LondonOrderHeaderStg tables).
- A customer can own one or more sites (LondonCustomerStg, LondonCustomerSiteStg tables).

Can anyone spot the one of the weaknesses in this model? We have no way of identifying which customer site the order belongs to. We will have to address this issue in our ODS. The logical data dictionary for the product table appears in Table 5.9.

Column	Data Type	Length	Description
Product No	Text	6	This is the unique identifier for the product.
Product Description	Text	256	This is the description for the product.
Package	Text	32	This is a description of how the product is packaged.
Wholesale	Decimal	5,2	This is the wholesale price of the product.

Table 5.9 - The London Product Table Data Dictionary

This table stores basic product information such as the product description, packaging description and wholesale price. There is a single primary key, the Product No column.

The data dictionary for the physical staging table that receives this data appears in Table 5.10.

Target Column	Target Data Type
Product No	nvarchar(6)
Product Description	nvarchar(255)
Package	nvarchar(255)
Wholesale	money

Table 5.10 - The London Product Staging Table (LondonInventoryStg) Data Dictionary

Notice the data types assigned by SQL Server. Again, I manually assigned the money data type to the wholesale column.

Next we turn our attention to the data dictionary for the London Customer database table. This data dictionary appears in Table 5.11.

Column	Data Type	Length	Description
Customer No	Text	5	This is the unique identifier for the customer.
Customer Name	Text	256	This is the customer's name.
Province	Text	256	This is the name of the province where the customer is located.
City	Text	256	This is the name of the city where the customer is located.
Main Telephone	Number	256	This is the customer's main telephone number.

Table 5.11 - The London Customer Data Dictionary

We have a single column primary key for this table. No problem here. We do have a flaw in the design in that we find the Province Name, City and Main Telephone Number columns. Main Telephone Number is probably OK but the Province and City columns should belong in the Customer Site table. They are redundant here and could cause data quality problems.

This is another design flaw we want to correct in the final ODS model. One possible solution is to include a Customer Site Type column in the Customer Site table or Customer Location table that could be used to differentiate customer sites as either being the main site, store sites, inventory sites or other types of sites.

The data dictionary for the staging table that was created to accept customer data from the Excel spreadsheet tab appears in Table 5.12.

Target Column	Target Data Type
Customer No	nvarchar(5)
Customer Name	nvarchar(255)
Province	nvarchar(255)
City	nvarchar(255)
Main Telephone	nvarchar(32)

Table 5.12 - The London Customer Staging Table (LondonCustomerStg) Data Dictionary

Notice the large lengths of the nvarchar columns that SQL Server assigned.

Next is the logical data dictionary for the London Customer Site table that was created using the physical data dictionary as a starting point. This appears in Table 5.13.

Column	Data Type	Length	Description
Customer No	Text	5	This is the unique identifier for the customer.
Site No	Number	3	This is a unique identifier for the customer site identifier.
Site Name	Text	128	This is the name of the customer site.
County	Text	128	This is county where the customer is located.
City	Text	64	This is the name of the city where the customer is located.
Postal Code	Text	32	This is the postal code for the customer's address.
Address	Text	256	This is the street address of the customer.
Telephone	Text	7	This is the customer's main telephone number.
Manager	Text	64	This is the full name of the customer site manager.

Table 5.13 - The London Customer Site Data Dictionary

We have a complex composite primary key. It is made up of two columns, Customer No and Site so as to support the rule that a customer can have one or more sites. The Customer No column also plays a role as the foreign key to the Customer table.

Notice the address information. Notice that we include a County attribute. Now if we refer back to the Customer table this might make sense that we include the Province column in the Customer table and the County column in the Customer Site table as a Province may contain one or more columns.

But what happens if a customer is located in more than one province? Then this design is still flawed. We definitely need to move the Province column to the Customer Site table. This design would support a customer being located in one or more provinces of a country and that a customer can have one or more sites in counties belonging to the province.

The data dictionary for the staging table that supports London Customer Site data appears in Table 5.14.

Target Column	Target Data Type
Customer No	nvarchar(5)
Site No	smallint
Site Name	nvarchar(255)
County	nvarchar(255)
City	nvarchar(255)
Postal Code	nvarchar(255)
Address	nvarchar(255)
Telephone	nvarchar(255)
Manager	nvarchar(255)

Table 5.14 - The London Customer Site Staging Table (LondonCustomerSiteStg) Data Dictionary

Again we see the default data type conversions that reflect mapping from one vendor database platform to another (In our case, Excel to SQL Server).

Let's now focus our attention to the order related tables, specifically the order header and order line tables. Table 5.15 below displays the logical data dictionary for the London Order Header table.

Column	Data Type	Length	Description
Customer No	Text	5	This is the unique identifier for the customer.
Order No	Text	8	This is the unique order number for a customer order.
Order Date	Date		This is the date that the customer placed the order.
Order Total	Decimal	10,2	This is the total price of the entire customer order.

Table 5.15 - The London Order Header Data Dictionary

As can be seen we have a single column primary key for this order table. It is the Order No column. We also have a foreign key that supports the relationship between the customer table and the order header table. It helps to enforce the rule that a customer can make one or more orders. Each time a customer enters an order a new unique Order No is generated.

If we wanted to reuse order numbers between customers we would have had to include the Customer No column as part of the primary key. We will need to see how the other databases implement the order number scheme. Fortunately for us we only need to worry about the Torino database in this simple example.

Sometimes, as part of the analysis, it is helpful to look at samples of the data. Table 5.16 shows us a sample of the order header data for the London Order Header table.

Customer No	Order No	Order Date	Order Total
10001	ORD-0001	10/1/2011	£579.98
10001	ORD-0002	10/1/2011	£339.63
10001	ORD-0003	10/1/2011	£935.28
10001	ORD-0004	10/1/2011	£1,483.90
10001	ORD-0005	10/2/2011	£543.40
10002	ORD-0006	10/2/2011	£862.13
10002	ORD-0007	10/2/2011	£1,238.33
10002	ORD-0008	10/2/2011	£418.00
10002	ORD-0009	10/2/2011	£1,186.08
10002	ORD-0010	10/2/2011	£538.18
10002	ORD-0011	10/2/2011	£1,139.05
10003	ORD-0012	10/3/2011	£156.75
10003	ORD-0013	10/3/2011	£1,719.03
10003	ORD-0014	10/3/2011	£2,126.58
10003	ORD-0015	10/3/2011	£1,285.35
10003	ORD-0016	10/3/2011	£360.53
10004	ORD-0017	10/4/2011	£731.50
10004	ORD-0018	10/4/2011	£1,429.04
10004	ORD-0019	10/4/2011	£2,006.40
10004	ORD-0020	10/4/2011	£642.68
10004	ORD-0021	10/4/2011	£530.34
10005	ORD-0022	10/5/2011	£203.78
10005	ORD-0023	10/5/2011	£1,606.69
10005	ORD-0024	10/5/2011	£794.20
10005	ORD-0025	10/5/2011	£1,193.91
10005	ORD-0026	10/5/2011	£721.05
			£24,771.73

Table 5.16 - London Customer Order Data Dump

Here we can clearly see the order number scheme we described. Notice that order numbers are all unique and are never repeated across customers. With this scheme and also with the way that the order number data element is structured, we can only support 9999 orders for each customer before we run out. Another design flaw we need to address in our ODS design.

Schema integration also surfaces design flaws as we have just seen. It is an opportunity to improve on the design and create an ODS that can support better business rules.

The physical data dictionary for the staging table that was used as the basis for the logical data dictionary appears in Table 5.17.

Target Column	Target Data Type
Customer No	nvarchar(5)
Order No	nvarchar(8)
Order Date	datetime
Order Total	money

Table 5.17 - The London Order Header Staging Table (LondonOrderHeaderStg) Data Dictionary

No worries here, just the usual data type conversions. Right now we simply wish to create buckets in the form of staging tables that will receive the raw data from the source database. The most we wish to accomplish is to make some simple data type conversions that support the underlying target data types. Again, in this case I manually assigned the money data type.

Last but certainly important is the logical data dictionary for the order line table. This appears in Table 5.18.

Column	Data Type	Length	Description
Order No	Text	8	This is the unique identifier for the customer.
Line Item	Number		This is the line item number for the customer. Together with the order number it makes up the primary key.
Product No	Text	6	This is the unique identifier for the product.
Quantity	Number		This is the quantity ordered on the line item.
Wholesale	Decimal	10,2	This is the wholesale price of the item ordered.
Retail	Decimal	10,2	This is the retail price of the item ordered.
Tax	Decimal	10,2	This is the tax amount on the item ordered.
Sub Total	Decimal	10,2	This is the sub total(retail amount plus tax).
Discount	Decimal	5,2	This is any discount applied to the item ordered.
Total	Decimal	10,2	This is the total amount of the line item (subtotal minus discount) multiplied by quantity.

Table 5.18 - The London Order Line Data Dictionary

The primary key for this table is a composite primary key composed of the Order No and Line Item columns. The data dictionary also shows that there is a foreign key implemented with the Product No column. This establishes a relationship with the product inventory table. We certainly would not want to generate an order line for an order without a product appearing in it. Our coffee company would never make any money!

This table has a lot of pricing information in it such as the wholesale and retail price of the product. It also contains tax, discount and sub-total information and total price information. The Total column is calculated as can been seen by the description for this column in the data dictionary.

A partial data dump report to help us with our analysis appears in Table 5.19.

Column	Data Type	Length	Description
Order No	Text	8	This is the unique identifier for the customer.
Line Item	Number		This is the line item number for the customer. Together with the order number it makes up the primary key.
Product No	Text	6	This is the unique identifier for the product.
Quantity	Number		This is the quantity ordered on the line item.
Wholesale	Decimal	10,2	This is the wholesale price of the item ordered.
Retail	Decimal	10,2	This is the retail price of the item ordered.
Tax	Decimal	10,2	This is the tax amount on the item ordered.
Sub Total	Decimal	10,2	This is the sub total(retail amount plus tax).
Discount	Decimal	5,2	This is any discount applied to the item ordered.
Total	Decimal	10,2	This is the total amount of the line item (subtotal minus discount) multiplied by quantity.

Table 5.19 - The London Order Line Data Dictionary

And finally, the physical data dictionary for the staging table that was used as the basis for the logical data dictionary appears in Table 5.20.

Target Column	Target Data Type
Order No	nvarchar(8)
Line Item	smallint
Product No	nvarchar(6)
Quantity	integer
Wholesale	money
Retail	money
Tax	money
Sub Total	money
Discount	decimal(5,2)
Total	money

Table 5.20 - The London Order line Staging Table (LondonOrderLineStg) Data Dictionary

I used the same approach as with the other spreadsheet tabs. Let SSIS create the default table DDL prior to loading the data. Make any manual name and/or data type changes, load the data and then create the logical data dictionary.

Reverse Engineering the Torino Database

Next we turn our attention to the database used by the company based in Torino. This is based on a series of Microsoft Access tables. Luckily for us there are only 3 tables. The physical data model for this database appears in Figure 5.3.

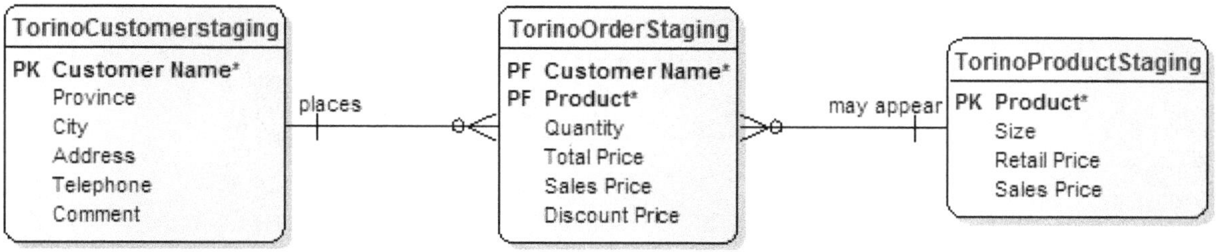

Figure 5.3 - The Order Data Model for Torino

As stated earlier, I cheated a bit in order to generate the data model. By using SQL Server's ETL tool, I can create ETL flows that load the spreadsheet tabs into raw relational staging tables. I can then generate the data models with SQL Server's built in model drawing tool and add relationships.

After the models are created I generate the physical data dictionaries and use them as the basis for the logical data dictionaries. It is the logical data dictionaries that we use in the schema integration process. Figure 5.4 depicts the SSIS tasks and connections I used to create the staging tables and load the data from the Access tables.

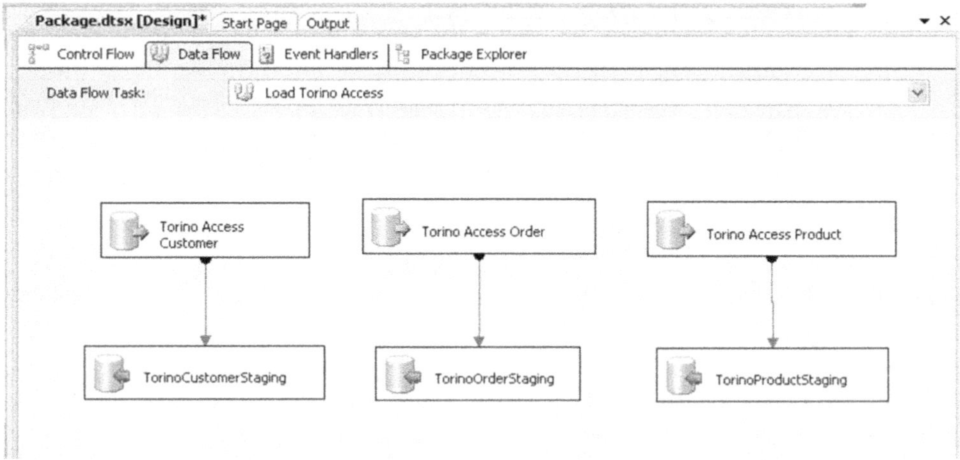

Figure 5.4 - Creating and Loading SQL Server Tables from Access

The boxes at the top of each flow allow you to define connections to the data source, in this case a tab in an Excel spreadsheet. The boxes at each end of the 3 flows allow you to define the target of the flow. In this case a relational table. The tool allows you to define the mappings between source and target data objects as shown in Figure 5.5.

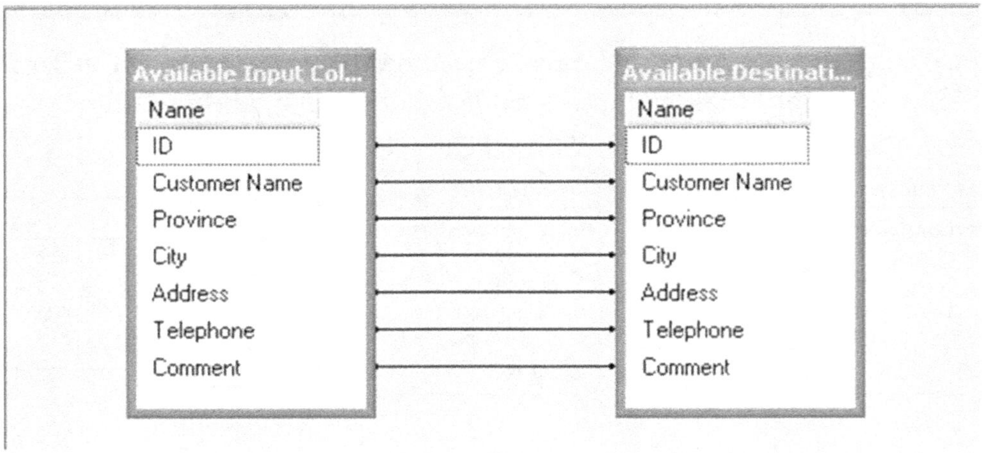

Figure 5.5 - Defining Mappings between the Spreadsheet Tab and the Destination Table

By double clicking on the green data flow lines we can map the source columns to the destination columns. As can be seen, the source and destination columns need not be in the same order. The data physical dictionary for the target table appears in Table 5.21.

Column	Data Type	Length	Description
Customer Name	Text	256	This is the name of the customer that places the order.
Province	Text	256	This is the name of the province where the customer resides.
City	Text	256	This is the name of the city where the customer resides.
Address	Text	256	This is the street address where the customer resides.
Telephone	Text	64	This is the telephone number for the customer.
Comment	Text	256	This is any comment related to the customer.

Table 5.21 - Torino Customer Data Dictionary

We assign a length of 256 to all the columns for now except for the telephone column which is assigned a length of 64.

The data dictionary for the physical staging table appears next. Notice the generated target data type and lengths so as to accommodate SQL Server data types.

We only have seven alphanumeric characters for the telephone number in the spreadsheet SQL Server assigned and nvarchar(7) data type for this column.

Therefore, we increase it to 64 characters in the logical data model in case we need to accommodate large numbers that include country and area codes.

Logical Column	Physical Column	Target Data Type
Customer Name	CUST_NAME	nvarchar(128)
Province	CUST_PROVINCE	nvarchar(128)
City	CUST_CITY	nvarchar(64)
Address	CUST_ADDRESS	nvarchar(128)
Telephone	CUST_TEL	nvarchar(7)
Comment	CUST_COMMENT	nvarchar(255)

Table 5.22 - The Customer Staging Table (TorinoCustomerStg) Data Dictionary

As a slight variation I also included an extra column to show the physical name. It is good practice to display the logical name and also the corresponding physical name. I only show it here as an alternative and will not do it for the other tables so as to save space.

Again, notice the change in data types to comply with SQL Server 2008 data types. The data types could change multiple times during the schema integration process in order to accommodate any differences in the data types found in the columns of subsequent schemas being integrated.

Next we look at the physical data dictionaries that were the basis for our logical data dictionaries for the product tables. The first data dictionary appears in Table 5.23.

Column	Data Type	Length	Description
Product Name	Text	256	This is the name of the product that appears on the order.
Size	Text	128	This is the size of the product.
Retail Price	decimal	10,2	This is the retail price of the product.
Sales Price	decimal	10,2	This is the wholesale price of the product.

Table 5.23 - The Product Data Dictionary

The corresponding physical data dictionary that was generated from the staging table appears in Table 5.24.

Target Column	Target Data Type
Product Name	nvarchar(255)
Size	nvarchar(255)
Retail Price	money
Sales Price	money

Table 5.24 - The Product Physical Staging Table (TorinoProductStaging) Data Dictionary

The approach of generating generic logical data dictionaries can be used to create a vendor agnostic data model. This way, if you decide to use a different target database, like let's say Oracle, you can assign Oracle data types once the final integrated ODS schema is completed.

Another valuable analysis tool is to also take sample data dumps so we have examples of what the data looks like. This will aid us in the analysis. (I did not do it for all the staging tables in the interest of saving space.)

Table 5.25 displays a sample data dump of the product spreadsheet.

Product Name	Size	Retail Price	Sales Price
Baci Perugina	12 Pieces	€ 6.00	€ 7.50
Baci Perugina	24 Pieces	€ 10.00	€ 12.50
Baci Perugina	32 Pieces	€ 20.00	€ 25.00
Baci Perugina	64 Pieces	€ 40.00	€ 50.00
Ganduiotti	12 Pieces	€ 6.00	€ 7.50
Ganduiotti	24 Pieces	€ 10.00	€ 12.50
Ganduiotti	32 Pieces	€ 20.00	€ 25.00
Ganduiotti	64 Pieces	€ 40.00	€ 50.00
Torrone	1/4 Kilogram	€ 6.00	€ 7.50
Torrone	1/2 Kilogram	€ 10.00	€ 12.50
Torrone	1 Kilogram	€ 20.00	€ 25.00
Baci Di Dama	Small Box	€ 10.00	€ 12.50
Baci Di Dama	Medium Box	€ 20.00	€ 25.00
Baci Di Dama	Large Box	€ 40.00	€ 50.00

Table 5.25 - Physical Data Dump of the Product Table

Sample data allows us to really understand the semantics behind each of the column names so we can better integrate the data with the other related tables that will be merged when additional schema are integrated.

A good set of design and analysis documentation includes data models, data dictionaries and sample data for starters. Additionally, you might want to give the analyst the capability to view or query the source data.

Next we turn our attention to the order table. The data dictionary for this table appears in Table 5.26. Recall that this table serves as both the order header and order line so we will need to perform some splitting of the data so as to load it into an order header table and an order line table.

Column	Data Type	Length	Description
Customer Name	Text	256	This is the name of the customer that placed the order.
Product	Text	256	This is the product that the customer ordered.
Quantity	Text		This is the quantity of the product ordered.
Total Price	Decimal	10,2	This is the total price of the product ordered. (Retails Price times Quantity)
Discount	Decimal	10,2	This is any discount applied to the order.
Sales Price	Decimal	10,2	This is the wholesale price of the product.
Order Date	Date	10,2	This is the date the order was placed.

Table 5.26 - The Order Data Dictionary

The physical data dictionary for the staging table appears in Table 5.27.

Target Column	Target Data Type
Customer Name	nvarchar(255)
Product	nvarchar(255)
Quantity	int
Total Price	money
Discount	decimal(5,2)
Sales Price	money
Order Date	datetime

Table 5.27 - The Order Physical Staging Table (TorinoOrderStaging) Data Dictionary

Notice how SQL Server retained the same names for the columns it found in the Access tables. For now this is OK as we want to easily be able to back track where the data came from in case there are any issues.

If you are using other database or ETL tools, expect the same type of behavior. The ETL tool will attempt to convert the source data types to default target data types for the columns. You have the choice to accept the default types or change them as required.

Reverse Engineering the Paris Database

Lastly we turn our attention to the database used by the company in Paris France called "Cakes of Europe" that will become part of the Café Magnifico Empire.

This company specializes in baking specialty cakes from France, Belgium, Munich, Austria, Switzerland and Italy. The cakes are baked at various locations, frozen and then placed in inventories. It's main customers are distributers that order the cakes and then resell them to restaurants, cafes and supermarkets. This is the biggest company being absorbed in the Cafe Magnifico Empire.

The database that is used in each of the locations is based on a MySQL open source database. Figure 5.6 contains the reverse engineered model for this.

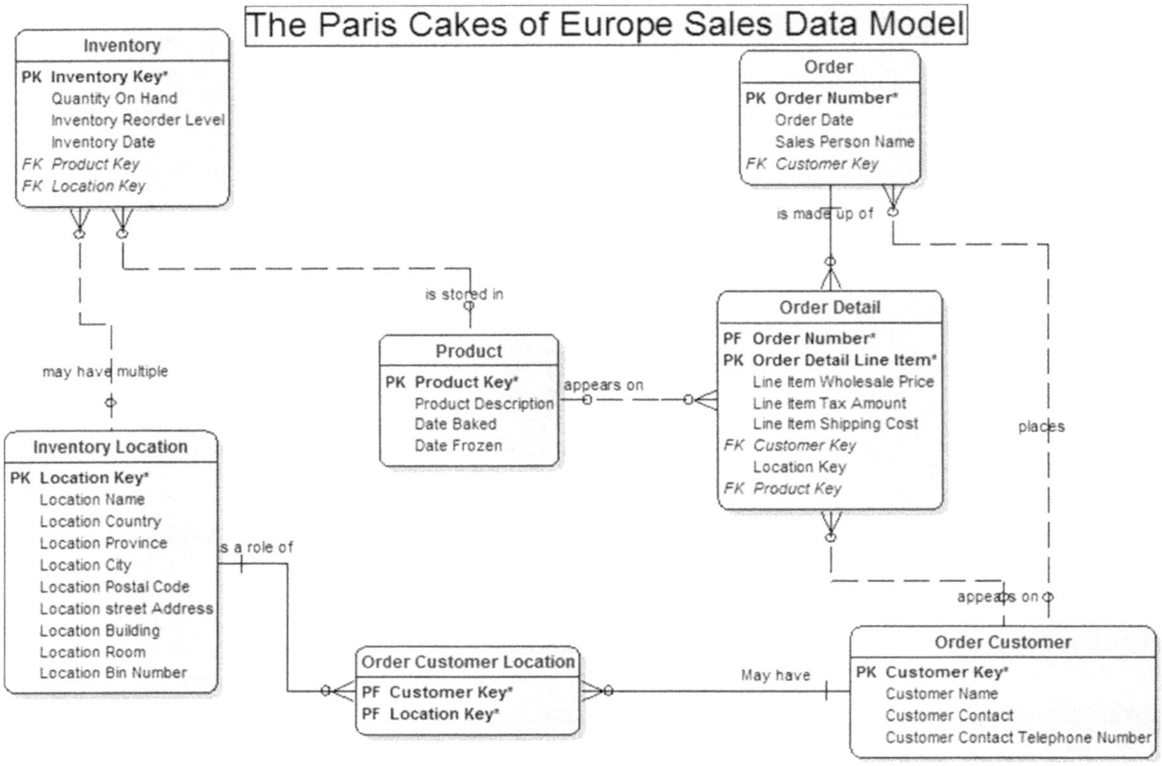

Figure 5.6 - The (Paris) Cakes of Europe Sales Data Model

Some areas of interest are apparent. Notice that we have a pretty detailed inventory subject area. By the relationships we can see that a product can be stored in one or more inventory locations. This is important because a cake baked in Belgium can be shipped to inventories in other countries so as to be available to local distributor customers. Also, an inventory may span more than one location if multiple warehouses for the cakes exist. Notice how the product table has columns for quality control. These columns show when the cake was baked and then frozen. Each cake has a frozen shelf life of three months so we want to make sure that the product is of highest quality for the customers.

The order table is also interesting. It only has the order number, order date, sales person name and the customer key. All details about the order are kept in the order detail table.

Also notice how the location table performs double duty. It identifies locations for the company's inventory locations but it also identifies locations for a customer's inventory location. The link table called Customer Location supports the business rule that a customer can have more than one location.

Lastly, notice that the customer key and customer location both appear in the Order Detail Table. This supports the rule that a customer can order a single item but that different quantities can be shipped to different customer sites.

Table 5.28 contains a data dictionary that lists the descriptions of each table in the database.

Table Name	Description
Product	This table stored identifiers, descriptions and all related information about a product.
Location	This table holds all attributes related to a location, for example, Country, Province, Address, etc.
Inventory	This table holds all inventory level information for a product. It also identifies where a product inventory location is.
Customer	This table holds all information related to a customer.
Order	This table holds all information related to a customer order header.
Customer Location	This table links customers to all its locations. It also links inventories to all their locations.
Order Detail	This table holds all information related to an order line item.

Table 5.28 - Descriptions of Each Table

So as to be consistent, Table 5.29 contains the data dictionary for the Product table.

Column Name	Data Type	Length	Description
Product Key	INT		This is a unique identifier for a product.
Product Description	VARCHAR	256	This is a description for the product.
Date Baked	DATETIME		This is the date that the product was baked.
Date Frozen	DATETIME		This is the date that the product was frozen.

Table 5.29 - Product Data Dictionary

The product data dictionary table is simple, only a primary key, a description column for the product and the two quality control dates. The data dictionary identifies which column is a key by not only the name but by underlying the column name.

Table 5.30 contains data dictionary for the Location table.

Column Name	Data Type	Length
Location Key	INT	
Location Name	VARCHAR	128
Location Country	VARCHAR	256
Location Province	VARCHAR	256
Location City	VARCHAR	128
Location Postal Code	VARCHAR	12
Location Street Address	VARCHAR	256
Location Building	VARCHAR	64
Location Room	VARCHAR	24
Location Bin Number	VARCHAR	24

Table 5.30 - Location Data Dictionary

The inventory data dictionary is next. It identifies the primary key, some simple inventory level attributes and keys to product and location tables.

Column Name	Data Type
Inventory Key	INT
Quantity On Hand	INT
Inventory Reorder Level	INT
Inventory Date	DATETIME
Product Key	INT
Location Key	INT

Table 5.31 - Inventory Data Dictionary

Notice that foreign key information is identified by italicized column names. The product key establishes the relationship with the product table and the location key establishes the relationship to the location table.

Next we examine the customer data dictionary. This can be seen in Table 5.32.

Column Name	Data Type	Length	Description
Customer Key	INT		This is a unique identifier for a customer.
Customer Name	VARCHAR	128	This is the name of the customer.
Customer Contact	VARCHAR	128	This is the name of the customer contact.
Customer Contact Telephone	VARCHAR	12	This is the telephone number of the customer contact.

Table 5.32 - Customer Data Dictionary

No surprises here, we see a primary key called Customer Key, and minimal customer information such as name, customer contact and customer contact telephone number.

The Order Header data dictionary is shown in Table 5.33. It shows basic order information and the foreign key to the Customer table so as to retrieve key customer data for any order sales document.

Column Name	Data Type	Length
Order Number	INT	
Order Date	DATETIME	
Sales Person Name	VARCHAR	128
Customer Key	INT	

Table 5.33 - Order (Header) Data Dictionary

We also see the Sales Person Name attribute included so we can associate an order to a member of the sales staff.

This next table is considered a bridge or "link" table. It is used to establish the fact that a customer can have one or more locations. We will see a design issue surface when we perform schema integration. Right now we can link the order header to the customer table without a problem. If we try to retrieve address information for a customer on an invoice we could have an issue. The problem is the link table. A customer can have one or more addresses. If we try to generate an order or an invoice for a customer that has multiple addresses how do we select the correct address in a join query used to create a sales document? This is an issue to be solved in the schema integration phase.

Next we look at the customer Location link table data dictionary.

Column Name	Data Type	Length	Description
Customer Key	INT		This is the unique identifier for the customer. It can be used to link to the customer table.
Location Key	INT		This is a unique key for the location. It can be used to link to the Location table to obtain the customer's address information.

Table 5.34 - Customer Location Data Dictionary

This is a typical link table used to resolve many to many relationships. A link table only contains keys and maybe a few codes to categorize the types of links. This supports the fact that a customer can have one or more locations. Also, a location could support one or more customers. For example, in New York you have stores that contain more than one vendor. The address is the same for both.

The Order Detail data dictionary is discussed next.

Column Name	Data Type	Length	Description
Order Number	INT		This is the unique identifier for an order. It can be used to link the order detail to the order table.
Order Detail Line Item	INT		This is column identifies the line item of an order. An order can have one or more line items.
Line Item Wholesale Price	DECIMAL(10,2)		This is the wholesale price for the product in the line item.
Line Item Tax Amount	DECIMAL(10,2)		This is the applicable shipping cost for the product in the line item.
Line Item Shipping Cost	DECIMAL(10,2)		This is the applicable tax amount for the product in the line item.
Customer Key	INT		This is the unique identifier for the customer. It can be used to link to the customer table.
Location Key	INT		This is a unique key for the location. It can be used to link to the Location table to obtain the customer's address information.
Product Key	INT		This is a unique identifier for a product.

Table 5.35 - Order Detail Data Dictionary

Like the other detail tables, this table contains basic order information plus keys to the customer, product, and location tables. Order documents and detailed reports can be generated by joining the tables of interest or creating views to support the details required by the particular document.

Summary

So we have successfully completed our reverse engineering exercise and generated a number of data dictionaries to support our project. Specifically we created a data model and a set of data dictionaries for:

- The London Excel model
- The Torino Access database
- The Munich SQL Server database
- The French MySQL database.

These design documents will be valuable tools for when we begin our schema integration process. Notice that the steps we followed in this chapter follow the methodology we discussed in Chapter 3. Also note that we discovered flaws in the data models and also missing data. This was done on purpose so that when we perform the schema data integration process we can simulate real world scenarios of working with less than perfect data models. One last item, all names and examples, addresses, etc. are fictional and do not represent any actual organizations, people or locations!

Having generated the necessary physical models and data dictionaries in Chapter 5, we now apply schema integration techniques to merge the models of the MS Access database and the model for the Excel spreadsheets into one model. This will be our first interim model which will be merged with the SQL Server physical model so as to produce the second interim schema which will be the basis for the ODS. We will follow the process introduced in Chapter 3 and generate the various data dictionaries that will be used to create the ETL logic for resolving the data conflicts.

We will then merge the interim schema with the Munich SQL Server 2008 schema in order to produce a second interim schema. We will leave the integration of the MySQL database schema to the reader as an exercise.

Reviewing the Data Models

We will begin by reviewing the physical data model for the Munich inventory database. This model is shown in Figure 6.1.

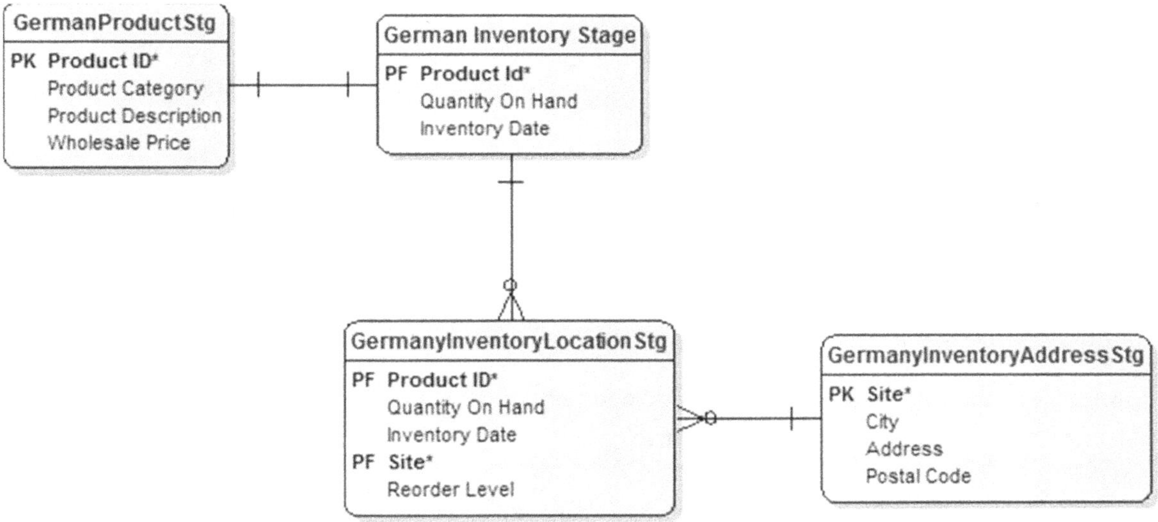

Figure 6.1 - The Munich Inventory Staging Schema

As can be seen this is a simple model with four tables. The product table stores basic product information such as product category, product description and wholesale price.

A product can appear in the inventory table which stores the quantity on hand and the date that inventory was taken.

A product also appears in the Inventory Location table. This table contains columns such as the product key, the site key, the quantity on hand at the physical location, the date that inventory was taken at the site. The primary key is a composite key made up of the product id and site id.

Next we see a relationship between the inventory and inventory location table. This relationship supports the fact that an inventory is made up of one or more physical locations. The main inventory table is used to store all inventory total product levels on hand.

Last but not least is the inventory address table. This table stores the physical location attributes of an inventory site such as City, Address and Postal Code.

In conclusion, this model supports the following business rules:

- An inventory is composed of one or more physical sites.
- A physical site has only one address.
- A physical address can support only one site. (This is a limitation as in real world situations an address could support more than one inventory site.)
- The total inventory levels for all sites for a product are stored in the inventory table.
- The total inventory levels for each physical site are stored in the inventory location.

This is a simple model but it does satisfy the basic requirements for an inventory database.

Next we turn our attention to the London Customer database which is implemented as a series of spreadsheets. This model appears in Figure 6.2.

This model is a bit more complex in that it contains five tables and is used to support customer orders, customers and inventory.

Starting with the customer table we see that it supports basic customer information such as customer number, customer name but also some partial customer location attributes. This could be a problem as they also appear in the customer site table.

We see from the model that a customer can place one or more orders. The order header table contains the minimal information for an order. It includes the order number, order date and order total. The primary key is the order number column and it contains the customer number in order to support the relationship between customers and orders.

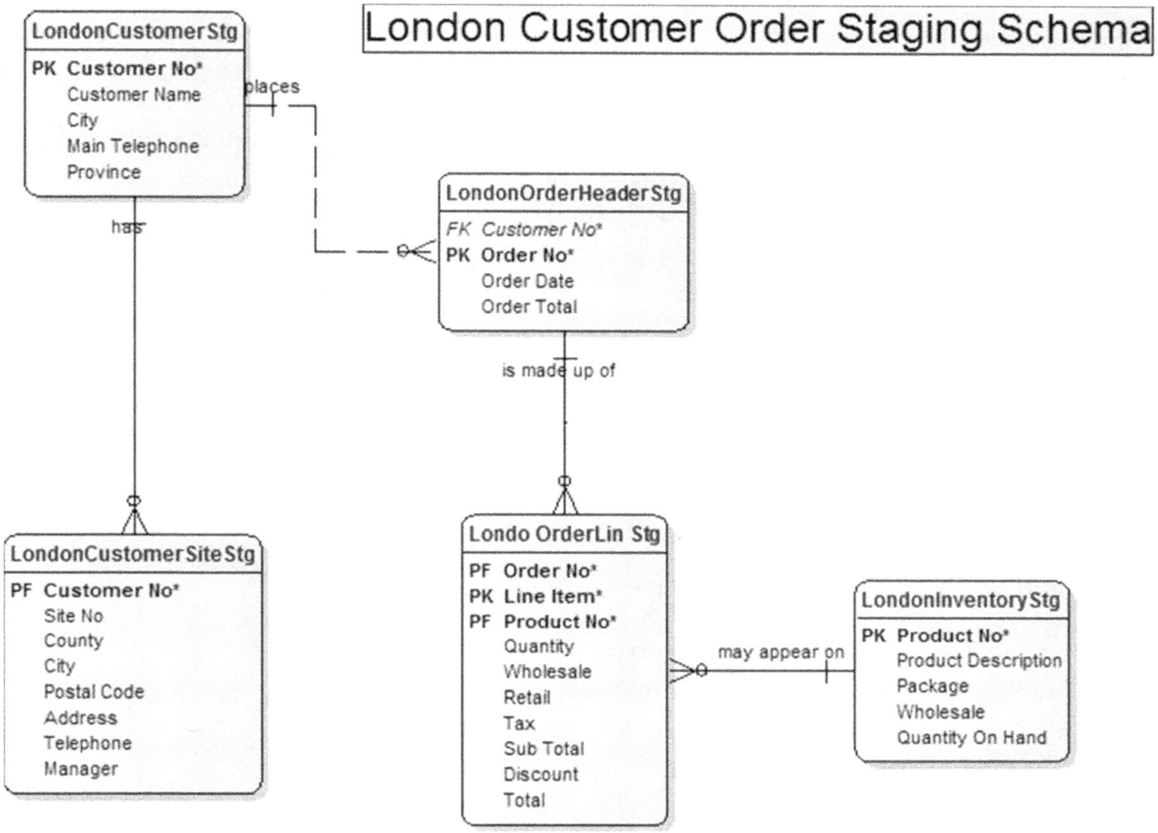

Figure 6.2 - The London Customer Staging Schema

Next, we see that an order is made up of one or more order lines. This is a typical structure for tables used to support orders. The order line table has a composite primary key composed of the order number and a line item number column. Additionally, we include the product number column so we can link a product to an individual order line. Lastly, we include basic order line information such as quantity, wholesales price, retail price, tax amount, subtotal, discount and the total for the order. The order subtotal is calculated as the product quantity times the retail price plus any tax amount. We also apply any discounts so as to calculate the total amount.

Next, the inventory table contains basic information such as product number (which is used as the primary key), the product description, the packaging type description and the wholesale price.

Right off the bat we see a few shortcomings in the model. The wholesale price appears in both the inventory table and order line table. We will consider removing it from the line item table as we can use a join between the inventory table and the line item table in case we need to create some sort of report that needs to display the wholesale price of the product.

We also mention again the partial address information in the customer table. As we have a customer site table that contains the address information for each customer, we can remove the address information from the customer table.

Lastly, examining the customer table we see the basic address information such as city, site number, site name, county, postal code, street address, telephone number and manager name. We notice that a country code or country name is missing. As this database is dedicated to London the country is always assumed to be the United Kingdom. This is a shortcoming though. What if we have customer sites not only in Wales, Scotland, England but also in Ireland and other countries on the European continent? We will have to correct this flaw as we integrate the models.

Summing up, the relationships supported by this model are:

- A customer can place one or more orders.
- An order is made up of one or more order lines.
- A product may appear on one or more order lines.
- A customer can have one or more physical sites.

Again, this is a very simple and basic model. We want all our models to be simple so when we go through the integration process we can apply the techniques against a small set of tables.

Our next database is the Torino Order database, implemented with Microsoft Excel. It appears in Figure 6.3.

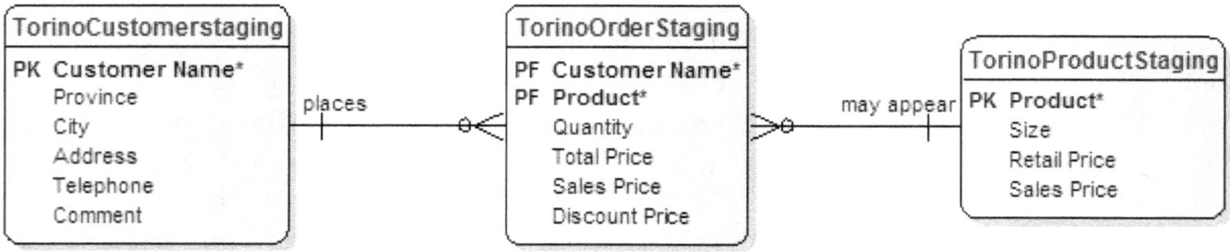

Figure 6.3 - The Torino Order Staging Schema

This is a simple model based on 3 tables. It supports the storing of basic customer, customer order and product information. Notice that there is no order header information, just order line information.

This is a fairly big flaw and demonstrates a structural conflict between this database schema and the London order model. Recall that the London order model was implemented with an order header table and an order line item table. This construct made it easy to sum up totals for each order that was made up of more than one line item.

Let's examine each table starting with the customer table. Here we see basic customer information such as customer name, basic address information plus a telephone column and a general purpose comment column to save comments associated with each customer.

Already we see flaws with this table design. The primary key is the customer's name. What happens if a customer has multiple sites? We need to add a customer number as the primary key. Also, no columns exist to store country information. Italy is implied but what if we start a mail order business that sells products to other customers such as Switzerland? We will have to add, at a minimum, a country name column. Ideally we would create a separate country table and use a country code column in the customer table as a foreign key that supports a relationship between the customer table and country table.

Next we look at the order table. As mentioned before this table is meant to support order lines. Basic information such as customer name (the primary key), product and quantity columns appear. Also, we see basic line item information such as total price, discount amount, sales price and order date.

This is another flawed design we need to fix when we integrate the database schema. The primary key is all wrong - there is no order number information to base the key on. The customer name primary key should be a foreign key used to establish a relationship with the customer table. (Remember that these tables were derived from a simple spreadsheet.) The product column can be used to establish a relationship between the order table and the product table but this should be some sort of product number, not a product name or description.

Last is the product table. This contains basic product information such as the size of the product, the retail and sales price of the product.

A very basic model indeed.

To summarize the business rules supported by the model we see that:

- A customer can place one or more individual orders for an item. (There is no structure to support an order header.)
- A product may appear on one or more orders.

Now that we have familiarized ourselves with the physical database models in scope, we can begin the integration process. Our first task is to analyze each model and identify the common tables and unique tables for each schema.

We did not cover the MySQL data model as we covered it in Chapter 5. Please refer back to Chapter 5 if you need a review of the model.

Defining the Integration Sequence

In order to define the integration sequence, we need to take inventory, so to say, of all the tables in scope. The simplest way to do this is to use a spreadsheet so we can list all the database tables against each of their schema and to assign a subject area name. This scheme is shown in Table 6.1 below.

Schema	Table	Subject Area
Munich	MunichInventoryAddressStg	Inventory
Munich	MunichInventoryLocationStg	Inventory
Munich	MunichInventoryStg	Inventory
Munich	MunichProductStg	Product
London	LondonCustomerSiteStg	Customer
London	LondonCustomerStg	Customer
London	LondonInventoryStg	Inventory
London	LondonOrderHeaderStg	Order
London	LondonOrderLineStg	Order
Torino	TorinoCustomerStg	Customer
Torino	TorinoOrderStaging	Order
Torino	TorinoProductStaging	Product

Table 6.1 - Tables by Schema

After we assign the subject areas we sort by subject area so as to generate the table list shown in Table 6.2.

Notice that this technique allows us to group the tables by subject area so as to suggest the sequence we will use to integrate the databases. The term "subject area" is used by the CA ERwin data modeling tool. It can be considered a term used to logically group tables in common business areas such as customer, inventory, orders, etc.

Schema	Table	Subject Area
London	LondonCustomerSiteStg	Customer
London	LondonCustomerStg	Customer
Torino	TorinoCustomerStg	Customer
Munich	MunichInventoryAddressStg	Inventory
Munich	MunichInventoryLocationStg	Inventory
Munich	MunichInventoryStg	Inventory
London	LondonInventoryStg	Inventory
London	LondonOrderHeaderStg	Order
London	LondonOrderLineStg	Order
Torino	TorinoOrderStaging	Order
Munich	MunichProductStg	Product
Torino	TorinoProductStaging	Product

Table 6.2 - Tables by Subject Area

Looking at our list, we start with the customer subject area. This category contains 3 tables that model the customer and the customer's sites.

By Customer Subject Area

Source	Interim Schema 1
LondonCustomerStg	IS1_Customer
TorinoCustomerStaging	IS1_Customer

Source	Interim Schema 1
LondonCustomerSiteStg	IS1_CustomerSite

Table 6.3 - Integration Sequence 1 - Customer Subject Area

Based on this information, we anticipate integrating the two customer tables and the customer site table will stand alone. We might want to create a simple model at this stage to give us an idea of what the integrated schema might look like. This is shown in Figure 6.4.

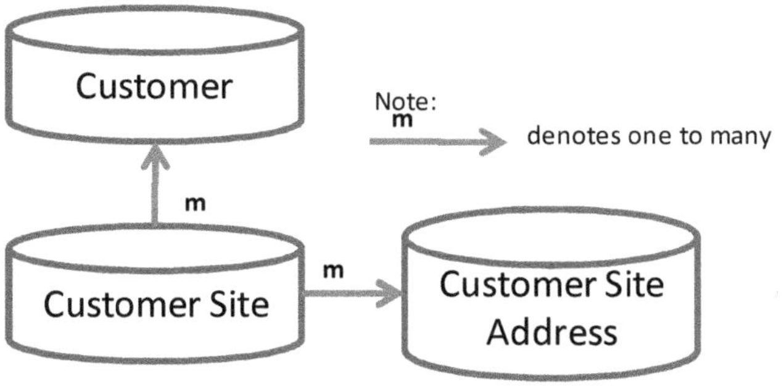

Figure 6.4 - Interim Schema 1 Customer Conceptual Model

We now remind ourselves that we need to support the rule that a physical address can support one or more customer sites.

Our second integration sequence will combine the two product tables. This part of the specification is shown in Table 6.4.

Source	Interim Schema 1
MunichProductStg	IS1_Product
TorinoProductStaging	IS1_Product

Table 6.4 - Integration Sequence 1 - Product Subject Area

No intermediate conceptual model is required here as it is clear we will merge the two product tables. So far, our first interim schema will include the customer tables and the product table.

Our next integration sequence involves the integration of the inventory tables. Luckily for us we have only two tables. Our specification is shown in Table 6.5.

Source	Interim Schema 1
MunichInventoryStg	IS1_Inventory
LondonInventoryStg	IS1_Inventory

Table 6.5 - Integration Sequence 1 - Inventory Subject Area

This concludes the tables and sequences we will use to derive interim schema 1. Our conceptual model at this stage appears in Figure 6.5.

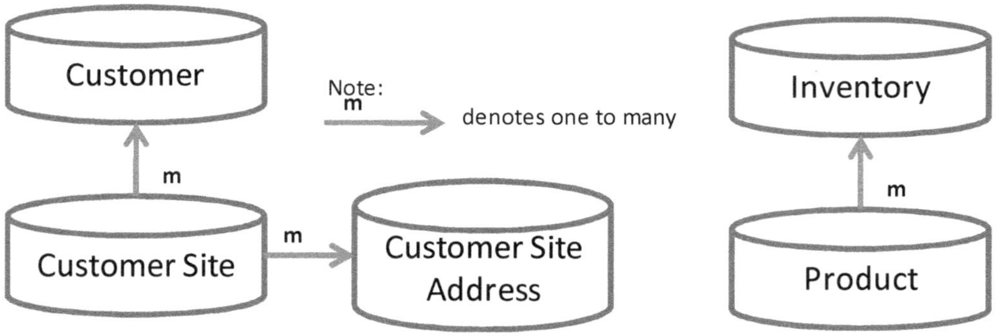

Figure 6.5 - Interim Schema 1 Customer, Product & Inventory Conceptual Model

Again, it is a good technique to create the small (or large) conceptual models as you define the integration sequence. Not only does it give you an indication of what the final integrated conceptual model will look like but it also gives you an opportunity to view your assumptions and make course corrections if a better integration sequence surfaces. A picture is worth a 1000 words!

Next, we examine Integration Sequence 4 which is shown in Table 6.6.

Source	Interim Schema 2
LondonOrderHeaderStg	IS2_Order
TorinoOrderStaging	IS2_Order

Table 6.6 - Integration Sequence 4 - Order Subject Area

Here we have the first of the order tables. We need to integrate orders from the London and Torino database models. Recall that the London model supports an order header/order line table structure while the Torino database model only supports an order line structure. We will address the order header portion for now in this integration sequence. The order line tables will be addressed in Integration Sequence 6.

Our conceptual model now looks appears in Figure 6.6.

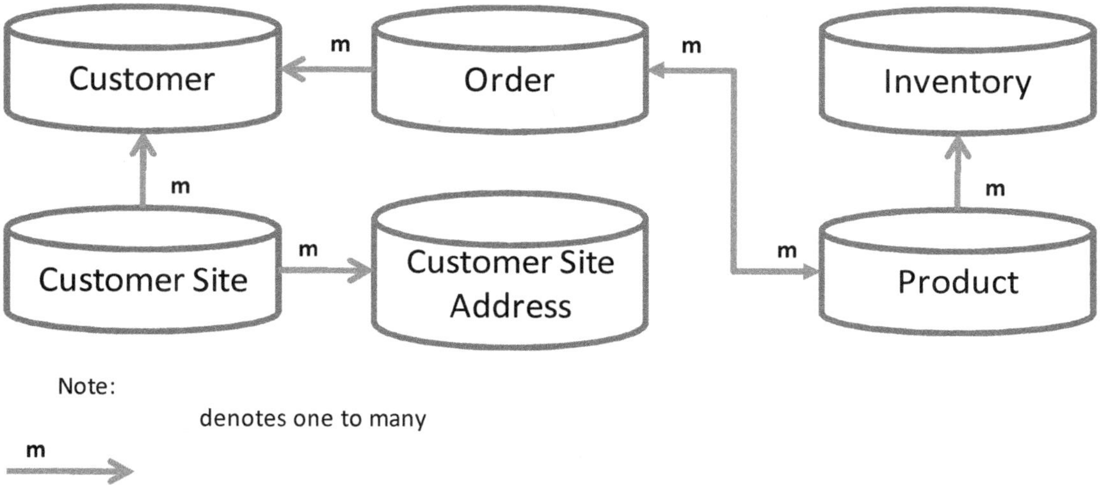

Figure 6.6 - Interim Schema 2: Customer, Product, Inventory & Order Conceptual Model

Our integration sequence is helping us derive our ODS model. The model so far supports the following rules:

- A customer can have one or more sites.
- A customer site address supports one or more customer sites.
- A customer can place one or more orders.
- A product appears in one or more orders.
- An order can include one or more products.
- Inventory records stock levels for one or more products.

So far so good. Let's expand on the inventory subject area with Integration Sequence 5 which is shown in Table 6.7.

By Inventory Subject Area

Source	Interim Schema 2
MunichInventoryAddressStg	IS2_InventoryAddress
MunichInventoryLocationStg	IS2_InventoryLocation

Table 6.7 - Integration Sequence 5 - Inventory Address and Location Subject Area

Here is where we address the location aspects of our inventory tables. Although we do not have to integrate these tables with other schemas we will need to come up with an ETL process to add London's inventory address information to these tables. Recall that the London database had only one table for inventory information while the Munich database has the inventory address information broken out into two tables.

Our revised conceptual model appears in Figure 6.7 (after being tidied up a bit).

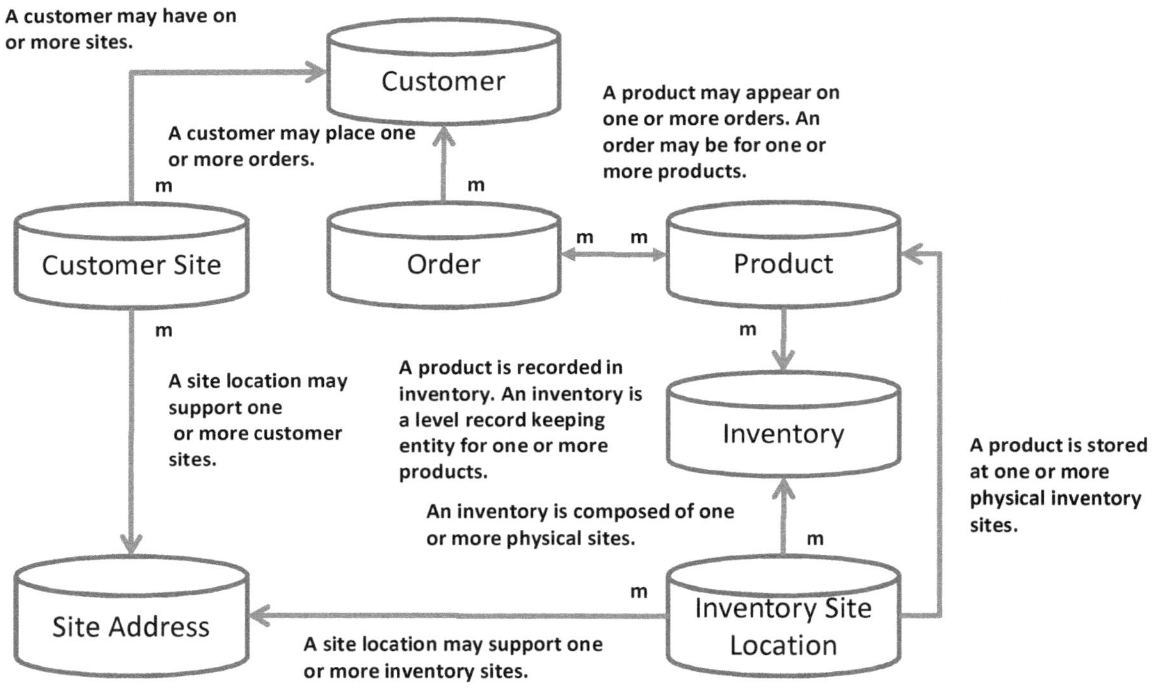

Figure 6.7 - Interim Schema 2: Customer, Product, Inventory, Site & Order Conceptual Model

At this stage the model can be made a bit more informative by adding business rules that describe the relationships between entities. Below is a summary of the business rules:

- A customer can place one or more orders.
- An order is placed by a customer.
- A customer may have one or more sites.
- A site address may support one or more customer sites.
- An order may reference one or more products.
- A product may appear on one or more orders.
- A product's on hand levels are stored in inventory.
- An inventory is composed of one or more physical inventory sites.
- A product may be stored in one or more inventory sites.
- An inventory site is a repository for one or more products.
- A site address may support one or more inventory sites.

Notice how we defined a generic Site Address table. This table can contain addresses for either customer sites or inventory sites. Notice also that there is a many to many relationship between orders and products. Our last integration sequence will resolve this many to many relationship by inserting an order line table.

Last but not least is Integration Sequence 6 which is depicted in Table 6.8. We now need to include the London Order Line table and the Torino Order table into our final interim schema.

Source	Interim Schema 2
LondonOrderLineStg	IS2_Order_Line
TorinoOrderStaging	IS2_Order_Line

Table 6.8 - Integration Sequence 6 - Order Line Subject Area

Recall that the order structure for London included an order header table and an order line table. The Torino database only had a single table that was basically a simple order line table. The Torino database was implemented as three Microsoft Access tables and represented a very basic design to support customer orders. The ETL processes that will load order information will need to split the Torino table into both the order header part and in this integration sequence the order line part.

Our final version (for now) of our conceptual model for our ODS is depict in Figure 6.8.

Our final conceptual model shows how everything should fall in place once we apply our integration sequences. Our model is a simple one but it does illustrate how all three of the source models where combined to form a final ODS structure. We began by reverse engineering the source models to get a lay of the land. The source models were based on an Excel spreadsheet, an Access database, a Microsoft SQL Server 2008 database and a MySQL database.

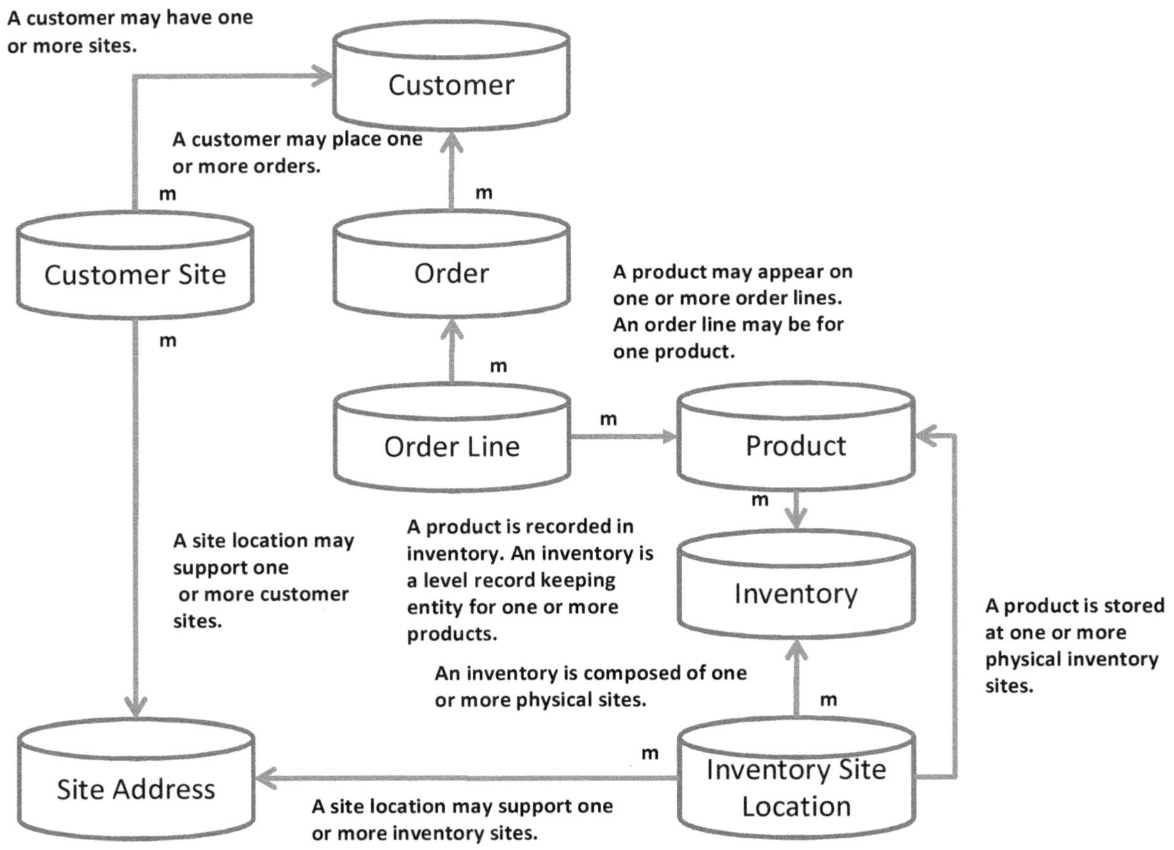

Figure 6.8 - The Final ODS Conceptual Schema

As we mentioned earlier, the fourth model, the MySQL database model we leave to you the reader to integrate it as an exercise. Just follow the steps we will discuss.

Now we are ready to apply the first step in the schema integration process by defining an integration sequence. This allows us to categorize the tables into subject areas. We decided to integrate the models by using the subject areas as our guide. We could have defined the integration sequence based on other criteria, such as meeting business goals or meeting reporting requirements. For example, a business goal would be to derive a global customer master that integrates customer information from various databases.

We now proceed in the integration process by:

- Defining the ETL processes
- Identifying the data conflicts (data type, semantic and structural)

- Developing a physical data dictionary for all the interim schema tables and final ODS tables.

At the end of the process, we will have all of the specifications required to create the tables and ETL code that will load our ODS.

Integration Sequence 1 - Analysis & Conflict Resolution for Customer

Figure 6.9 shows the first of a series of data flow diagrams that specify the ETL processes required to integrate our data.

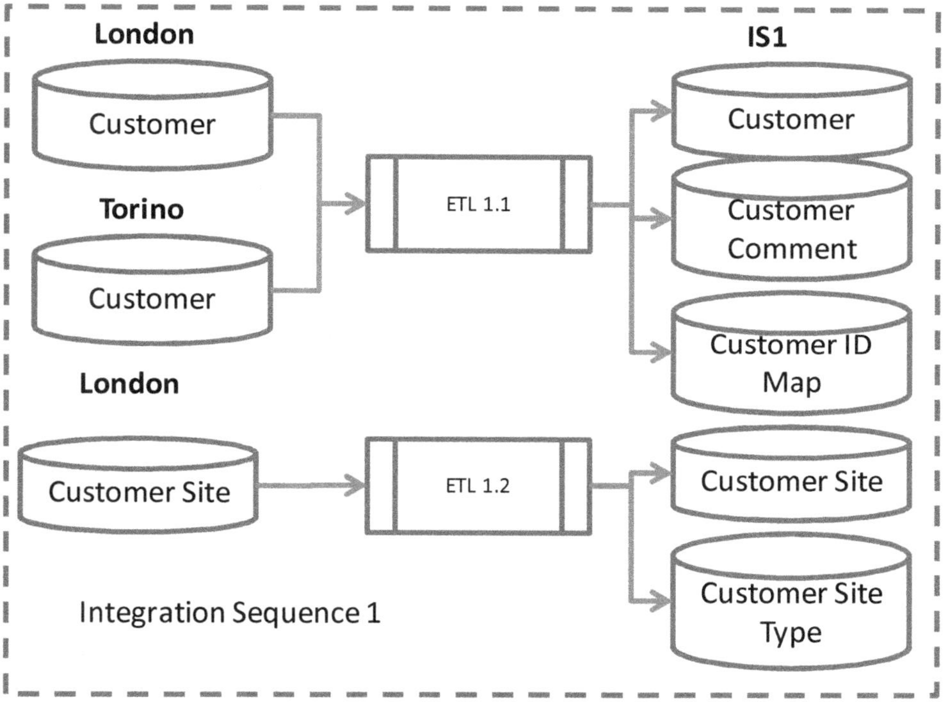

Figure 6.9 - Data Flow for Customer Integration Sequence

Our first integration sequence is for customer data, we identify the source tables on the left side and the target tables on the right side. There are two main ETL processes in the data flow. ETL 1.1 will split out the customer information based on the contents of each table. In addition to basic customer data, we see we need a customer comment table and also a mapping table that will link new customer numbers to old customer numbers. Lastly, we need to load customer site information into a customer site table and also a table that has codes to identify the customer site type. This is addressed by ETL 1.2.

Another data model is called for to provide us with a clear picture of the integrated customer subject area. This is shown in Figure 6.10.

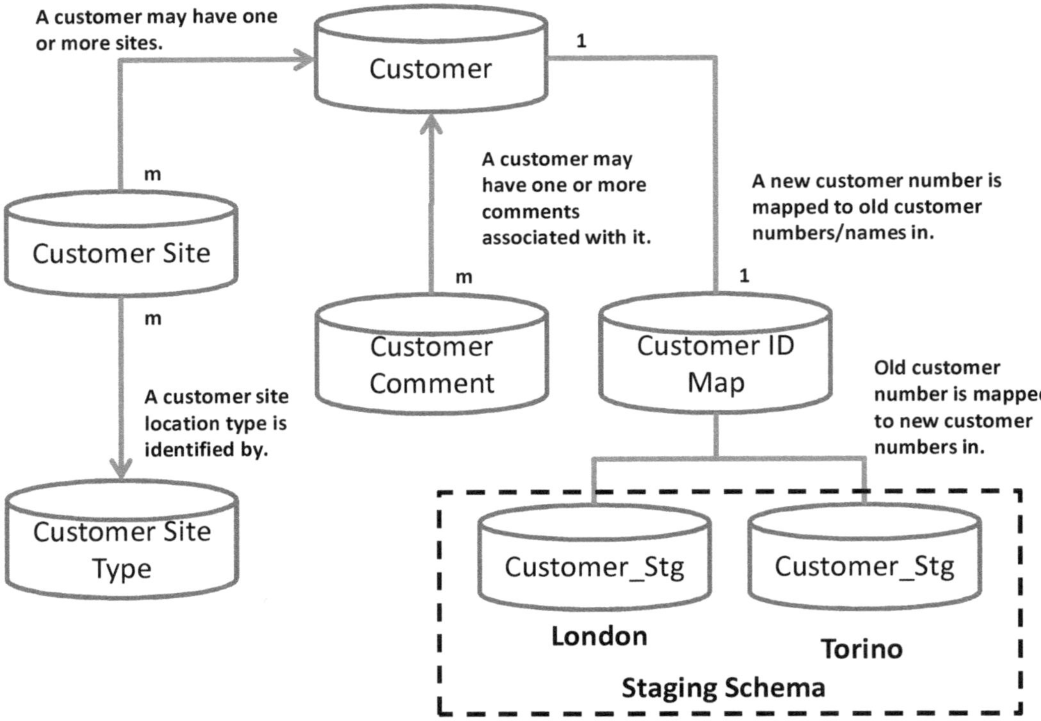

Figure 6.10 - The Enhanced Customer Subject Area in IS1

As can be seen we added two more tables. We now have a customer site type table to help us identify a customer site. This could be a store, inventory location or home address for example. A customer site could also be a restaurant, pub or other type of establishment that sells or purchases our products.

We also added a customer id map table. This mapping table records the mapping between newly generated customer numbers against the old customer numbers. We want a brand new customer numbering schema in our ODS.

Lastly, we include the customer staging tables from London and Torino just to show what customer numbers or names need to be mapped to new customer numbers.

Now, we need to perform our conflict identification and resolution analysis for this subject area. This entails looking at the schema table pair for the customer tables and then identifying the common and unique columns for each pair. For common columns, we need to identify any data conflicts and document them. Columns unique to their schema we leave alone and revisit in the next integration level.

Table 6.9 identifies the source staging tables and then the common/unique column reports.

TorinoCustomerStg

Target Column	Target Data Type
Customer Name	nvarchar(255)
Province	nvarchar(255)
City	nvarchar(255)
Address	nvarchar(255)
Telephone	float
Comment	nvarchar(255)

LondonCustomerStg

Target Column	Target Data Type
Customer No	float
Customer Name	nvarchar(255)
Province	nvarchar(255)
City	nvarchar(255)
Main Telephone	float

LondonCustomerSiteStg

Target Column	Target Data Type
Customer No	float
Site No	nvarchar(255)
Site Name	float
County	nvarchar(255)
City	nvarchar(255)
Postal Code	nvarchar(255)
Address	nvarchar(255)
Telephone	nvarchar(255)
Manager	nvarchar(255)

Table 6.9 - Customer Subject Area Conflict Resolution Analysis

The report is easy to read. (I split the report into two sections for easier readability.)

For reference we include the staging table schema. The common column report contains the most important information. We identify the source schema, the column name, its data type and then the conflict.

Here we see that the Torino and London tables have customer name in common. The conflict is that the Torino table has no primary key whereas the London table has a primary key associated with the customer name. We could say that the Torino table uses the customer name as the primary key in which case we would have a semantic conflict. In this case we identify it as a structural conflict in that one table has a primary key and the other does not.

Common Columns

Schema	Column Name	Data Type	Conflict
Torino	Customer Name	nvarchar(255)	Structural, no PK
London	Customer Name	nvarchar(255)	Structural, has PK
Torino	Province	nvarchar(255)	minor data type
London	Province	nvarchar(255)	minor data type
Torino	City	nvarchar(255)	minor data type
London	City	nvarchar(255)	minor data type
Torino	Telephone	float	Naming, Data Type
London	Main Telephone	float	Naming, Data Type

Schema Unique Columns

Schema	Column Name	Data Type	Conflict
Torino	Comment	nvarchar(255)	minor data type
Torino	Address	nvarchar(255)	minor data type
London	Customer No	nvarchar(5)	Structural, used as PK

Table 6.9a - Customer Subject Area Conflict Resolution Analysis

The remaining conflicts are minor data type or naming conflicts which will be address in the data dictionaries below. As stated earlier, the unique schema columns we leave alone and pass on for analysis in the next integration layer.

Having created the data flow diagram, the supporting data model and the conflict resolution report for this integration sequence, we now need to create data dictionaries for the target IS1 tables. These are shown in Table 6.10.

This data dictionary shows the information we need to create the DDL commands to create the target tables for the interim schema. We also resolve any naming comments and data type conflicts by selecting appropriate data types that will support the loading of the data from both tables.

Customer - Interim Schema 1

Schema	Column Name	Data Type
IS1	**Customer No**	nvarchar(5)
IS1	Customer Name	nvarchar(255)

Customer ID Map - Interim Schema 1

Schema	Column Name	Data Type
IS1	**Customer No**	nvarchar(5)
IS1	Old Customer No	nvarchar(255)
IS1	Schema Name	nvarchar(255)

Customer Comment - Interim Schema 1

Schema	Column Name	Data Type
IS1	**Customer No**	nvarchar(5)
IS1	**CustomerComment No**	nvarchar(5)
IS1	Customer Comment	nvarchar(255)
IS1	Comment Date	Date
IS1	Employee Name	nvarchar(128)

Table 6.10 - Customer, Customer ID Map and Customer Comment Data Dictionary

Next is the data dictionary for the customer site and customer site type IS1 tables. This appears in Table 6.11.

Customer Site - Interim Schema 1

Schema	Column Name	Data Type
IS1	**Customer No**	nvarchar(5)
IS1	**Site No**	smallint
IS1	Site Name	nvarchar(64)
IS1	County	nvarchar(64)
IS1	City	nvarchar(128)
IS1	Postal Code	nvarchar(32)
IS1	Address	nvarchar(128)
IS1	Telephone	nvarchar(7)
IS1	Manager	nvarchar(32)
IS1	***Site Type***	smallint

Customer Site Type - New Interim Schema 1 Table

Schema	Column Name	Data Type
IS1	**Site Type**	smallint
IS1	Site Type Description	nvarchar(255)

Table 6.11 - The Integrated Customer Site Tables

Notice the simple notation I used to identify key information. Primary keys are identified in bold, underlined font. Foreign keys are identified in bold italicized font.

The data dictionaries above represent the minimal information you need to create a table DDL statement, for example:

```
CREATE TABLE [Customer Site]
(
[Customer No]      nvarchar(5) not null,
[Site No]          smallint    not null,
[Site Name]        nvarchar(64),
[County]           nvarchar(64),
[City]             nvarchar(128),
[Postal Code]      nvarchar(32),
[Address]          nvarchar(128),
[Telephone]        nvarchar(7),
[Manager]          nvarchar(32),
[Site Type]        smallint
)
GO
```

Let's proceed with Integration Sequence 2 where we integrate the product tables.

Integration Sequence 2 - Analysis & Conflict Resolution for Product

The ETL process to integrate the two product tables is fairly simple. This is shown in the data flow diagram in Figure 6.11 below.

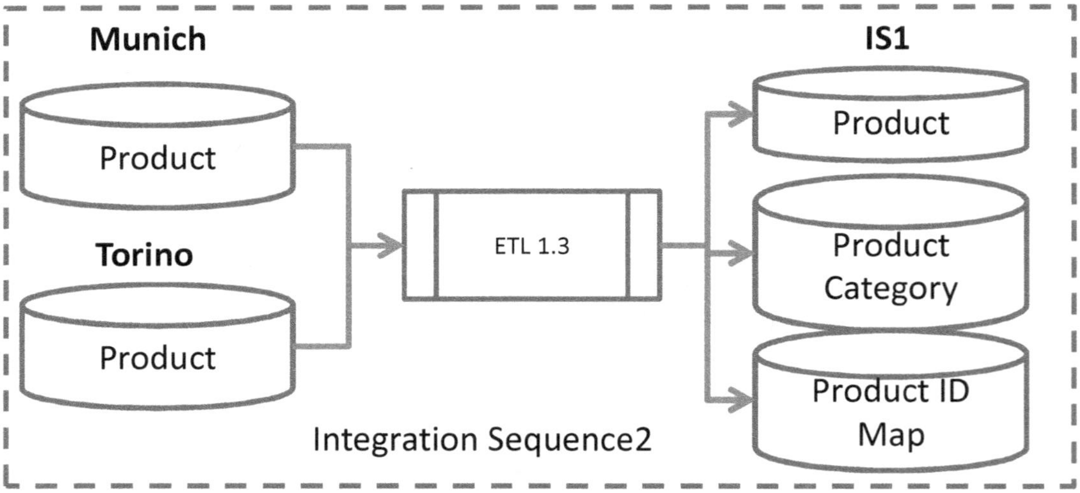

Figure 6.11 - Data Flow for Product Integration Sequence

Data from both tables flows into ETL process ETL 1.3. This step splits out the data into 3 tables: the product table, a product category table and a product id map table. The product id map table works much like the customer id map table. It takes any old product number or name and maps it to a new global product code that will be used in the ODS. The ETL logic will generate the new product number and load it into the mapping table with the old product number. It will also use it in the row that gets loaded into the integrated product table.

The product category table is a new table that contains codes to categorize each product. Lastly, the product table is our basic table that stores product names, characteristics and descriptions.

As before, our next step is to prepare the conflict resolution report shown in Table 6.12.

TorinoProductStaging

Target Column	Target Data Type
Product Name	nvarchar(255)
Size	nvarchar(255)
Retail Price	money
Sales Price	money

MunichProductStg

Target Column	Target Data Type
Product Category	nvarchar(255)
Product ID	nvarchar(9)
Product Description	nvarchar(255)
Wholesale Price	money

Table 6.12 - Unique/Common Product Columns Between Schema Pair for Products

Common Columns

Schema	Column Name	Data Type	Conflict
Munich	Wholesale Price	money	Naming
Torino	Sales Price	money	Naming, semantic

Schema Unique Columns

Schema	Column Name	Data Type	Conflict
Torino	Product Name	nvarchar(255)	Structural, no PK
Torino	Size	nvarchar(255)	none, unique to schema
Torino	Retail Price	money	none, unique to schema
Munich	Product Category	nvarchar(255)	structural, unique
Munich	Product ID	nvarchar(9)	none, unique to schema
Munich	Product Description	nvarchar(255)	none, unique to schema

Table 6.12a - Unique/Common Product Columns Between Schema Pair for Products

Here we are in luck. We have only two common columns. But the data conflicts are messy. We have a naming and semantic conflict between the wholesale price and the sales price columns. In the Munich schema wholesale price implies just that, the wholesale price of the product. In the Torino database the Sales price implies retail price but in actuality it is the wholesale price.

We notate this conflict and make sure data from both columns gets loaded into a target wholesale price column in the integrated table.

The unique columns do have some conflicts or issues related to their implementation in the source database. Notice the product category column. It is a 255 character column but has no primary key associated with it. It contains descriptions of the product categories but has no associated codes for each description.

That is why we created a new product category table so we can associate a new product category code to each description. This product category code will also appear in the product table.

Again we see that the Torino database did not use unique keys with its principal data objects. In this case we have a product name column but no associated product number that we could use as the primary key. This is identified as a structural conflict that is resolved by generating a new product number for the product, inserting it into the new integrated table but also mapping it to the old product name in the product id map table.

It is always good practice to create these types of tables as not only do they assist in creating new keys but also provide a valuable archiving or audit track in case issues arise when loading data into the ODS for the first time or in case of audit requests, like going back and resolving old order issues.

Table 6.13 presents the data dictionaries for the integrated product tables that will appear in interim schema 1 (IS1).

Product - Interim Schema 1

Schema	Column Name	Data Type
IS1	**Product No**	nvarchar(9)
IS1	Product Name	nvarchar(255)
IS1	Product Description	nvarchar(255)
IS1	Product Size	nvarchar(255)
IS1	Product Wholesale Price	money
IS1	Product Retail Price	money
IS1	Product Packaging	nvarchar(255)
IS1	***Product Category***	smallint

Product Category - Interim Schema 1

Schema	Column Name	Data Type
IS1	<u>**Product Category**</u>	smallint
IS1	Product Category Description	nvarchar(255)

Product ID Map - Interim Schema 1

Schema	Column Name	Data Type
IS1	<u>**Product No**</u>	<u>**Product No**</u>
IS1	Old Product No	nvarchar(255)
IS1	Schema Name	nvarchar(255)

Table 6.13 - The Integrated Product Schema

For the sake of completeness let's generate a product subject area model. This is shown in Figure 6.12.

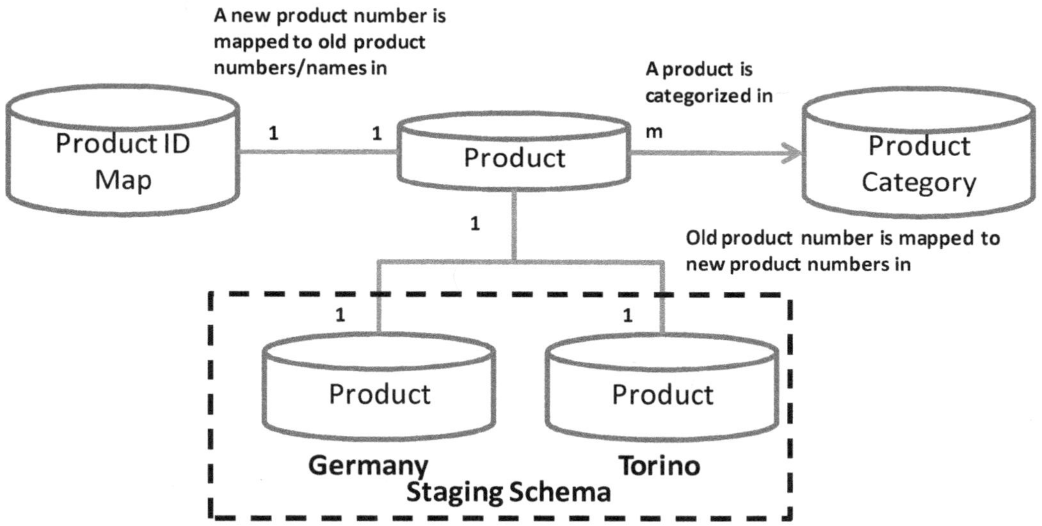

Figure 6.12 - IS1 Product Subject Area

Now that we have the product tables sorted out, we can proceed to address the inventory tables.

Integration Sequence 3 - Analysis & Conflict Resolution

Associated with the product subject area is the inventory subject area. The data flow diagram depicted in Figure 6.13 below shows the integration process we need to follow.

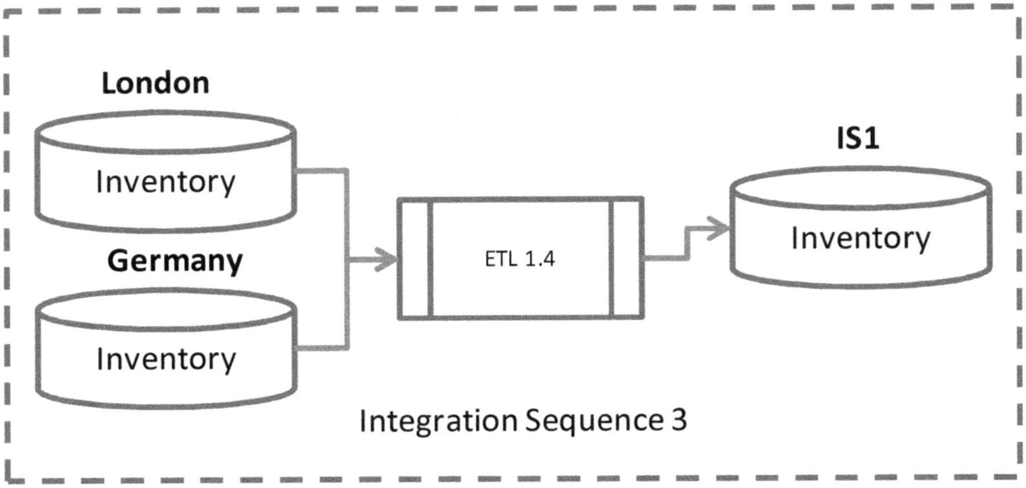

Figure 6.13 - Integration Sequence 3 - Integrating Inventory Data

Recall that the London and Munich databases both have inventory data. This step is simple in that we need to integrate only two tables. ETL process ETL1.4 is used to load data from both tables into staging tables and then perform the mapping and any required conflict resolution steps such as data type conversion or resolution of structural conflicts.

The conflict resolution report is shown in Table 6.14 below.

LondonInventoryStg

Target Column	Target Data Type
Product No	nvarchar(255)
Product Description	nvarchar(255)
Package	nvarchar(255)
Wholesale	money

MunichInventoryStg

Target Column	Target Data Type
Product ID	nvarchar(9)
Quantity On Hand	float
Inventory Date	datetime

MunichInventoryLocationStg

Target Column	Target Data Type
Product ID	nvarchar(9)
Quantity On Hand	float
Inventory Date	datetime
Site	nvarchar(255)
Reorder Level	float

MunichInventoryAddressStg

Target Column	Target Data Type
Site	nvarchar(255)
City	nvarchar(255)
Address	nvarchar(255)
Postal Code	nvarchar(255)
Contact	nvarchar(255)

Table 6.14 - Unique/Common Inventory Columns Between Schema Pair

Common Columns - Inventory

Schema	Column Name	Data Type	Conflict
London	Product No	nvarchar(255)	Naming, data type
Munich	Product ID	nvarchar(255)	Naming, data type

Schema Unique Columns - Inventory

Schema	Column Name	Data Type	Conflict
London	Product Description	nvarchar(255)	Structural, Move to product table
London	Package	nvarchar(255)	Structural, Move to product table
London	Wholesale	money	Structural, Move to product table
Munich	Quantity On Hand	float	Unique
Munich	Inventory Date	datetime	Unique
Munich	Site	nvarchar(255)	Does not exists in London
Munich	City	nvarchar(255)	Does not exists in London
Munich	Address	nvarchar(255)	Does not exists in London
Munich	Postal Code	nvarchar(255)	Does not exists in London
Munich	Contact	nvarchar(255)	Does not exists in London

Table 6.14a - Unique/Common Inventory Columns Between Schema Pair

As before, the source staging tables are presented to the left for reference. We are in luck again as we have only one pair of common columns. London has a Product No column to identify its products and Munich has a Product ID column. This is a minor naming and data type conflict which is easy to solve.

We do have some issues with the unique columns. In the London inventory tables we have product related information which is more suitable for the product table. I call it a structural conflict as we need to move these columns (product description, package and wholesale) out of the inventory table and into the product table.

Lastly, Munich has some unique columns and some address related columns that identify inventory locations that London does not have. We will address how to resolve these in the chapter where we develop specifications for the ETL processes that resolve the conflicts. For now we just want to identify the conflicts, prepare supporting data flow diagrams and some more detailed conceptual models when required.

The data dictionary for the target tables is shown in Table 6.15. Notice the final selection of data types as to the data types in the original staging tables.

Inventory - Interim Schema 1

Schema	Column Name	Data Type
IS1	**Product No**	nvarchar(9)
IS1	Total Quantity On Hand	integer
IS1	Inventory Date	datetime

Inventory Location - Interim Schema 1

Schema	Column Name	Data Type
IS1	**Product No**	nvarchar(9)
IS1	**Site Identifier**	smallint
IS1	Local Quantity On Hand	integer
IS1	Inventory Date	datetime
IS1	Reorder Level	integer

Inventory Address - Interim Schema 1

Schema	Column Name	Data Type
IS1	**Inventory Site Identifier**	smallint
IS1	Inventory Site Name	nvarchar(32)
IS1	Inventory Site City	nvarchar(64)
IS1	Inventory Site Address	nvarchar(255)
IS1	Inventory Site Postal Code	nvarchar(32)
IS1	Inventory Contact	nvarchar(64)

Table 6.15 - The Integrated Inventory Location and Address Schema

Next we look at a detailed conceptual model that relates products to inventory as shown in Figure 6.14.

Having completed all of our reference data (Customer, Product, etc.) we now proceed to the order data.

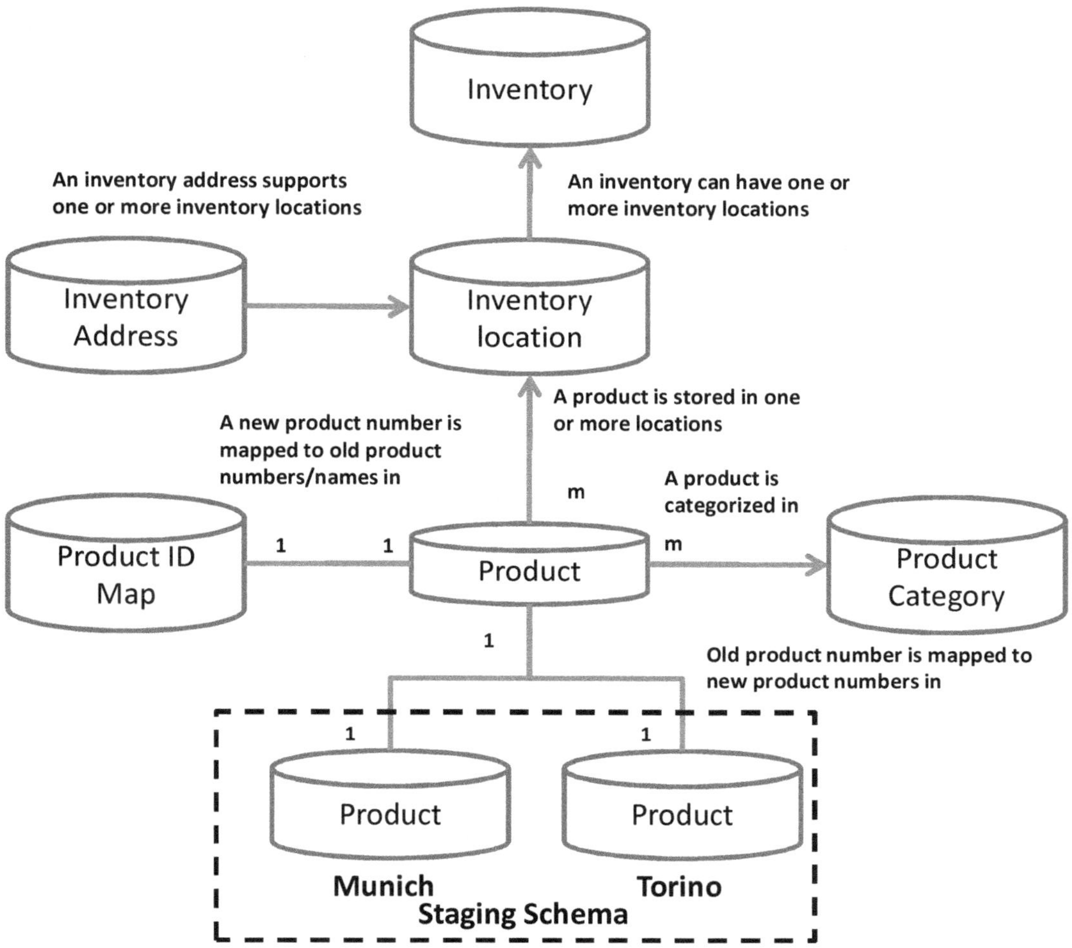

Figure 6.14 - Inventory and Product Subject Areas

Integration Sequence 4 - Analysis & Conflict Resolution

We will revisit the inventory related tables in Integration Sequence 5 but we now turn our attention to the order header subject area in Integration Sequence 4. Figure 6.15 shows the data flow diagram for integrating the order header data.

Recall that we have order information in the London database and in the Torino database. Also recall that the Torino database is implemented as a simple Access database and the order table is really for order lines. No order header is used in this model.

As with customer and product data we will need to generate new order numbers and map them to the old order numbers by using a mapping table. Our data flow diagram shows that we will input the data from both staging tables and merge it into one order (header) table. We will generate new order numbers and insert them together with the old order numbers in the new order id map table.

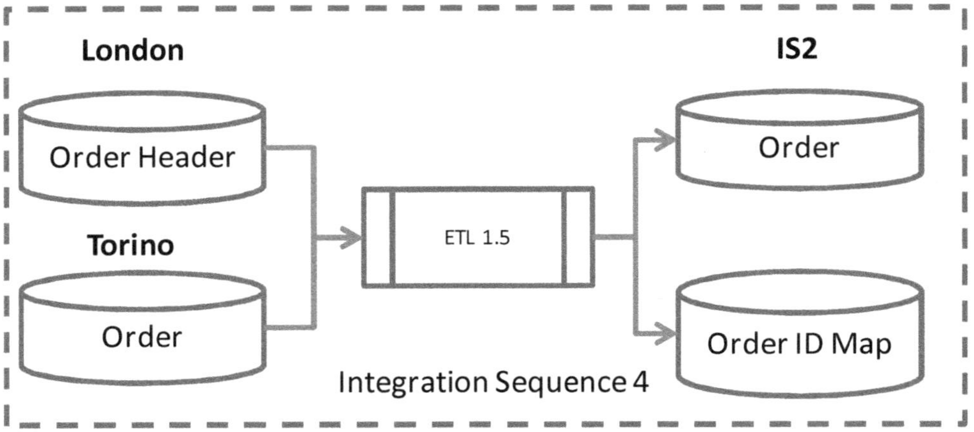

Figure 6.15 - Integration Sequence 4 - Integrating Order Header Data

The data conflict report appears in Table 6.16.

LondonOrderHeaderStg

Target Column	Target Data Type
Customer No	nvarchar(5)
Order No	nvarchar(255)
Order Date	datetime
Order Total	money

LondonOrderLineStg

Target Column	Target Data Type
Order No	nvarchar(255)
Line Item	float
Product No	nvarchar(255)
Quantity	float
Wholesale	money
Retail	money
Tax	money
Sub Total	money
Discount	float
Total	money

TorinoOrderStaging

Target Column	Target Data Type
Customer Name	nvarchar(255)
Product	nvarchar(255)
Quantity	float
Total Price	money
Discount	float
Sales Price	money
Order Date	datetime

Table 6.16 - Unique/Common Order Header Columns Between Schema Pair

Here we have mainly semantic and structural conflicts in that we have missing order number data or have customer names (in the case of the Torino database) that are used as identifiers. This is illustrated in the common column section of our report.

Common Columns - Order

Schema	Column Name	Data Type	Conflict
London	Customer No	nvarchar(5)	semantic & structural (PK)
Torino	Customer Name	nvarchar(255)	semantic & structural (PK)

Schema Unique Columns - Order Header

Schema	Column Name	Data Type	Conflict
London	Order No	nvarchar(255)	semantic & structural (PK)
London	Order Date	datetime	missing in Torino
London	Order Total	money	missing in Torino

Table 6.16a - Unique/Common Order Header Columns Between Schema Pair

London uses a customer number to uniquely identify customers whereas Torino uses the customer name. We will need to look up the new customer number key in the customer id mapping table. This scenario also illustrates how we will need to load all the customer and product reference data first before we load the order related data and the inventory data. We want all our new keys to be generated.

Lastly, as stated earlier, Torino has no concept of an order header or of an order number so we consider this as a semantic and structural conflict as the definition of an order number is missing and that we will have to generate a new one when we load the integrated order header table.

The data dictionary for the target order header table appears in Table 6.17.

Order - Interim Schema 2

Schema	Column Name	Data Type
IS2	**Customer No**	nvarchar(5)
IS2	**Order No**	nvarchar(12)
IS2	Order Date	datetime
IS2	Order Total	money

Order ID Map - Interim Schema 1

Schema	Column Name	Data Type
IS2	**Order No**	nvarchar(12)
IS2	Old Order No	nvarchar(255)
IS2	Schema Name	nvarchar(255)

Table 6.17 - The Integrated Order Header Data Dictionary

Although simple it solves a lot of problems. The order header has a composite primary key composed of the customer number and the order number. This allows us to reuse order numbers for each unique customer as depicted in Table 6.18.

Customer No	Order No	Order Date	Order Total
10001	1	10/1/2011	£579.98
10001	2	10/1/2011	£339.63
10001	3	10/1/2011	£935.28
10001	4	10/1/2011	£1,483.90
10001	5	10/2/2011	£543.40
10002	1	10/2/2011	£862.13
10002	2	10/2/2011	£1,238.33
10002	3	10/2/2011	£418.00
10002	4	10/2/2011	£1,186.08

Table 6.18 - Reusing Order Numbers for Customers

This schema has the advantage in that we can quickly see how many orders a customer has placed by simply looking for the largest order number:

```
SELECT [Customer No], MAX([Order No]) AS Orders To Date

FROM Orders

Group By [Customer No]
```

We will defer a conceptual data model for this subject area until we address the integration and conflict report for the order line tables.

Integration Sequence 5 - Analysis & Conflict Resolution for Inventory Address

Next, we look at Integration Sequence 5 which addresses the ETL we need to resolve the conflict resolution issues we identified for inventory location and inventory address data. Figure 6.16 contains the process flow diagram for this integration sequence.

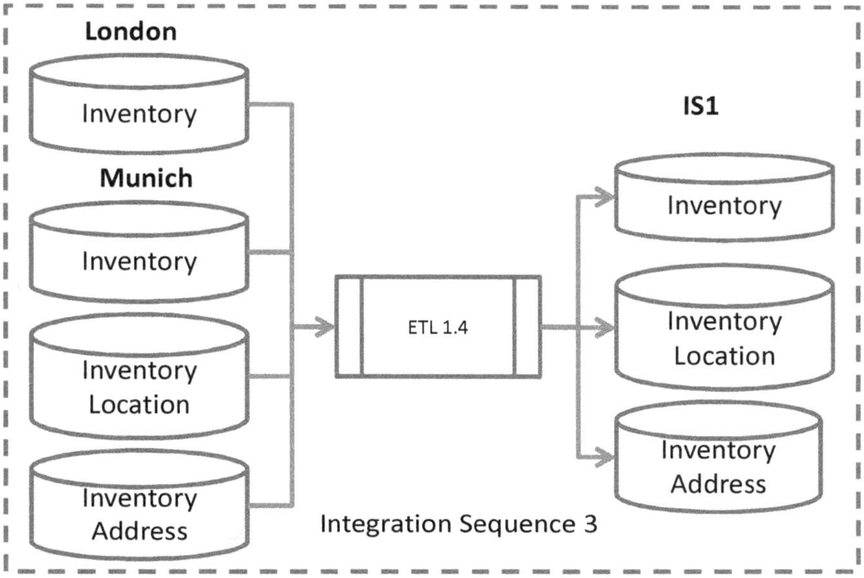

Figure 6.16 - Integration Sequence 5 - integrating Inventory Address Data

As can be seen, we are loading inventory location related data from both the London inventory database and the Munich inventory database. A single ETL process, ETL 1.4 is assigned the task of implementing the logic to load, resolve data conflicts and merge the data.

As there are no similar tables in the London database, we will migrate these tables to the final ODS database schema as per the data dictionary above.

Table 6.19 shows the data dictionaries for the inventory location and address tables.

Inventory - Interim Schema 1

Schema	Column Name	Data Type
IS1	**Product No**	nvarchar(9)
IS1	Total Quantity On Hand	integer
IS1	Inventory Date	datetime

Inventory Location - Interim Schema 1

Schema	Column Name	Data Type
IS1	**Product No**	nvarchar(9)
IS1	**Site Identifier**	smallint
IS1	Local Quantity On Hand	integer
IS1	Inventory Date	datetime
IS1	Reorder Level	integer

Table 6.19 - The Inventory Location and Inventory Address Data Dictionary

Integration Sequence 6 - Analysis & Conflict Resolution for Order Line

Our last and final integration sequence deals with integrating order line data and is shown in Figure 6.17 below.

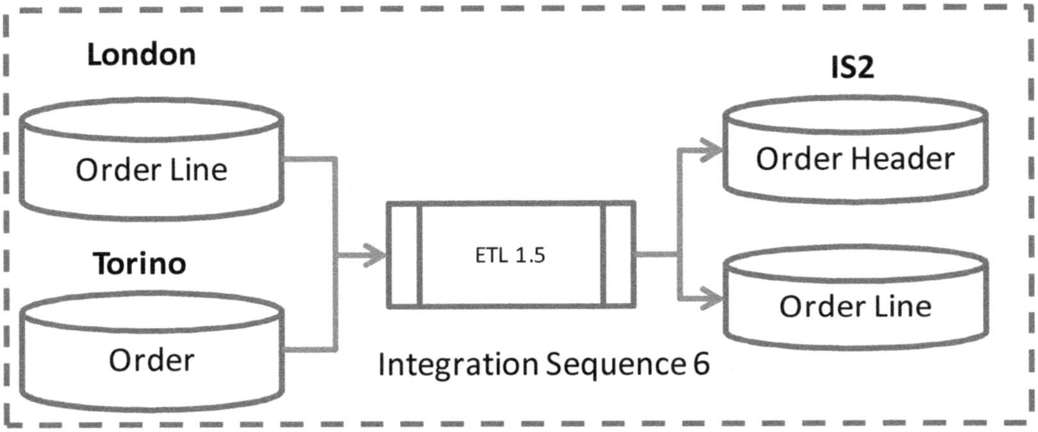

Figure 6.17- Integration Sequence 6 - Integrating Order Line Data

We are going to integrate order line data from the London order line table and the Torino Order table. Recall that the Torino order information for both header and order line is stored in a single Access table so we will need to load this into a staging table and extract the order line data out so we can load it and then also create a new order header row in the target order table.

Table 6.20 shows the Order Line Conflict Report.

Inventory - Interim Schema 1

Schema	Column Name	Data Type
IS1	**Product No**	nvarchar(9)
IS1	Total Quantity On Hand	integer
IS1	Inventory Date	datetime

Inventory Location - Interim Schema 1

Schema	Column Name	Data Type
IS1	**Product No**	nvarchar(9)
IS1	**Site Identifier**	smallint
IS1	Local Quantity On Hand	integer
IS1	Inventory Date	datetime
IS1	Reorder Level	integer

Table 6.20 - The Order Line Conflict Report

Right away we see some semantic and structural conflicts. Notice that in the London table we have a primary key for products called Product No whereas in the Torino table we only have a product name. Additionally, we see the issues around the order line structures. The London table includes the order number in its design. It also has a corresponding Line Item attribute that together with the Order No attribute can be used in a composite primary key. The Torino table does not include a primary key for order information.

We see a naming conflict related to pricing information. In the London database we see an attribute called Retail. This is indeed the Retail Price for a product. We also see a Wholesale Price attribute in the London database. In the Torino database we see a Sales Price attribute. This is actually the Wholesale Price so we have a naming and semantic conflict.

We also see a whole bunch of attributes in the London table that are missing in the Torino table. Table 6.21 below shows the target schema that we are aiming for once the data is integrated.

Order - Interim Schema 2

Schema	Column Name	Data Type
IS2	**Order No**	nvarchar(12)
IS2	**Line Item**	smallint
IS2	***Product No***	*nvarchar(9)*
IS2	Quantity	integer
IS2	Retail Price	money
IS2	Wholesale	money
IS2	Discount	float
IS2	Tax	money
IS2	Sub Total	money
IS2	Total Price	money

Table 6.21 - The Integrated Order Line Data Dictionary

As can be seen, this is a more robust order line table design. It contains all the main attributes required to record an order line and also contains the proper primary keys and foreign keys used to link it to the order header table and the order line table.

The Final Conceptual Model

Figure 6.18 below shows the conceptual model for our level 2 integrated schema.

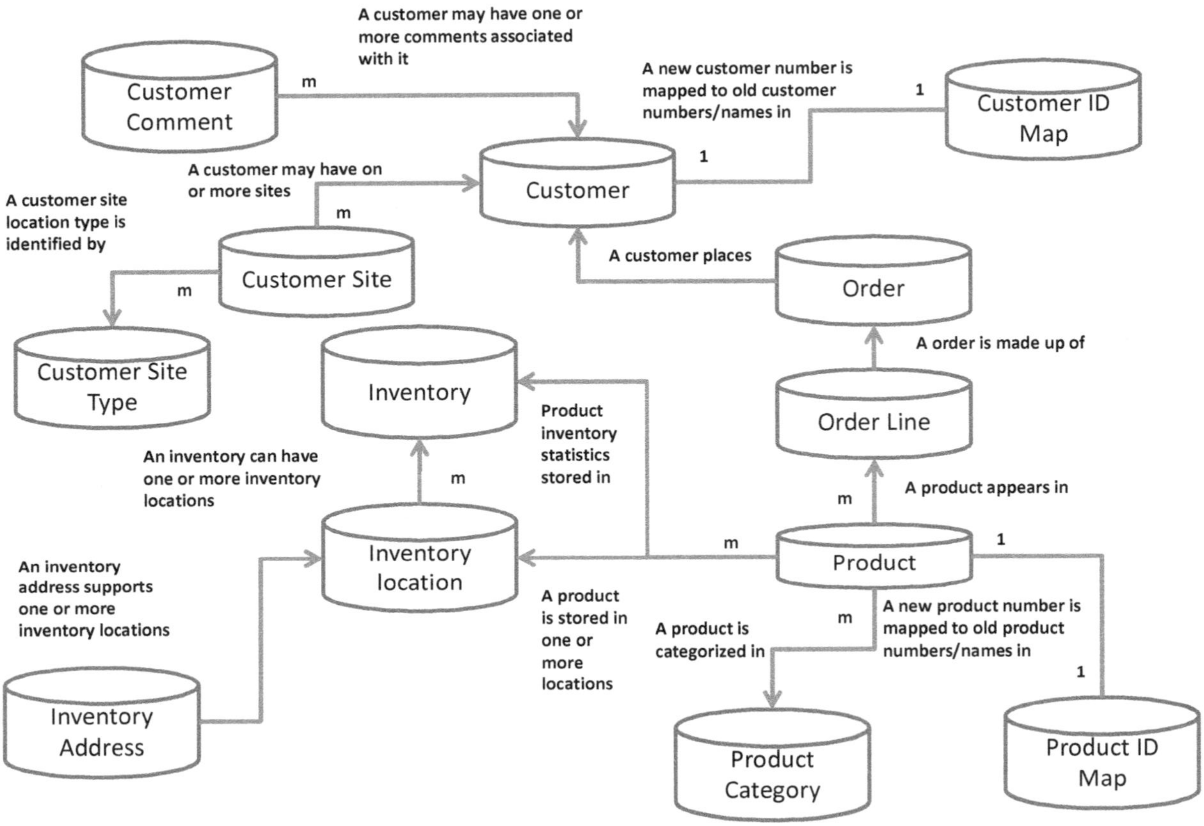

Figure 6.18 - IS2 (Integration Schema 2) Conceptual Model

As can be seen, the model for our ODS is starting to take shape. We have a model that supports customers, customer sites, comments and customer type information. We can link a customer to their orders and detailed order lines. Lastly, we have a solid product subject area and also an inventory subject area.

Summary

This was our chapter on integrating schema to derive an interim model. You can consider this as a sort of tutorial as it will set the standard for the subsequent phase of the integration process dealing with the MySQL database which you will do on your own as an exercise.

The model and data dictionary for the MySQL database is in Chapter 5. We suggest that you now attempt to integrate that schema into the schema we just created prior to continuing to Chapter 7.

As we proceeded to combine common tables and columns, not only did we identify and resolve data conflicts but we also found opportunities to improve on names and create a new table or two to support existing and anticipated business rules.

We concentrated mainly on the data side of things. We will use the conflict resolution specs we identified to create the ETL logic required to implement the data transformation in a later chapter.

I think we can agree that the small data dictionaries and data flow diagrams we generated are an important tool in the process. Notice how we followed the process introduced in Chapter 3.

Having generated the necessary physical models and data dictionaries in Chapter 5 and having generated our interim schema in Chapter 6, we are ready to create the ETL specifications for our processes that will load the data, resolve any data conflicts and finally merge the data into the ODS database.

Our ETL specifications will be based on three types of process diagrams and one type of report that describes the ETL logic required to resolve the conflicts we discovered in Chapter 6. Specifically we will create:

- A data flow diagram that depicts the flow of information and identifies the tasks that need to occur.
- A process hierarchy diagram that shows the different levels of processes and tasks in the overall ETL process.
- A process dependency diagram that shows the sequence of process execution over time. In other words what process has to execute before the next process can execute.

We will dedicate a section to each of the main processes for each of the main subject areas:

- Customer ETL Specifications
- Product ETL Specifications
- Inventory ETL Specifications
- Order Header ETL Specifications
- Order Line ETL Specifications.

The divide and conquer approach allows us to develop a set of specifications at a time and also build the actual ETL processes so we can test them individually before we integrate them into one ETL system.

Lastly, we will start with the Customer and Product ETL specifications first as some of the other ETL processes require that we have these two reference data sets loaded first.

The Customer ETL Specifications

We start with the ETL specification that loads the customer data from our Torino and London customer data sources. The diagram we use is called a data flow diagram. It identifies the data stores (depicted by computer disk icons), data flows (depicted by arrows) and process (depicted by process symbols boxes). The process symbols are decomposed to show the individual tasks that each process must perform. These tasks are described in the ETL specification tables that accompany each diagram.

Figure 7.1 shows the first data flow diagram that will be used to load and merge customer data.

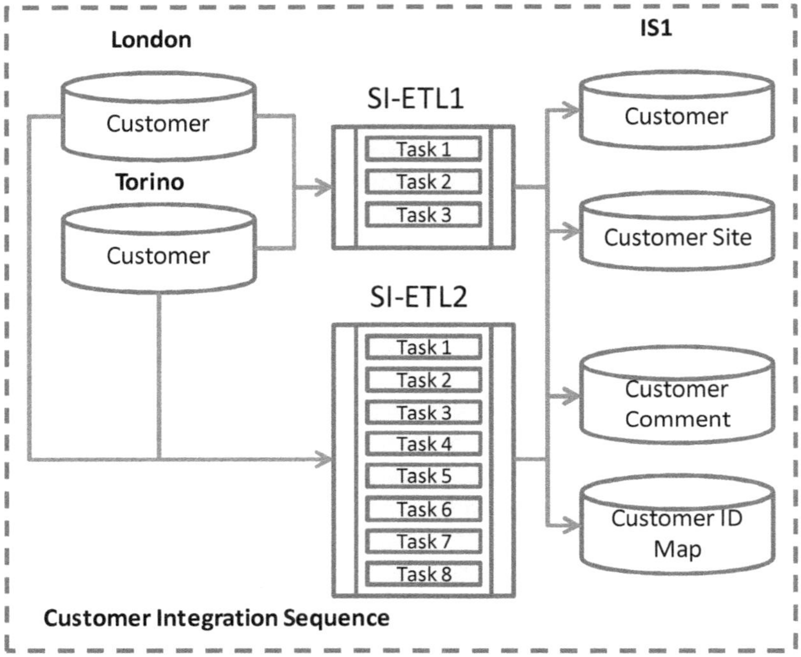

Figure 7.1 - Customer Load and Integration Data Flow

As we only have customer data in the London and Customer data sources we do not need to refer to the Munich data source. Recall that the Munich data source only has inventory and product information.

Our inputs are the London customer spreadsheet and the Torino Access customer table. Our output is the merged customer table, a new customer comment table and a customer ID mapping table. This last table is used to map the newly generated customer numbers to the old customer numbers. As the London Customer spreadsheet and Torino customer table have different customer number schemes, we wish to standardize on one consistent numbering scheme. As rows are loaded into the new customer table we generate a new number and insert the new number and old number into the mapping table so we have an audit trail of the old customer numbers.

We also need to parse out the customer comments from the Torino customer table and load them into the new customer comment table while using the new customer number that was generated.

Lastly, we want to extract the customer site information from the London spreadsheet and the Torino customer table and insert it into the new Customer Site table using the new customer number that was generated when we inserted London customer rows into the new customer table. The customer site table will hold all customer address related information.

The ETL specification to load customer data from both the Torino and London data sources is shown in Table 7.1.

Schema	Column Name	Data Type	Conflict	ETL Spec	Task
Torino	Customer Name	nvarchar(255)	Structural, no PK	SI-ETL1	Task 1
London	Customer Name	nvarchar(255)	Structural, has PK	SI-ETL1	Task 2
London	Customer No	nvarchar(5)	Structural, used as PK	SI-ETL1	Task 3

Table 7.1 - Customer Integration Specification SI - ETL1

Task	Description
Task 1	Torino schema has no primary key, move row to new customer table that has a primary key and generate a new primary key.
Task 2	Move to new customer table and generate a new primary key. Create a new customer key mapping table and insert the new primary key and old primary key in the mapping table.
Task 3	Move to new customer table and generate a new primary key. Create a new customer key mapping table and insert the new primary key and old primary key in the mapping table.

Table 7.1a - Customer Integration Specification SI - ETL1

Our first specification is easy. We simply need to extract the customer number and name so we can insert it into the new customer table. The only twist is that for each row extracted, we need logic to generate a new customer number. After the new number is generated, it is inserted in the customer table and also in the mapping table along with the old customer number so we can go back and identify the old customer numbers in case of bugs or errors.

Once all of the customers from London and Torino are loaded we need to load the address information for both into the new customer site table. We also need to parse out the customer comments from the Torino table and insert them into the new customer comments table.

As can be seen, the ETL process has nine tasks. The specifications together with the task descriptions for these ETL tasks is shown below in Table 7.2:

Schema	Column Name	Data Type	Conflict	ETL Spec	Task
Torino	Province	nvarchar(255)	None, minor data type	SI-ETL2	Task 1
London	Province	nvarchar(255)	None, minor data type	SI-ETL2	Task 2
Torino	City	nvarchar(255)	None, minor data type	SI-ETL2	Task 3
London	City	nvarchar(255)	None, minor data type	SI-ETL2	Task 4
Torino	Telephone	float	Naming, Data Type	SI-ETL2	Task 5
London	Main Telephone	float	Naming, Data Type	SI-ETL2	Task 6
Torino	Address	nvarchar(255)	None	SI-ETL2	Task 7
Torino	Comment	nvarchar(255)	None	SI-ETL2	Task 8
London	Address	nvarchar(255)	None	SI-ETL3	Task 9

Task	Description
Task 1	Move to new customer table and convert the data type to nvarchar(128).
Task 2	Move to new customer table and convert the data type to nvarchar(128).
Task 3	Move to new customer table and convert the data type to nvarchar(128).
Task 4	Move to new customer table and convert the data type to nvarchar(128).
Task 5	Move to new customer table and convert the data type to nvarchar(24).
Task 6	Move to new customer table and convert the data type to nvarchar(24).
Task 7	Move to new customer table and convert the data type to nvarchar(256).
Task 8	Move to new customer comment table using the new customer key as a unique primary key for the row.
Task 9	Move to new customer table and convert the data type to nvarchar(256).

Table 7.2 - Customer Site Integration Specification SI - ETL2

Luckily we have only some minor naming and data type conversions to perform in these sets of ETL tasks. As we parse out the customer comments, we need to retrieve the new customer number from the mapping table using the old customer number as a lookup key.

Also none of the data sources specified the country that the sites are located in. As part of the logic we will need to add a hardcoded country name for each source once we created the SQL statement that will be used to insert the rows into this table.

A more complex solution would be to create a country code table that contains the two and three character ISO country codes. We could then insert the country codes into the address information.

Some of you might find the specification tables a bit repetitive and verbose as we proceed with the chapter. Keep in mind that in real world projects you might be assigned the task of preparing these specifications for a developer that is in a different location then you. You want to make sure that the specifications are as complete and accurate as possible so that the remote developer can deliver correct results.

Next we develop the ETL specifications for product data.

The Product ETL Specifications

The ETL specifications dealing with product data will pull data from the Munich and Torino product data tables and London inventory spreadsheet tab. Although the London data source has product data stored in the inventory spreadsheet tab we will address the ETL for pulling product data from the London source at this time.

The specifications for the product ETL is shown in Figure 7.2.

As can be seen, we have three input tables and three output tables. We need to merge basic product data and insert it into a new product table. As with the customer data, we need to generate a new product number while retaining the mapping between the new and old product number. For this purpose we create a new product id map table. As we generate and insert a new product row into the product table, we save the old product number and insert it together with the new product number into the product id map table.

Munich product data also has product categories. We insert the product categories together with new product category codes into a product category code table. No need for a mapping table this time as the Munich data had only product category descriptions and no codes.

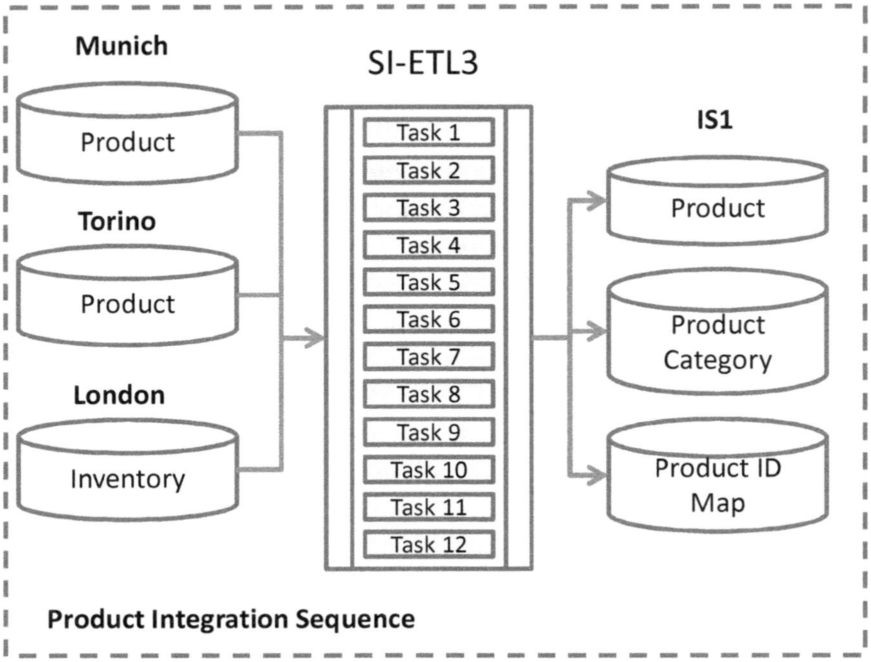

Figure 7.2 - Product Load and Integration Data Flow

This ETL specification has 12 tasks that are identified in Table 7.3 below.

Product Integration- Specification SI - ETL3

Schema	Column Name	Data Type	Conflict	ETL Spec	Task
Munich	Wholesale Price	money	Naming	SI-ETL3	Task 1
Torino	Sales Price	money	Naming, semantic	SI-ETL3	Task 2
Torino	Product Name	nvarchar(255)	Structural, no PK	SI-ETL3	Task 3
Torino	Size	nvarchar(255)	unique to schema	SI-ETL3	Task 4
Torino	Retail Price	money	unique to schema	SI-ETL3	Task 5
Munich	Product Category	nvarchar(255)	structural, unique	SI-ETL3	Task 6
Munich	Product ID	nvarchar(9)	unique to schema	SI-ETL3	Task 7
Munich	Product Description	nvarchar(255)	unique to schema	SI-ETL3	Task 8
London	Product No	nvarchar(255)	Naming, data type	SI-ETL3	Task 9
London	Product Description	nvarchar(255)	Structural, Move to product	SI-ETL3	Task 10
London	Package	nvarchar(255)	Structural, Move to product	SI-ETL3	Task 11
London	Wholesale	money	Structural, Move to product	SI-ETL3	Task 12

Task	Description
Task 1	Move to new product table, retain name, data type and semantic meaning of this column.
Task 2	Move to new product table and insert into wholesale price column.
Task 3	Torino schema has no primary key, move row to new product table that has a primary key and generate a new primary key.
Task 4	Move to new product table, retain name.
Task 5	Move to new product table, renaming column to Product Size.
Task 6	Replace product category description with the code from the new product category table.
Task 7	Move to new product table and generate a new product number. Create a product id mapping table and insert the new product number and old product id map.
Task 8	Move to new product table, retain name.
Task 9	Move to new product table and generate a new product number. Create a product id mapping table and insert the new product number and old product id map.
Task 10	Replace with the product id for this description. Product table needs to be loaded prior to this table.
Task 11	This data needs to be in the product table and replaced with the new product key.
Task 12	This data needs to be in the product table and replaced with the new product key.

Table 7.3 - Product Integration Specification SI - ETL3

Some interesting conflicts need to be resolved. The sales price column name implies the final sales price. It really stores the wholesale price of the product so we need to load it into a new Wholesale Price column. Torino product data source has no product number, only product names so we need to generate a new product number for these.

London has product descriptions but no product numbers. We move these out of the London inventory spreadsheet and insert them into the new product table, generating a new product number. The same goes for the package and wholesale price attributes. We need to store these in the product table as it is dedicated to store all product related information.

When the developer creates the code for these ETL processes, most of the tasks can be combined into one statement, such as when converting from one data type to the other. Let's take a look at a simple example. Assume that we have some basic product category as shown in Table 7.4.

Product Category	Product ID	Product Description	Wholesale Price
Coffee Grinder	ITEM-0001	Small capacity coffee grinder	40.00 €
Coffee Grinder	ITEM-0002	Medium capacity coffee grinder	50.00 €
Coffee Grinder	ITEM-0003	Large capacity coffee grinder	70.00 €

Table 7.4 - Product Category Staging Data

All columns are stored as text strings. We need to perform some basic transformation steps. The interesting transformation requires us to convert the wholesale price value to a money value. As we can see we have the "Euro" currency code as part of the price. We need to pull this out prior to the conversion.

The SQL DML statement below does the trick:

```
SELECT CONVERT(varchar(64),[Product Category])  as [Product Category]
      ,CONVERT(varchar(9),[Product ID])          as [Product ID]
      ,CONVERT(varchar(256),[Product Description])as [Product Description]
      ,CONVERT(money,(REPLACE([Wholesale Price],' €',''))) as [Wholesale
Price]
 FROM [CafeMagnificoStagingArea].[dbo].[German Product Staging]
```

Notice the embedded functions such as CONVERT and REPLACE which allow us to convert from one data type to another and to eliminate unwanted characters.

The set of specifications we are developing will come in handy for the ETL developer.

Table 7.5 contains the output of the statement executed above.

Product Category	Product ID	Product Description	Wholesale Price
Coffee Grinder	ITEM-0001	Small capacity coffee grinder	40
Coffee Grinder	ITEM-0002	Medium capacity coffee grinder	50
Coffee Grinder	ITEM-0003	Large capacity coffee grinder	70
Coffee Grinder	ITEM-0004	Industrial capacity coffee grinder	100
Espresso Machine	ITEM-0005	2 station espresso maker	70

Table 7.5 - Product Category Converted Staging Data

All we need to do is add an INSERT clause so we can insert it into the target table:

```
INSERT INTO PRODUCT_CATEGORY_CODE
SELECT CONVERT(varchar(64),[Product Category]) as [Product Category]
      ,CONVERT(varchar(9),[Product ID]) as [Product ID]
      ,CONVERT(varchar(256),[Product Description])as [Product Description]
      ,CONVERT(money,(REPLACE([Wholesale Price],' €',''))) as [Wholesale
Price]
FROM [CafeMagnificoStagingArea].[dbo].[German Product Staging]
GO
```

The Inventory ETL Specifications

We now turn our attention to the data and tables that are part of the inventory subject area. Both the London data source and the Munich data source have inventory tables. These can be seen in the data flow diagram shown in Figure 7.3.

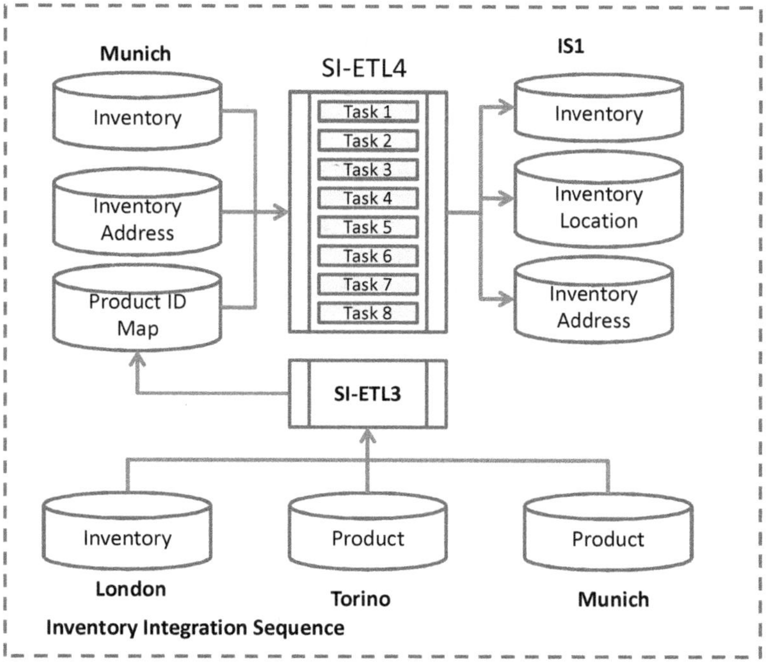

Figure 7.3 - Inventory Load and Integration Data Flow

Notice the inclusion of the product ID map table we discussed earlier. We need the information in this table so we can retrieve the new product numbers based on the old product identifiers and descriptions.

Notice that we have three input tables. Also notice that we also have ETL process SI-ETL3. We realize that this process needs to execute first so it can generate the new product codes.

There are three output tables, the main inventory table, the inventory location table and the inventory address table. Our ODS database model will support the business rule that a product inventory can have one or more physical sites and each physical site is located in one and only one address.

Now the above rule may be limiting. It is possible that a single physical address can support multiple inventory sites, such as a warehouse with multiple rooms and shelves to store products. Each room could be considered an inventory site.

This ETL process has eight sub tasks which are described in Table 7.6.

Schema	Column Name	Data Type	Conflict	ETL Spec	Task
Munich	Product ID	nvarchar(255)	Naming, data type	SI-ETL4	Task 1
Munich	Quantity On Hand	float	Unique, data type	SI-ETL4	Task 2
Munich	Inventory Date	datetime	Unique	SI-ETL4	Task 3
Munich	Site	nvarchar(255)	None, unique	SI-ETL4	Task 4
Munich	City	nvarchar(255)	None, unique	SI-ETL4	Task 5
Munich	Address	nvarchar(255)	None, unique	SI-ETL4	Task 6
Munich	Postal Code	nvarchar(255)	None, unique	SI-ETL4	Task 7
Munich	Contact	nvarchar(255)	None, unique	SI-ETL4	Task 8

ETL Spec	Task	Description
SI-ETL4	Task 1	Generate new product number, insert old and new number in mapping table.
SI-ETL4	Task 2	Move to new inventory table and convert to integer data type.
SI-ETL4	Task 3	Move to new inventory table.
SI-ETL4	Task 4	Move to new inventory table and convert to nvarchar(32).
SI-ETL4	Task 5	Move to new inventory table and convert to nvarchar(64).
SI-ETL4	Task 6	Move to new inventory table and convert to nvarchar(255).
SI-ETL4	Task 7	Move to new inventory table and convert to nvarchar(32).
SI-ETL4	Task 8	Move to new inventory table and convert to nvarchar(64).

Table 7.6 - Inventory Specification SI-ETL 4.1

These are all rather straightforward. We simply perform some minor data type conversions and load the data into their respective inventory, inventory location and inventory address tables.

These sub tasks can be considered the specifications for the logic that is used to create the stored procedures that will load and populate the ODS tables. Stored procedures are programming units found in database products such as SQL Server, Oracle and Sybase.

The Order Header ETL Specifications

Next we turn our attention to the ETL specifications dealing with the order header. This can be seen in Figure 7.4.

This diagram contains the data flow steps for loading orders from the London and Torino data sources into the new Order Header table. Notice that in addition to the order data we now also use the product ID map and customer ID map tables so as to retrieve the new generated product numbers and customer numbers. The ETL logic will do this by matching the customer and product numbers in the data sources against the equivalent values in the mapping tables.

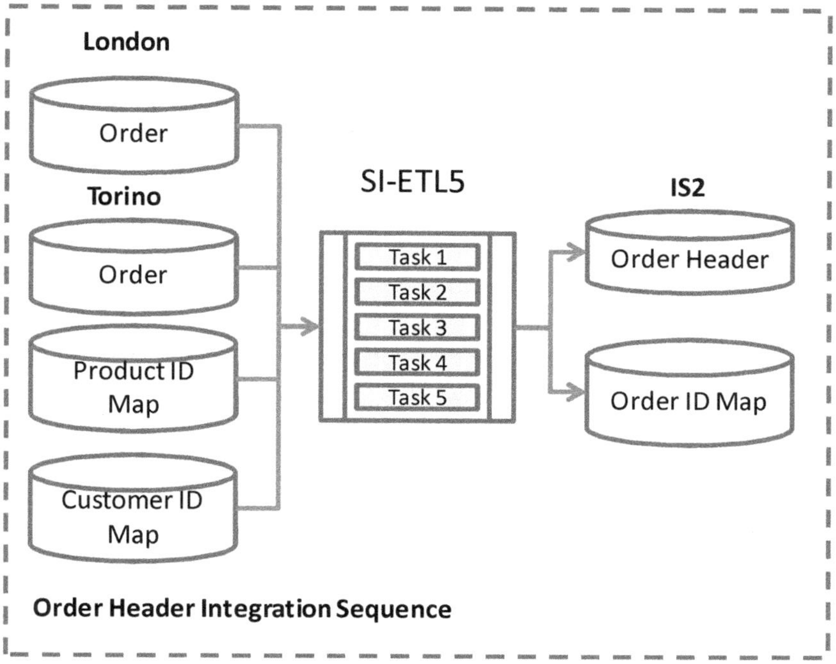

Figure 7.4 - Order Header Load and Integration Data Flow

This ETL specification contains five tasks and they are described in Table 7.7.

Schema	Column Name	Data Type	Conflict	ETL Spec	Task
London	Customer No	nvarchar(5)	semantic & structural (PK)	SI-ETL5	Task 1
Torino	Customer Name	nvarchar(255)	semantic & structural (PK)	SI-ETL5	Task 2
London	Order No	nvarchar(255)	semantic & structural (PK)	SI-ETL5	Task 3
London	Order Date	datetime	missing in Torino	SI-ETL5	Task 4
London	Order Total	money	missing in Torino	SI-ETL5	Task 5

ETL Spec	Task	Description
SI-ETL5	Task 1	Retrieve new customer number from mapping table and insert into new order header row.
SI-ETL5	Task 2	Omit in new Order Header.
SI-ETL5	Task 3	Generate a new order number and insert it into the order no mapping table with the old order number. Use the new order number in the order header table row being inserted.
SI-ETL5	Task 4	Move to new order table as is.
SI-ETL5	Task 5	Move to new order table as is.

Table 7.7 - Order Header Integration Specification SI - ETL5

Notice the semantic and structural conflicts. This is due to the fact that we need to map old primary keys to new primary keys. In the case of the Torino data there is no customer number in the original data, only the customer name so we need to use the name against the mapping table to retrieve the new customer number and use it as a foreign key in the order header table.

Sometimes a picture is worth a thousand words. Figure 7.5 depicts a flow chart that shows more detailed steps that need to be executed in the ETL flow.

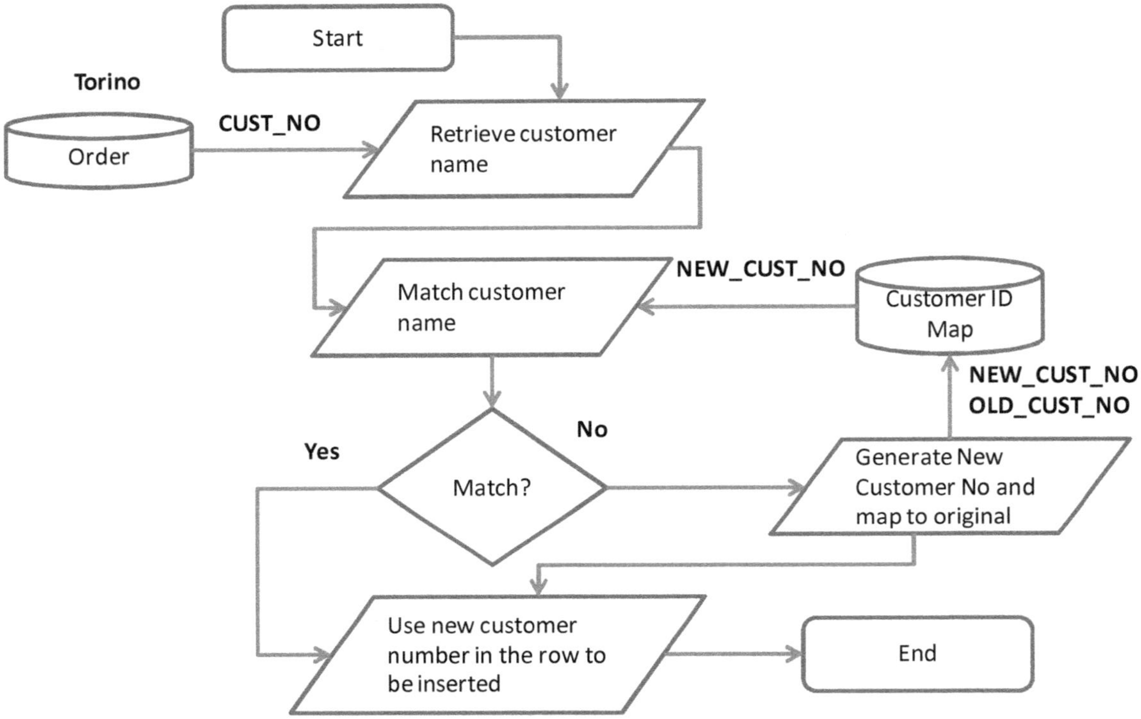

Figure 7.5 - Flow Chart for Retrieving New Customer Numbers

Sometimes we need to enhance our ETL specifications by including flow charts that illustrate or describe the logic that the developer needs to use when developing code that will execute the desired ETL process or task.

Figure 7.5 showed the logic for retrieving the new customer numbers that will be included in the row that gets inserted into the new order header table. We retrieve the customer name or number from the source data and attempt to match it by querying the mapping table.

If we find a match we retrieve the new customer number and use it in the INSERT statement. If we do not find a match we generate a new number and insert it into the mapping table. We then use the new number in the INSERT statement.

Next we turn our attention to the order line ETL specifications.

The Order Line ETL Specifications

Figure 7.6 displays the data flow or process flow diagram that will be used to implement the ETL process used to load the order line table and order id mapping table.

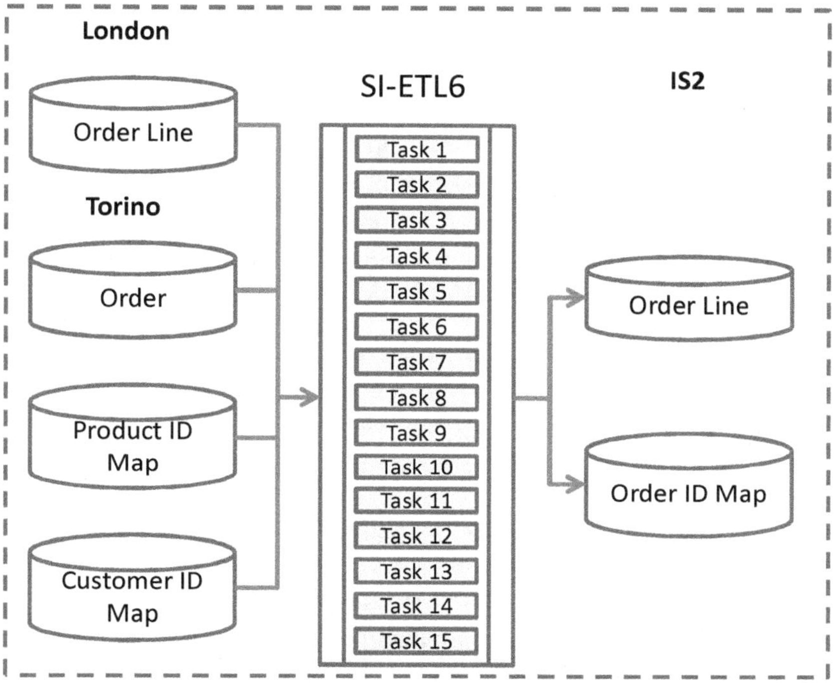

Figure 7.6 - Order Line Load and Integration Data Flow

Four tables are used as input. The first table is the London Order Line table and the second is the Torino Order table. Additionally two reference tables are required: Product ID Map and Customer ID Map. The last two tables are required as we want to include the new generated product numbers and customer numbers.

Output is the Order Line table plus any new generated order numbers which get loaded into the Order ID Map mapping table.

Notice that there are 15 individual tasks in the process that either resolve the data integration conflicts we identified earlier or perform some sort of data conversion steps. Table 7.8 below contains the specifications for each task:

Schema	Column Name	Data Type	Conflict	ETL Spec	Task
London	Product No	nvarchar(255)	Semantic & structural	SI-ETL6	Task 1
Torino	Product	nvarchar(255)	Semantic & structural	SI-ETL6	Task 2
London	Quantity	float	none	SI-ETL6	Task 3
Torino	Quantity	float	none	SI-ETL6	Task 4
London	Retail	money	naming	SI-ETL6	Task 5
Torino	Sales Price	money	naming	SI-ETL6	Task 6
London	Discount	float	none	SI-ETL6	Task 7
Torino	Discount	float	none	SI-ETL6	Task 8
London	Total	money	naming	SI-ETL6	Task 9
Torino	Total Price	money	naming	SI-ETL6	Task 10
London	Order No	nvarchar(255)	structural	SI-ETL6	Task 11
London	Line Item	float	structural	SI-ETL6	Task 12
London	Wholesale	money	missing in Torino	SI-ETL6	Task 13
London	Tax	money	missing in Torino	SI-ETL6	Task 14
London	Sub Total	money	missing in Torino	SI-ETL6	Task 15

ETL Spec	Task	Description
SI-ETL6	Task 1	Retrieve new product number from product id mapping table and use in the new row.
SI-ETL6	Task 2	Retrieve new product number from product id mapping table and use in the new row.
SI-ETL6	Task 3	Convert to integer when inserting into new order line row.
SI-ETL6	Task 4	Convert to integer when inserting into new order line row.
SI-ETL6	Task 5	Insert into retail price column in new order line table.
SI-ETL6	Task 6	Insert into wholesale price column in new order line table.
SI-ETL6	Task 7	Convert to decimal(5,2) when inserting into new order line table row.
SI-ETL6	Task 8	Convert to decimal(5,2) when inserting into new order line table row.
SI-ETL6	Task 9	Insert into Total Price column in new order line table.
SI-ETL6	Task 10	Insert into Total Price column in new order line table.
SI-ETL6	Task 11	Retrieve new order number from the order id mapping table and use in the new row.
SI-ETL6	Task 12	Convert to integer when inserting into new order line row.
SI-ETL6	Task 13	Insert into Wholesale Price column in the new order line table.
SI-ETL6	Task 14	Insert into the Tax column in the new order line table.
SI-ETL6	Task 15	Insert into Sub Total column in the new order line table.

Table 7.8 - Order Line Integration Specification SI - ETL6

So far, we presented 2 important sets of diagrams that an ETL developer will use when it is time to create the ETL processes. We presented a series of data flow diagrams and ETL specification spreadsheets. In the next section we create the process hierarchy or process decomposition diagram that shows the different layers of the ETL processes we need to implement.

Process Hierarchy Diagram

Process Hierarchy diagrams are diagrams that depict the hierarchical structure of the different tasks and sub tasks that compose the ETL process needed to integrate the data that will be loaded in the Cafe Magnifico ODS. Figure 7.7 shows this type of diagram.

As can be seen we have the six main processes called S1 - ETL1 through 6. Each process is then decomposed into its own individual steps. Each of the steps or tasks corresponds to the tasks in the specifications we just created.

If necessary, each task could be further documented by adding flow charts that describe the logic of the task as we saw earlier in the chapter. Next, we create our last diagram, the process dependency diagram. This diagram shows the flow of the steps over time and identifies which step is dependent on other steps to successfully execute before it can execute.

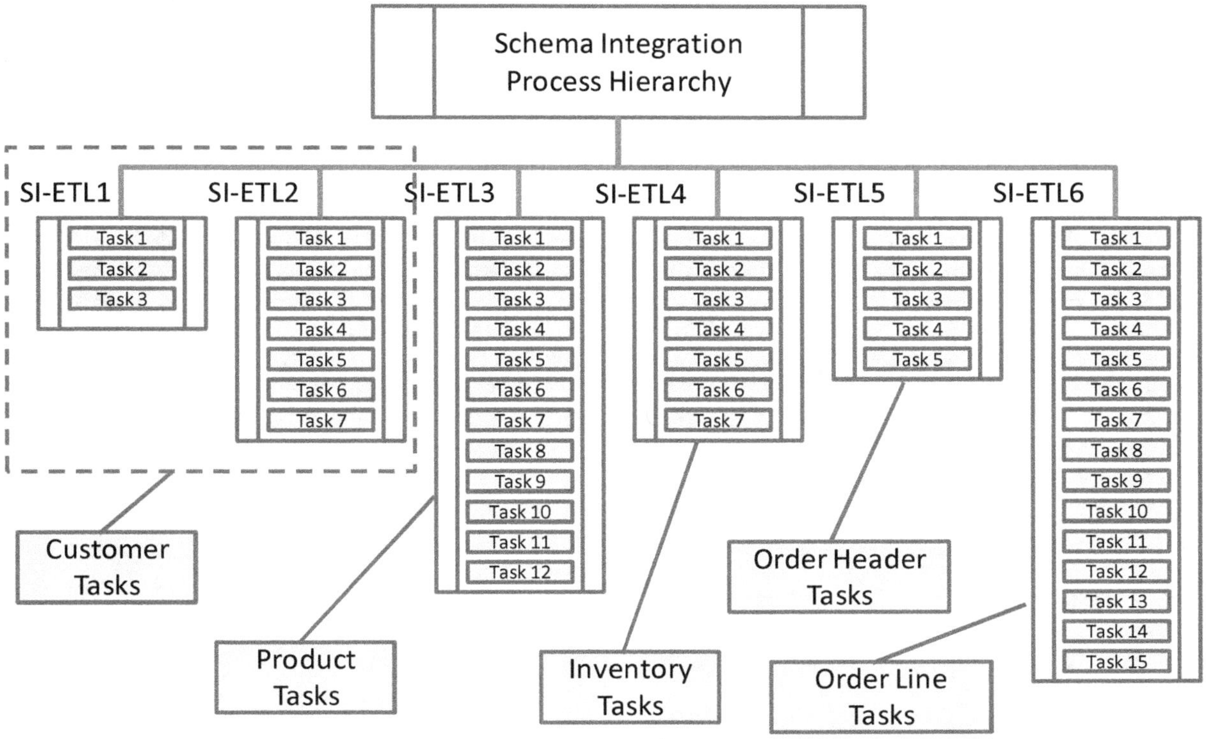

Figure 7.7 - ETL Process Decomposition Diagram

Process Dependency Diagram

Figure 7.8 displays the Process Dependency Diagram (PDD) that shows the flow of the ETL steps over time.

We have three time slices identified, T1, T2 and T3. T1 clearly shows that there are three ETL tasks that can occur in parallel. SI - ETL1 and SI - ETL2 are the two steps that load customer data. Process SI - ETL3 loads the product data. The three processes can occur in parallel in time slice T1.

Next we execute ETL process SI - ETL 5 which loads the order header data. Notice that it is dependent on steps SI ETL 1 and 2 to complete first as it needs to include customer data in the records such as customer number keys.

Step SI ETL 4 can execute in parallel as it will load inventory data. This process is dependent on process SI - ETL 3 to complete as it needs the product reference data and keys in order to properly load the inventory data.

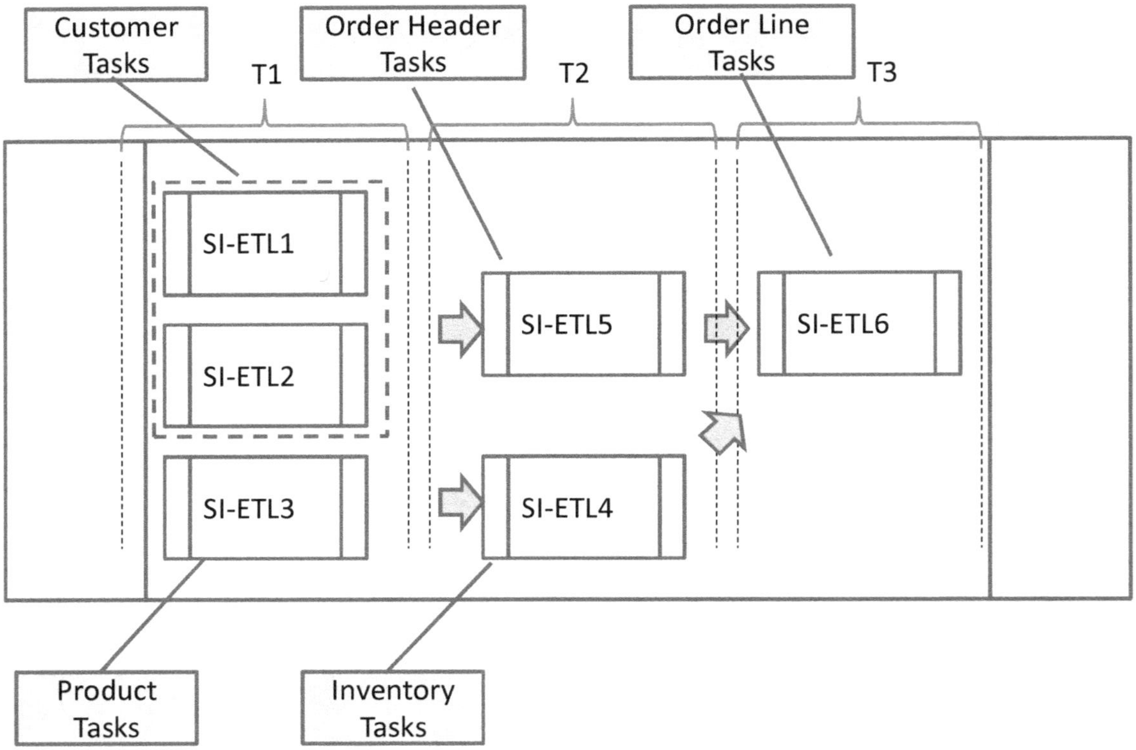

Figure 7.8 - ETL Process Dependency Diagram

Last but not least is process SI - ETL 6 which is used to load the order line specific data. This step is dependent on not only process SI ETL 5 (load order header) but it is also dependent on steps SI ETL 1 & 2 (load customer data) and step SI ETL 3 (load product) data so that it has all the reference data it needs for when the order line table is loaded.

Summary

We are now finished with the creation of our specification documents. We have created the following sets of documents so a developer can get a complete view of the processes he or she needs to develop.

To summarize, we have created a set of:

- Process Flow Diagrams as a set of MS PowerPoint slides
- ETL Process Specification Document as a set of MS Excel spreadsheets
- ETL Process Hierarchy diagram as a PowerPoint slide
- ETL Process Dependency Diagram as a PowerPoint Slide.

A complete set of data models showing entities, attributes and relationships were also created.

We can now forge ahead and create the physical database tables and the ETL process flows for our ODS.

Having generated the necessary physical models and data dictionaries in Chapter 5 for the source database and having generated ODS schema in Chapter 7, we now create the physical database model. In this chapter we will present models for each of the main subject area and then display the final model. This chapter also includes the data dictionaries that map the logical entity and attribute names to the physical names we will use in the ODS.

Let's start by assigning physical names to the logical table names and also include descriptions so we can easily identify the purpose of the table. Table 8.1 below is used for this purpose.

Physical TableName	Description
INVENTORY_TBL	This table holds all product inventory levels such as quantity on hand for all inventory sites.
INVENTORY_LOCATION_TBL	This table holds all inventory product levels such as quantity on hand for an individual site.
INVENTORY_ADDRESS_TBL	This table contains the address information for an individual inventory site.
PRODUCT_TBL	This table holds details related to a product such as unit weight, price information and packaging description.
PRODUCT_CATEGORY_TBL	This table contains all the category codes for a product.
PRODUCT_ID_MAPPING_TBL	This table is used to map new product identifiers to the old product identifiers.
CUSTOMER_TBL	This table contains customer related information such as customer name and unique identifier.
CUSTOMER_SITE_TBL	This table contains address information for a customer site.
CUSTOMER_SITE_TYPE_TBL	This table contains codes that identify the type of customer site.
CUSTOMER_ID_MAPPING_TBL	This table is used to map a new customer identifier to the old customer identifier.
CUSTOMER_COMMENT_TBL	This table contains any comments related to a customer.
ORDER_HEADER_TBL	This table contains order information such as the date the order was placed and the customer identifier for the customer that placed the order.
ORDER_LINE_TBL	This table contains individual line items that make up an order.
ORDER_ID_MAPPING_TBL	This table is used to map a new order identifier to the old order identifier.

Table 8.1 - The Physical Table Data Dictionary

Next we define some business rules that uncover the relationships between the tables:

- An inventory can have multiple locations.
- A location is at one and only one address.
- A product can be stored in one or more inventory locations.
- The sum of all product quantities can be stored in the main inventory location.
- A product category identifies the type or category of a product.
- A product mapping table will be used to map the old product identifiers to new product identifiers.
- A product appears in one or more line items.
- An order is made up of one or more line items.
- A customer can place one or more orders.
- An order mapping table will be used to map the old order numbers to the new order numbers.
- A customer mapping table will be used to map old customer numbers to new customer numbers.
- A customer can have one or more sites.
- One or more comments can be stored for a customer.
- A customer site type table identifies the type of customer site. (Stores, warehouses or distribution centers for example.)

The report in Table 8.2 together with the physical table description data dictionary, the physical column data type report and the models presented in this chapter deliver the minimal set of information that a developer or DBA needs to create the ODS.

Parent Table Name	Primary Key	Child Table Name	Foreign Key
INVENTORY_TBL	PRODUCT_NO	INVENTORY_LOCATION_TBL	PRODUCT_NO
INVENTORY_TBL	PRODUCT_NO	PRODUCT_TBL	PRODUCT_NO
PRODUCT_CATEGORY_TBL	PRODUCT_CATEGORY_CODE	PRODUCT_TBL	PRODUCT_CATEGORY_CODE
PRODUCT_TBL	PRODUCT_NO	PRODUCT_ID_MAPPING_TBL	PRODUCT_NO
INVENTORY_LOCATION_TBL	PRODUCT_NO	PRODUCT_TBL	PRODUCT_NO
INVENTORY_ADDRESS_TBL	INV_SITE_ID	INVENTORY_LOCATION_TBL	INV_SITE_ID
PRODUCT_TBL	PRODUCT_NO	ORDER_LINE_TBL	PRODUCT_NO
ORDER_HEADER_TBL	ORDER_NO	ORDER_LINE_TBL	ORDER_NO
ORDER_HEADER_TBL	ORDER_NO	ORDER_ID_MAPPING_TBL	ORDER_NO
CUSTOMER_TBL	CUSTOMER_NO	ORDER_HEADER_TBL	CUSTOMER_NO
CUSTOMER_TBL		CUSTOMER_ID_MAPPING_TBL	CUSTOMER_NO
CUSTOMER_TBL	CUSTOMER_NO	CUSTOMER_SITE_TBL	CUSTOMER_NO
CUSTOMER_TBL	CUSTOMER_NO	CUSTOMER_COMMENT_TBL	CUSTOMER_NO
CUSTOMER_SITE_TYPE_TBL	CUSTOMER_NO	CUSTOMER_SITE_TBL	CUSTOMER_NO

Table 8.2 - The Table Relationship Data Dictionary

The report is divided into three sections:

- The first section describes the primary key side of the relationship.
- The second section is the relationship business rule description between the parent and child tables. (This is not shown in the table so as to conserve space.)
- The third section is the foreign key side of the relationship.

The relationships are shown below:

- An inventory can be made up of one or more locations.
- An inventory lists stock information for one or more products.
- A product category code is used to identify the product category.
- A new product identifier is mapped to an old product identifier.
- An inventory location lists stock information for one or more products for an individual physical site location.
- An inventory location has only one address (see note 1).
- A product appears on one or more order lines.
- An order has one or more order line items where products purchased are listed together with price and quantity information.
- A new order number is mapped to an old order number.
- A customer number appears on an order.
- A new customer number is mapped to an old customer number.
- A customer has one or more sites.
- One or more customer comments can be stored for a customer.
- A customer type code identifies the type of customer (restaurant, coffee shop, pastry shop, etc.).

Notice that the table names together with the primary key information and relationship description provide the DBA with enough information to define the referential constraints between tables.

One thing to notice is that an inventory location is supported by one and only one address. This might be a limiting business rule. It is very possible that there can be one or more physical inventories at a single physical address. To support this requirement we might want to add a link table that maps addresses to multiple sites.

Customer Physical Model and DDL

Let's examine each subject area in more detail and prepare the required design documents. We start with the Customer subject area first. Figure 8.1 below identifies the critical tables and relationships that will allow us to create the SQL DDL (Data Declaration Language) statements required to create the physical table in our ODS.

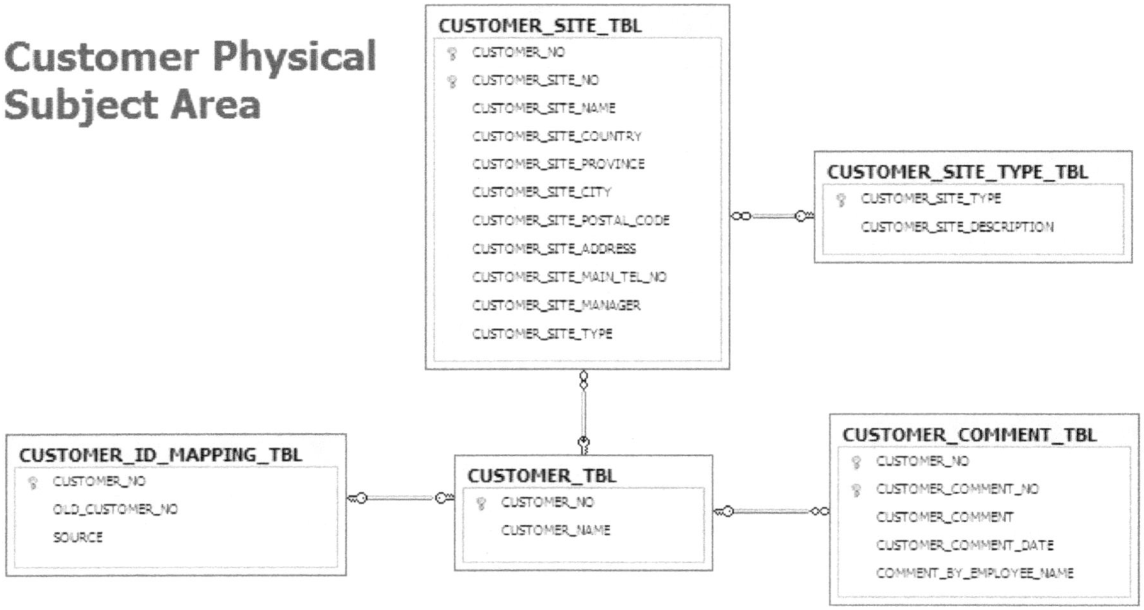

Figure 8.1 - The Customer Physical Subject Area Data Model

This model has five tables related to the customer subject area. Notice how the business relationship rules we identified earlier are used to establish the relationships between tables. The table column report in Table 8.2 below helps identify the primary keys, foreign keys and data type for each column in the table. Recall the simple notation I use:

- Primary keys are in bold type face and underlined.
- Foreign keys are in bold type face and in italics.

The primary key for the CUSTOMER_ID_MAPPING_TBL table is only the new CUSTOMER_NO column as there is a one to one mapping between it and the CUSTOMER_TBL. The old OLD_CUSTOMER_NO column is kept for archiving purposes and is dependent on the new cusomter key.

Please also note that due to size limitations I have kept the models and reports as small and simple as possible while still conveying the importance of each design document.

Table 8.3 shows the data dictionary for the customer table.

Logical Entity Name	Physical Table Name
Customer	CUSTOMER_TBL

Logical Column Name	Physical Column Name	Data Type
Customer No	**CUSTOMER_NO**	Integer
Customer Name	CUSTOMER_NAME	nvarchar(255)

Table 8.3 - The Customer Table Data Dictionary

Notice that the primary key is the CUSTOMER_NO column with a data type of integer. We only include the customer name in this table as other customer data will be stored in supporting customer tables.

Table 8.4 shows the data dictionary for the customer site table. It also uses the CUSTOMER_NO column as part of the primary key together with the CUSTOMER_SITE_NO column.

Logical Entity Name	Physical Table Name
Customer Site	CUSTOMER_SITE_TBL

Logical Column Name	Physical Column Name	Data Type
Customer No	**CUSTOMER_NO**	Integer
Site No	**CUSTOMER_SITE_NO**	smallint
Site Name	CUSTOMER_SITE_NAME	nvarchar(64)
Country	CUSTOMER_SITE_COUNTRY	nvarchar(64)
Province	CUSTOMER_SITE_PROVINCE	nvarchar(64)
City	CUSTOMER_SITE_CITY	nvarchar(128)
Postal Code	CUSTOMER_SITE_POSTAL_CODE	nvarchar(32)
Address	CUSTOMER_SITE_ADDRESS	nvarchar(128)
Telephone	CUSTOMER_SITE_MAIN_TEL_NO	nvarchar(7)
Manager	CUSTOMER_SITE_MANAGER	nvarchar(32)
Site Type	***CUSTOMER_SITE_TYPE***	smallint

Table 8.4 - The Customer Site Data Dictionary

The composite primary key combination above allows us to reuse the site number values for different customers. For example if Customer A has a customer number of 1000 and has five locations and customer B has a customer number of 1001 but only 2 locations a dump of the composite key data would look like what appears in Table 8.5.

Customer No	Site No
1000	1
1000	2
1000	3
1000	4
1000	5
1001	1
1001	2

Table 8.5 - Composite Primary Key Example for Customer Sites

Looking back at the data dictionary, notice also that we have a single foreign key: CUSTOMER_SITE_TYPE. This foreign key column contains codes that allow us to identify the type of customer we are dealing with. For example it could be a restaurant, coffee shop, pastry shop or pub just to name a few.

Table 8.6 below shows the data dictionary for the table that will be used to store customer site type codes and descriptions.

Logical Entity Name	Physical Table Name
Customer Site Type	CUSTOMER_SITE_TYPE_TBL

Logical Column Name	Physical Column Name	Data Type
Site Type	**CUSTOMER_SITE_TYPE**	smallint
Site Type Description	CUSTOMER_SITE_DESCRIPTION	nvarchar(255)

Table 8.6 - The Customer Site Type Data Dictionary

This table only has a primary key which we identified as a foreign key in the customer site table. An example data dump for this table is shown in Table 8.7.

CUSTOMER_SITE_TYPE	CUSTOMER_SITE_DESCRIPTION
1000	Restaurant
2000	Coffee Bar
3000	Coffee Shop
4000	Pastry Shop
5000	Baker

Table 8.7 - Customer Site Type Data Dump

As we are merging customer information from various source databases, we have introduced a mapping table that will allow us to generate brand new customer numbers for all the customers while allowing us to retain the old customer numbers for archival and debugging purposes.

The data dictionary in Table 8.8 will help us build the table structure we need to support this mapping requirement.

Logical Entity Name	Physical Table Name
Customer ID Map	CUSTOMER_ID_MAPPING_TBL

Logical Column Name	Physical Column Name	Data Type
Customer No	CUSTOMER_NO	Integer
Old Customer No	OLD_CUSTOMER_NO	nvarchar(255)
Schema Name	SOURCE	nvarchar(255)

Table 8.8 - The Customer ID Map Data Dictionary

As before, it is helpful to look at a data dump so we can visualize the mapping of new to old customer numbers. The data dump report is shown in Table 8.9.

CUSTOMER_NO	OLD_CUSTOMER_NO	SOURCE
1	10001	London
2	10002	London
3	10003	London
4	10004	London
5	10005	London
6	Maria Brunetti	Torino
7	Anna Sapienza	Torino
8	Suzi Maggiore	Torino
9	Anna Vittorio	Torino
10	Valentina Vespa	Torino
11	Angelo Modugno	Torino
12	Carla Gambretti	Torino
13	Govanni Alberti	Torino

Table 8.9 - Customer Number Mapping Data Dump

Keep in mind that not only does this table store historical customer number mapping, but it also allows us to retrieve the new customer numbers when we load the orders from London and Torino into the new order header table. It also identifies the source of the old customer numbers.

We also want to be able to store comments related to a customer. For this we have to create a new table in the ODS that will allow us to not only store comments, but to also identify who made the comments and the date that the employee made the comment.

Table 8.10 has the data dictionary we will use to create the comment table.

Logical Entity Name	Physical Table Name
Customer Comment	CUSTOMER_COMMENT

Logical Column Name	Physical Column Name	Data Type
Customer No	CUSTOMER_NO	Integer
Customer Comment No	CUSTOMER_COMMENT_NO	nvarchar(5)
Customer Comment No	CUSTOMER_COMMENT	nvarchar(255)
Comment Date	CUSTOMER_COMMENT_DATE	Date
Employee Name	COMMENT_BY_EMPLOYEE_NAME	nvarchar(128)

Table 8.10 - The Customer Comment Table Data Dictionary

This table will have a composite key made up of the CUSTOMER_NO and CUSTOMER_COMMENT_NO columns. It supports the rule that a customer can have one or more comments associated with it. Let's take a look at a data dump report for this data. This is shown in Table 8.11.

CUSTOMER_NO	CUSTOMER_COMMENT_NO	CUSTOMER_COMMENT
1	1	Customer ordered chocolate again
1	2	Customer ordered chocolate again
1	3	Customer ordered our dark chocolate

CUSTOMER_COMMENT_DATE	COMMENT_BY_EMPLOYEE_NAME
10/10/2011	Giovanni
10/11/2011	Giovanni
10/12/2011	Susi

Table 8.11 - Customer Comment Table (split in two parts for easier reading)

Notice that not only does this table allow us to store important comments related to a customer but it also contains important demographic and buying pattern data. This customer apparently likes dark chocolates so we can target her for marketing campaigns when we have specials on dark chocolate products.

Let's take a look at the SQL DDL code that was created with the data dictionary information for the customer tables and also the data model for this subject area:

```
/****************/
/* CUSTOMER_TBL */
/****************/

CREATE TABLE CUSTOMER_TBL
(
CUSTOMER_NO       NVARCHAR(5) NOT NULL,
```

```
CUSTOMER_NAME      NVARCHAR(255)
)
GO

/*************************/
/* Define the primary key */
/*************************/

ALTER TABLE CUSTOMER_TBL WITH NOCHECK
ADD CONSTRAINT PK_CUSTOMER_CUSTOMER_NO
      PRIMARY KEY CLUSTERED (CUSTOMER_NO)
WITH (FILLFACTOR = 75, ONLINE = ON, PAD_INDEX = ON);
GO

/*************************************************/
/* Define the foreign key between the customer table  */
/* and the customer id mapping table                  */
/*************************************************/

ALTER TABLE CUSTOMER_TBL
WITH CHECK ADD
CONSTRAINT FK_CUSTOMER_TBL_TO_CUSTOMER_ID_MAPPING_TBL
FOREIGN KEY(CUSTOMER_NO)
REFERENCES CUSTOMER_ID_MAPPING_TBL (CUSTOMER_NO)
GO

/********************/
/* CUSTOMER_SITE_TBL */
/********************/

CREATE TABLE CUSTOMER_SITE_TBL
(
CUSTOMER_NO                    NVARCHAR(5) NOT NULL,
CUSTOMER_SITE_NO               SMALLINT    NOT NULL,
CUSTOMER_SITE_NAME             NVARCHAR(64),
CUSTOMER_SITE_COUNTY           NVARCHAR(64),
CUSTOMER_SITE_CITY             NVARCHAR(128),
CUSTOMER_SITE_POSTAL_CODE      NVARCHAR(32),
CUSTOMER_SITE_ADDRESS          NVARCHAR(128),
CUSTOMER_SITE_MAIN_TEL_NO      NVARCHAR(7),
CUSTOMER_SITE_MANAGER          NVARCHAR(32),
CUSTOMER_SITE_TYPE             SMALLINT
)
GO

/*************************/
/* Define the primary key */
/*************************/

ALTER TABLE CUSTOMER_SITE_TBL WITH NOCHECK
ADD CONSTRAINT PK_CUSTOMER_SITE_CUSTOMER_NO_CUSTOMER_SITE_NO
      PRIMARY KEY CLUSTERED (CUSTOMER_NO,CUSTOMER_SITE_NO)
```

```
WITH (FILLFACTOR = 75, ONLINE = ON, PAD_INDEX = ON);
GO

/**********************************************************/
/* Define the foreign key between the customer site table   */
/* and the customer site type table                          */
/**********************************************************/

ALTER TABLE CUSTOMER_SITE_TBL
WITH CHECK ADD
CONSTRAINT FK_CUSTOMER_SITE_TBL_TO_CUSTOMER_SITE_TYPE_TBL
FOREIGN KEY(CUSTOMER_SITE_TYPE)
REFERENCES CUSTOMER_SITE_TYPE_TBL(CUSTOMER_SITE_TYPE)
GO

/**********************************************************/
/* Define the foreign key between the customer site table   */
/* and the customer table                                 */
/**********************************************************/

ALTER TABLE CUSTOMER_SITE_TBL
WITH CHECK ADD
CONSTRAINT FK_CUSTOMER_SITE_TBL_TO_CUSTOMER_TBL
FOREIGN KEY(CUSTOMER_NO)
REFERENCES CUSTOMER_TBL(CUSTOMER_NO)
GO

/**************************/
/* CUSTOMER_SITE_TYPE_TBL */
/**************************/

CREATE TABLE CUSTOMER_SITE_TYPE_TBL
(
CUSTOMER_SITE_TYPE            SMALLINT    NOT NULL,
CUSTOMER_SITE_DESCRIPTION     NVARCHAR(255)
)
GO

/**************************/
/* Define the primary key */
/**************************/

ALTER TABLE CUSTOMER_SITE_TYPE_TBL WITH NOCHECK
ADD CONSTRAINT PK_CUSTOMER_SITE_TYPE_CUSTOMER_SITE_TYPE
      PRIMARY KEY CLUSTERED (CUSTOMER_SITE_TYPE)
WITH (FILLFACTOR = 75, ONLINE = ON, PAD_INDEX = ON);
GO

/***************************/
/* CUSTOMER_ID_MAPPING_TBL */
/***************************/

CREATE TABLE CUSTOMER_ID_MAPPING_TBL
```

```
(
CUSTOMER_NO              NVARCHAR(5) NOT NULL,
OLD_CUSTOMER_NO          NVARCHAR(255),
SOURCE                   NVARCHAR(255)
)
GO

/*************************/
/* Define the primary key */
/*************************/

ALTER TABLE CUSTOMER_ID_MAPPING_TBL WITH NOCHECK
ADD CONSTRAINT PK_CUSTOMER_ID_MAPPING_CUSTOMER_NO
      PRIMARY KEY CLUSTERED (CUSTOMER_NO)
WITH (FILLFACTOR = 75, ONLINE = ON, PAD_INDEX = ON);
GO

/***********************/
/* CUSTOMER_COMMENT_TBL */
/***********************/

CREATE TABLE CUSTOMER_COMMENT_TBL
(
CUSTOMER_NO                   NVARCHAR(5) NOT NULL,
CUSTOMER_COMMENT_NO           NVARCHAR(5) NOT NULL,
CUSTOMER_COMMENT              NVARCHAR(255),
CUSTOMER_COMMENT_DATE         DATETIME,
COMMENT_BY_EMPLOYEE_NAME      NVARCHAR(128)
)
GO

/*************************/
/* Define the primary key */
/*************************/

ALTER TABLE CUSTOMER_COMMENT_TBL WITH NOCHECK
ADD CONSTRAINT PK_CUST_COMMENT_CUST_NO_CUST_COMM_NO
      PRIMARY KEY CLUSTERED (CUSTOMER_NO,CUSTOMER_COMMENT_NO)
WITH (FILLFACTOR = 75, ONLINE = ON, PAD_INDEX = ON);
GO

/*************************************************************/
/* Define the foreign key between the customer comment table    */
/* and the customer table                                     */
/*************************************************************/

ALTER TABLE CUSTOMER_COMMENT_TBL
WITH CHECK ADD
CONSTRAINT FK_CUSTOMER_COMMENT_TBL_TO_CUSTOMER_TBL
FOREIGN KEY(CUSTOMER_NO)
REFERENCES CUSTOMER_TBL(CUSTOMER_NO)
GO
```

As can be seen the data dictionaries were used to create these tables and the primary to foreign key constraints. I included just the bare minimum information necessary for the DBA to get the job done!

The syntax for this DDL is based on SQL Server 2008 syntax but it can be easily converted to other target databases like Oracle, Sybase or DB2 with minimal effort.

Last but not least we need some sort of design document that shows us how the source tables map to the target interim schema tables. Once again, we utilize a spreadsheet so as to create a simple mapping specification. This is shown in Tables 8.12a and 8.12b.

Schema	Source Table	Source Column Name	Data Type
Torino	TorinoCustomerStg	Customer Name	nvarchar(255)
Torino	TorinoCustomerStg	Province	nvarchar(255)
Torino	TorinoCustomerStg	City	nvarchar(255)
Torino	TorinoCustomerStg	Address	nvarchar(255)
Torino	TorinoCustomerStg	Telephone	float
Torino	TorinoCustomerStg	Comment	nvarchar(255)

Schema	Source Table	Source Column Name	Data Type
London	LondonCustomerStg	Customer No	float
London	LondonCustomerStg	Customer Name	nvarchar(255)
London	LondonCustomerStg	Province	nvarchar(255)
London	LondonCustomerStg	City	nvarchar(255)
London	LondonCustomerStg	Main Telephone	float

Schema	Source Table	Source Column Name	Data Type
London	LondonCustomerSiteStg	Customer No	float
London	LondonCustomerSiteStg	Site No	nvarchar(255)
London	LondonCustomerSiteStg	Site Name	float
London	LondonCustomerSiteStg	County	nvarchar(255)
London	LondonCustomerSiteStg	City	nvarchar(255)
London	LondonCustomerSiteStg	Postal Code	nvarchar(255)
London	LondonCustomerSiteStg	Address	nvarchar(255)
London	LondonCustomerSiteStg	Telephone	nvarchar(255)
London	LondonCustomerSiteStg	Manager	nvarchar(255)

Table 8.12a - The Customer Mapping Spreadsheet (source tables)

Schema	Target Table Name	Target Column Name	Target Data Type
IS1	Customer	Customer Name	nvarchar(255)
IS1	Customer Site	Province	nvarchar(64)
IS1	Customer Site	City	nvarchar(128)
IS1	Customer Site	Address	nvarchar(128)
IS1	Customer Site	Telephone	nvarchar(7)
IS1	Customer Comment	Customer Comment	nvarchar(255)

Schema	Target Table Name	Target Column Name	Target Data Type
IS1	Customer	Customer No	nvarchar(5)
IS1	Customer	Customer Name	nvarchar(255)
IS1	Customer Site	Province	nvarchar(64)
IS1	Customer Site	City	nvarchar(128)
IS1	Customer Site	Telephone	nvarchar(7)

Schema	Target Table Name	Target Column Name	Target Data Type
IS1	Customer	Customer No	nvarchar(5)
IS1	Customer Site	Site No	smallint
IS1	Customer Site	Site Name	nvarchar(64)
IS1	Customer Site	Province	nvarchar(64)
IS1	Customer Site	City	nvarchar(128)
IS1	Customer Site	Postal Code	nvarchar(32)
IS1	Customer Site	Address	nvarchar(128)
IS1	Customer Site	Telephone	nvarchar(7)
IS1	Customer Site	Manager	nvarchar(32)

Table 8.12b - The Customer Mapping Spreadsheet (Target tables)

Simple but it does the trick. The source schema is identified, the source tables, columns and data types are mapped to their targets.

This document together with the physical data model and ETL specifications will allow us to create the ETL processes required to load our interim schema and ODS.

Product Physical Model and DDL

The next ODS subject area we examine is the Product subject area. Figure 8.2 shows the physical data model for this part of the ODS database.

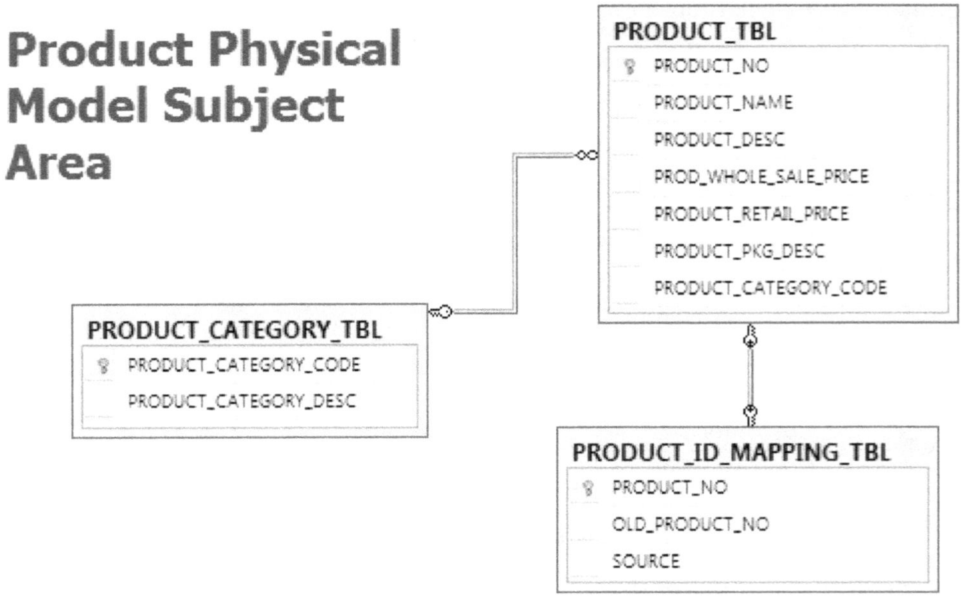

Figure 8.2 - The Product Physical Subject Area Data Model

There are only three tables in this subject area. We have the product table (PRODUCT_TBL) to store basic product information and the product category table (PRODUCT_CATEGORY_TBL) that contains codes and descriptions for each of the product categories. Lastly, we have the product id mapping table (PRODUCT_ID_MAPPING_TBL) to link the new product key with the old product key. Only the new PRODUCT_NO column is assigned as the primary key because there is a one to one relationship with the new PRODUCT_TBL. The OLD_PRODUCT_NO column is a non key attribute functionally dependent on the primary key.

The relationships are:

- The product category table has a one to many relationship with the product table.
- The product table has a one to one relationship with the product id mapping table that maintains the mapping between the new product numbers and the old product numbers.

The physical data dictionary for the product table is shown in Table 8.13.

Logical Entity Name	Physical Table Name
Product	PRODUCT_TBL

Logical Column Name	Physical Column Name	Data Type
Product No	**PRODUCT_NO**	nvarchar(9)
Product Name	PRODUCT_NAME	nvarchar(255)
Product Description	PRODUCT_DESC	nvarchar(255)
Product Wholesale Price	PROD_WHOLE_SALE_PRICE	money
Product Retail Price	PRODUCT_RETAIL_PRICE	money
Product Packaging	PRODUCT_PKG_DESC	nvarchar(255)
Product Category	***PRODUCT_CATEGORY_CODE***	smallint

Table 8.13 - The Product Table Data Dictionary

Examining the data dictionary, we can see that the primary key is based on the PRODUCT_NO column and there is one foreign key: PRODUCT_CATEGORY_CODE that is used to establish the relationship with the product category table.

The data dictionary for the product category table is examined next and is shown in Table 8.14.

Logical Entity Name	Physical Table Name
Product Category	PRODUCT_CATEGORY_TBL

Logical Column Name	Physical Column Name	Data Type
Product Category	**PRODUCT_CATEGORY_CODE**	smallint
Product Category Description	PRODUCT_CATEGORY_DESC	nvarchar(255)

Table 8.14 - The Product Category Table Data Dictionary

This is a simple table that contains the codes and descriptions for the product categories. The primary key is based on the PRODUCT_CATEGORY_CODE column. A sample dump of this table is shown in Table 8.15.

PRODUCT_CATEGORY_CODE	PRODUCT_CATEGORY_DESC
1	Coffee Grinder
2	Espresso Machine
3	Industrial Coffee Maker
4	Personal Coffee Maker

Table 8.15 - The Product Category Table Data Dump

As new product categories are added to the sales catalog, we can add them to this table by generating a new category id and description.

Next we look at the data dictionary for the product id mapping table. This is shown in Table 8.16.

Logical Entity Name	**Physical Table Name**
Product ID Map	PRODUCT_ID_MAPPING_TBL

Logical Column Name	**Physical Column Name**	**Data Type**
Product No	**PRODUCT_NO**	nvarchar(9)
Old Product No	OLD_PRODUCT_NO	nvarchar(255)
Schema Name	SOURCE	nvarchar(255)

Table 8.16 - The Product Id Mapping Table Data Dictionary

This is similar to the corresponding mapping table used for customer identifiers which we examined earlier. Here we want to maintain the link between the new product number and the old product number. We also have a column called SOURCE so we can identify the original source table.

As stated earlier, the OLD_PRODUCT_NO column is not part of the primary key for this table.

A sample dump report to give us a good idea of what this data looks like is shown in Table 8.17.

PRODUCT_NO	OLD_PRODUCT_NO	SOURCE
1001	10001	London
1002	10002	London
1003	10003	London
1004	10004	London
1005	10005	London
1006	P10001	Torino
1007	P10002	Torino
1008	P10003	Torino
1009	P10004	Torino
1010	PN1234	Torino
1011	PN1235	Torino
1012	PN1236	Torino
1013	PN1237	Torino

Table 8.17 - The Product ID Mapping Table Data Dump

As we design our physical database model and data dictionaries it is always good practice to examine sample data so we can make sure that not only do we understand the data structures but we also design the supporting tables correctly.

Below is the DDL for these sets of tables:

```
/***************/
/* PRODUCT_TBL */
/***************/

CREATE TABLE PRODUCT_TBL
(
PRODUCT_NO               VARCHAR(9)  NOT NULL,
PRODUCT_NAME             NVARCHAR(255),
PRODUCT_DESC             NVARCHAR(255),
PROD_WHOLE_SALE_PRICE    MONEY,
PRODUCT_RETAIL_PRICE     MONEY,
PRODUCT_PKG_DESC         NVARCHAR(255),
PRODUCT_CATEGORY_CODE    SMALLINT
)
GO

/*************************/
/* Define the primary key */
/*************************/

ALTER TABLE PRODUCT_TBL WITH NOCHECK
ADD CONSTRAINT PK_PRODUCT_PRODUCT_NO
      PRIMARY KEY CLUSTERED (PRODUCT_NO)
WITH (FILLFACTOR = 75, ONLINE = ON, PAD_INDEX = ON);
GO

/********************************************/
/* Define the foreign key between product table */
/* and the product category table            */
/********************************************/

ALTER TABLE PRODUCT_TBL
WITH CHECK ADD
CONSTRAINT FK_PRODUCT_TBL_TO_PRODUCT_CATEGORY_TBL
FOREIGN KEY(PRODUCT_CATEGORY_CODE)
REFERENCES PRODUCT_CATEGORY_TBL (PRODUCT_CATEGORY_CODE)
GO

/********************************************/
/* Define the foreign key between product table */
/* and the product id mapping table          */
/********************************************/

ALTER TABLE PRODUCT_TBL
WITH CHECK ADD
CONSTRAINT FK_PRODUCT_TBL_TO_PRODUCT_ID_MAPPING_TBL
FOREIGN KEY(PRODUCT_NO)
REFERENCES PRODUCT_ID_MAPPING_TBL (PRODUCT_NO)
GO
```

```
/************************/
/* PRODUCT_CATEGORY_TBL */
/************************/

CREATE TABLE PRODUCT_CATEGORY_TBL
(
PRODUCT_CATEGORY_CODE   SMALLINT    NOT NULL,
PRODUCT_CATEGORY_DESC   NVARCHAR(255)
)
GO

/**************************/
/* Define the primary key */
/**************************/

ALTER TABLE PRODUCT_CATEGORY_TBL WITH NOCHECK
ADD CONSTRAINT PK_PRODUCT_CATEGORY_PRODUCT_CATEGORY_CODE
      PRIMARY KEY CLUSTERED (PRODUCT_CATEGORY_CODE)
WITH (FILLFACTOR = 75, ONLINE = ON, PAD_INDEX = ON);
GO

/**************************/
/* PRODUCT_ID_MAPPING_TBL */
/**************************/

CREATE TABLE PRODUCT_ID_MAPPING_TBL
(
PRODUCT_NO         NVARCHAR(9) NOT NULL,
OLD_PRODUCT_NO     NVARCHAR(255),
SOURCE             NVARCHAR(255)
)
GO

/**************************/
/* Define the primary key */
/**************************/

ALTER TABLE PRODUCT_ID_MAPPING_TBL WITH NOCHECK
ADD CONSTRAINT PK_PRODUCT_ID_MAPPING_PRODUCT_NO
      PRIMARY KEY CLUSTERED (PRODUCT_NO)
WITH (FILLFACTOR = 75, ONLINE = ON, PAD_INDEX = ON);
GO
```

Lastly, the mapping spreadsheet that will help us define the ETL tasks to load the product tables appears in Tables 8.18a and 8.18b.

Schema	Source Table	Source Column Name	Data Type
Torino	TorinoProductStaging	Product Name	nvarchar(255)
Torino	TorinoProductStaging	Size	nvarchar(255)
Torino	TorinoProductStaging	Retail Price	money
Torino	TorinoProductStaging	Sales Price	money

Schema	Source Table	Source Column Name	Data Type
Munich	MunichProductStg	Product Category	nvarchar(255)
Munich	MunichProductStg	Product ID	nvarchar(9)
Munich	MunichProductStg	Product Description	nvarchar(255)
Munich	MunichProductStg	Wholesale Price	money

Table 8.18a - The Product Mapping Spreadsheet (Source)

Schema	Target Table Name	Target Column Name	Target Data Type
IS1	Product	Product Name	nvarchar(255)
IS1	Product	Product Size	nvarchar(255)
IS1	Product	Product Retail Price	money
IS1	Product	Product Wholesale Price	money

Schema	Target Table Name	Target Column Name	Target Data Type
IS1	Product Category	Product Category Description	nvarchar(255)
IS1	Product ID Map	Old Product No	nvarchar(255)
IS1	Product	Product Description	nvarchar(255)
IS1	Product	Product Wholesale Price	money

Table 8.18b - The Product Mapping Spreadsheet (Target)

I would recommend that after you have created the physical tables in the database, you reverse engineer them with a tool such as Toad or other modeling tool so you can compare the resulting physical model to your original model to make sure you got the relationships correct.

Inventory Physical Model and DDL

Our next subject area deals with the physical inventory for Cafe Magnifico's ODS. Inventory information needs to be stored both at the local shop or distribution level but also as a total aggregate level.

Figure 8.3 below shows the tables that are part of this subject area.

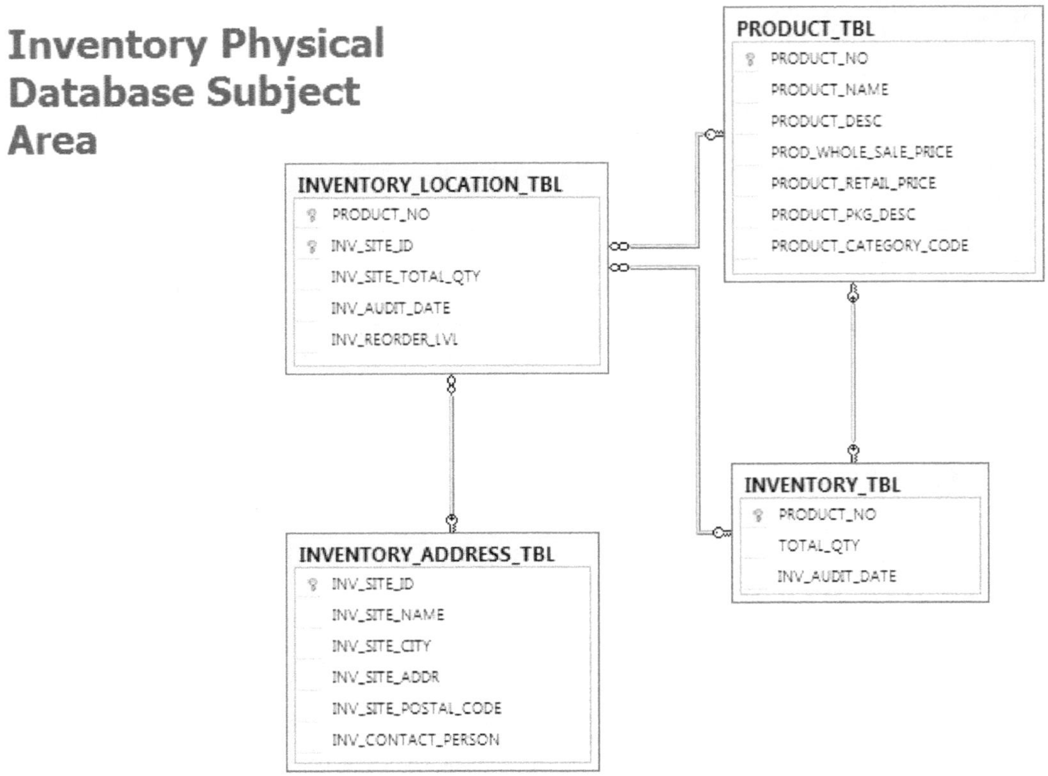

Figure 8.3 - The Inventory Physical Subject Area Data Model

One thing stands out. There is a one to one relationship between product and inventory. Recall that the inventory table will store aggregates of all the product levels such as total quantity on hand.

As it stands, a physical location address can only support one inventory site. In real world situations, it is possible to have multiple inventory sites at one address. We would need to make some modifications to our design to support these business requirements.

One easy fix would be to add an extra key, such as LOCATION_ID to the INVENTORY_LOCATION table. This would produce a composite key with three columns: PRODUCT_NO, LOCATION_ID and INV_SITE_ID. A more robust design would include room number information, building name and even rack, bin or shelf information. For now we wish to keep things simple.

Let's look at the data dictionaries for this subject area starting with the inventory subject area. This data dictionary is shown in Table 8.19.

Logical Entity Name	Physical Table Name
Inventory	INVENTORY_TBL

Logical Column Name	Physical Column Name	Data Type
Product No	**PRODUCT_NO**	nvarchar(9)
Total Quantity On Hand	TOTAL_QTY	integer
Inventory Date	INV_AUDIT_DATE	datetime

Table 8.19 - The Inventory Table Data Dictionary

A very simple table indeed. All that is included is the primary key, the total quantity on hand for a product and the date that all the inventory site totals were taken. We could enhance this table by at least adding the name of the person that took the inventory counts.

Next is the Inventory Location table. This is shown in Table 8.20 below.

Logical Entity Name	Physical Table Name
Inventory Location	INVENTORY_LOCATION_TBL

Logical Column Name	Physical Column Name	Data Type
Product No	**PRODUCT_NO**	nvarchar(9)
Site Identifier	***INV_SITE_ID***	smallint
Local Quantity On Hand	INV_SITE_TOTAL_QTY	integer
Inventory Date	INV_AUDIT_DATE	datetime
Reorder Level	INV_REORDER_LVL	integer

Table 8.20 - The Inventory Table Data Dictionary

This table is used to store the inventory level counts at each local site. We have a composite primary key consisting of the PRODUCT_NO and INV_SITE_ID columns. Notice also that the INV_SITE_ID column is a foreign key as it is both underlined and in italic font. (Recall that this is the simple methodology we use in this book). The INV_SITE_ID column serves as a foreign key to the INVENTORY_ADDRESS_TBL so we can retrieve the physical address components for the inventory site.

Our last data dictionary describes the Inventory Address table we will create. This is where a site's physical address attributes are stored.

Recall that this particular model supports the rule that a physical address can support only one inventory site, not many. This data dictionary appears in Table 8.21.

Logical Entity Name	Physical Table Name
Inventory Address	INVENTORY_ADDRESS_TBL

Logical Column Name	Physical Column Name	Data Type
Inventory Site Identifier	**INV_SITE_ID**	smallint
Inventory Site name	INV_SITE_NAME	nvarchar(32)
Inventory Site City	INV_SITE_CITY	nvarchar(64)
Inventory Site Address	INV_SITE_ADDR	nvarchar(255)
Inventory Site Postal Code	INV_SITE_POSTAL_CODE	nvarchar(32)
Inventory Contact	INV_CONTACT_PERSON	nvarchar(64)

Table 8.21 - The Inventory Address Table Data Dictionary

As you would expect, the usual suspects appear in the address table. We have a primary key (INV_SITE_ID), the name of the site, the city, address, postal code and a main contact person. We could have included a main telephone number and fax number also. We also might want to consider designing a separate table to hold telephone information for each site in case the contact person has a phone number, fax number and cell phone number.

Below are the DDL statements to create these tables:

```
/*****************/
/* INVENTORY_TBL */
/*****************/

CREATE TABLE INVENTORY_TBL
(
PRODUCT_NO          NVARCHAR(9) NOT NULL,
TOTAL_QTY           INT,
INV_AUDIT_DATE      DATETIME
)
GO

ALTER TABLE INVENTORY_TBL WITH NOCHECK
ADD CONSTRAINT PK_INVENTORY_
      PRIMARY KEY CLUSTERED (PRODUCT_NO)
WITH (FILLFACTOR = 75, ONLINE = ON, PAD_INDEX = ON);
GO

ALTER TABLE INVENTORY_TBL
WITH CHECK ADD
CONSTRAINT FK_INVENTORY_TBL_TO_PRODUCT_TBL
FOREIGN KEY(PRODUCT_NO)
REFERENCES PRODUCT_TBL (PRODUCT_NO)
GO
```

```
/*************************/
/* INVENTORY_LOCATION_TBL */
/*************************/

CREATE TABLE INVENTORY_LOCATION_TBL
(
PRODUCT_NO              NVARCHAR(9) NOT NULL,
INV_SITE_ID             SMALLINT    NOT NULL,
INV_SITE_TOTAL_QTY      INT,
INV_AUDIT_DATE          DATETIME,
INV_REORDER_LVL         INT
)
GO

/*************************/
/* Define the primary key */
/*************************/

ALTER TABLE INVENTORY_LOCATION_TBL WITH NOCHECK
ADD CONSTRAINT PK_INVENTORY_LOCATION_PRODUCT_NO
      PRIMARY KEY CLUSTERED (PRODUCT_NO,INV_SITE_ID)
WITH (FILLFACTOR = 75, ONLINE = ON, PAD_INDEX = ON);
GO

/************************************************************/
/* Define the foreign key between inventory location and inventory */
/************************************************************/

ALTER TABLE INVENTORY_LOCATION_TBL
WITH CHECK ADD
CONSTRAINT FK_INVENTORY_LOCATION_TBL_TO_INVENTORY_TBL
FOREIGN KEY(PRODUCT_NO)
REFERENCES INVENTORY_TBL (PRODUCT_NO)
GO

/**********************************************************/
/* Define the foreign key between inventory location and product */
/**********************************************************/

ALTER TABLE INVENTORY_LOCATION_TBL
WITH CHECK ADD
CONSTRAINT FK_INVENTORY_LOCATION_TBL_TO_PRODUCT_TBL
FOREIGN KEY(PRODUCT_NO)
REFERENCES PRODUCT_TBL (PRODUCT_NO)
GO

/**********************************************************/
/* Define the foreign key between inventory location and address */
/**********************************************************/

ALTER TABLE INVENTORY_LOCATION_TBL
WITH CHECK ADD
```

```
CONSTRAINT FK_INVENTORY_LOCATION_TBL_TO_INVENTORY_ADDRESS_TBL
FOREIGN KEY(INV_SITE_ID)
REFERENCES INVENTORY_ADDRESS_TBL (INV_SITE_ID)
GO

/************************/
/* INVENTORY_ADDRESS_TBL */
/************************/

CREATE TABLE INVENTORY_ADDRESS_TBL
(
INV_SITE_ID              SMALLINT    NOT NULL,
INV_SITE_NAME            NVARCHAR(32),
INV_SITE_CITY            NVARCHAR(64),
INV_SITE_ADDR            NVARCHAR(255),
INV_SITE_POSTAL_CODE     NVARCHAR(32),
INV_CONTACT_PERSON       NVARCHAR(64)
)
GO

ALTER TABLE INVENTORY_ADDRESS_TBL WITH NOCHECK
ADD CONSTRAINT PK_INVENTORY_ADDRESS_INV_SITE_ID
      PRIMARY KEY CLUSTERED (INV_SITE_ID)
WITH (FILLFACTOR = 75, ONLINE = ON, PAD_INDEX = ON);
GO
```

Our mapping spreadsheet for inventory-related tables appears in Tables 8.22a and 8.22b.

Schema	Source Table	Source Column Name	Data Type
London	LondonInventoryStg	Product No	nvarchar(255)
Munich	MunichInventoryStg	Product ID	nvarchar(255)

Schema	Source Table	Source Column Name	Data Type
London	LondonInventoryStg	Product Description	nvarchar(255)
London	LondonInventoryStg	Package	nvarchar(255)
London	LondonInventoryStg	Wholesale	money

Schema	Source Table	Source Column Name	Data Type
Munich	MunichInventoryStg	Product ID	nvarchar(9)
Munich	MunichInventoryStg	Quantity On Hand	float
Munich	MunichInventoryStg	Inventory Date	datetime

Schema	Source Table	Source Column Name	Data Type
Munich	MunichInventoryLocationStg	Product ID	nvarchar(9)
Munich	MunichInventoryLocationStg	Quantity On Hand	float
Munich	MunichInventoryLocationStg	Inventory Date	datetime
Munich	MunichInventoryLocationStg	Site	nvarchar(255)
Munich	MunichInventoryLocationStg	Reorder Level	float

Schema	Source Table	Source Column Name	Data Type
Munich	MunichInventoryAddressStg	Site	nvarchar(255)
Munich	MunichInventoryAddressStg	City	nvarchar(255)
Munich	MunichInventoryAddressStg	Address	nvarchar(255)
Munich	MunichInventoryAddressStg	Postal Code	nvarchar(255)
Munich	MunichInventoryAddressStg	Contact	nvarchar(255)

Table 8.22a - The Inventory Address Table Data Dictionary (source)

Schema	Target Table Name	Target Column Name	Target Data Type
IS1	Product	Product No	nvarchar(9)
IS1	Product	Product No	nvarchar(9)

Schema	Target Table Name	Target Column Name	Target Data Type
IS1	Product	Product Description	nvarchar(255)
IS1	Product	Product Packaging	nvarchar(255)
IS1	Product	Product Wholesale Price	money

Schema	Target Table Name	Target Column Name	Target Data Type
IS1	Inventory	Product No	nvarchar(9)
IS1	Inventory	Total Quantity On Hand	integer
IS1	Inventory	Inventory Date	datetime

Schema	Target Table Name	Target Column Name	Target Data Type
IS1	Inventory Location	Product No	nvarchar(9)
IS1	Inventory Location	Local Quantity On Hand	integer
IS1	Inventory Location	Inventory Date	datetime
IS1	Inventory Location	Site Identifier	smallint
IS1	Inventory Location	Reorder Level	integer

Schema	Target Table Name	Target Column Name	Target Data Type
IS1	Inventory Address	Inventory Site name	nvarchar(255)
IS1	Inventory Address	Inventory Site City	nvarchar(32)
IS1	Inventory Address	Inventory Site Address	nvarchar(64)
IS1	Inventory Address	Inventory Site Postal Code	nvarchar(32)
IS1	Inventory Address	Inventory Contact	nvarchar(64)

Table 8.22b - The Inventory Address Table Data Dictionary (target)

The table is split in two sections for better legibility. As an exercise for the reader, see if you can enhance the model to support the following rules:

- A physical address supports one or more inventory sites

- An inventory site has one or more contacts
- Each inventory site contact can have one or more telephones (such as main office or cell)
- An inventory site has a main telephone number and also a fax number
- A contact person may have multiple phone numbers (main, fax, cell, etc.).

See if you can also design an employee table that contains the following attributes:

- Employee Last Name
- Employee First Name
- Employee Title
- Employee Hire Date.

These enhancements would greatly improve our ODS model.

Order Header Physical Model and DDL

Next we turn our attention to the order subject area. The physical data model for this subject area appears in Figure 8.4.

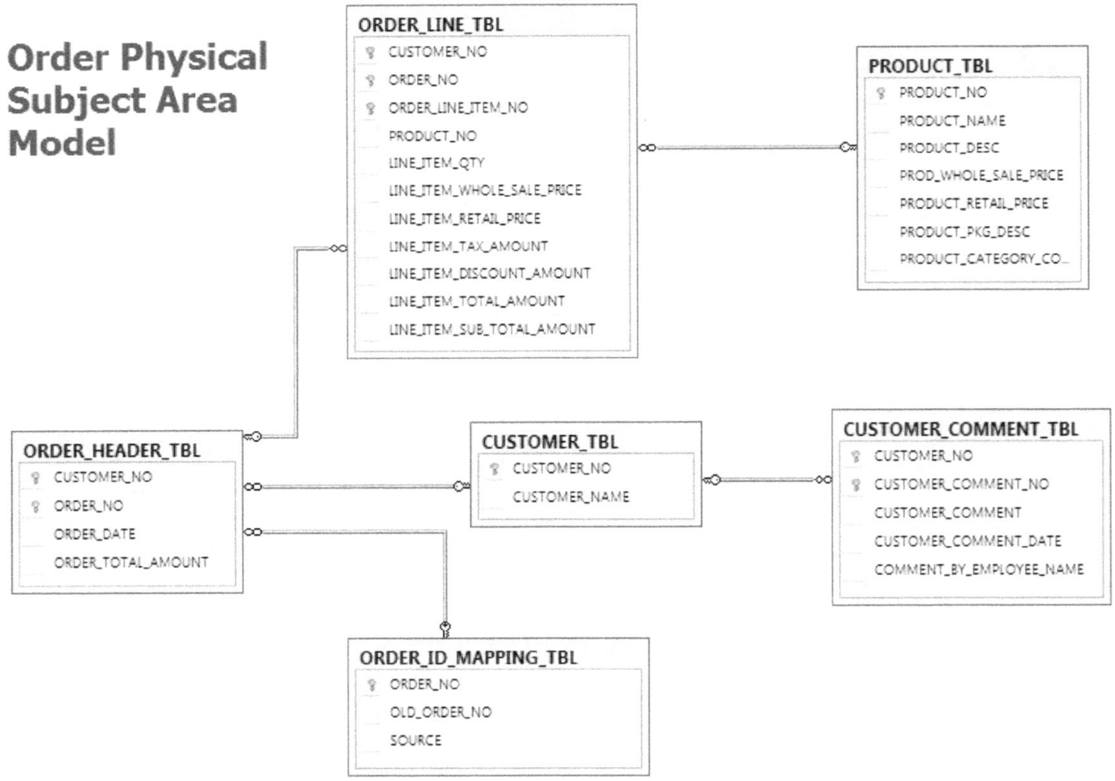

Figure 8.4 - Order Physical Subject Area Data Model

We have included the product, customer and customer comment tables as they are related to orders. Business subject areas can overlap as far as which tables are shown in each. This gives the modeler or anyone that needs to understand the model a perspective of how the business subject areas relate to each other.

As can be seen this model supports the following business rules:

- A customer may place one or more orders
- A customer may have one or more comments entered relating to the ordering process
- An order header is composed of one or more order line items
- A product appears on one or more line items.

Let's take a look at the data dictionaries for each of the tables in the subject area starting with the order table shown in Table 8.23.

Logical Entity Name	Physical Table Name
Order	ORDER_HEADER_TBL

Column Name	Physical Column Name	Data Type
Customer No	CUSTOMER_NO	Integer
Order No	ORDER_NO	nvarchar(12)
Order Date	ORDER_DATE	datetime
Order Total	ORDER_TOTAL_AMOUNT	money

Table 8.23 - The Order Header Table Data Dictionary

Notice the composite key for this table. It includes the Customer Number column and the Order Number column. This allows us the flexibility of using repeating, sequential order numbers for each customer but at the cost of a more complex key. Let's take a closer look. Our old scheme looked like the one shown in Table 8.24.

Customer No	Order No	Order Date	Order Total
10001	ORD-0001	10/1/2011	£579.98
10001	ORD-0002	10/1/2011	£339.63
10001	ORD-0003	10/1/2011	£935.28
10001	ORD-0004	10/1/2011	£1,483.90
10001	ORD-0005	10/2/2011	£543.40
10002	ORD-0006	10/2/2011	£862.13
10002	ORD-0007	10/2/2011	£1,238.33
10002	ORD-0008	10/2/2011	£418.00
10002	ORD-0009	10/2/2011	£1,186.08

Table 8.24 - The Old Order Number Sequential Scheme

The new ordering scheme appears in Table 8.25.

Customer No	Order No	Order Date	Order Total
10001	1	10/1/2011	£372.24
10001	2	10/1/2011	£330.88
10001	3	10/1/2011	£930.60
10001	4	10/1/2011	£1,456.70
10001	5	10/2/2011	£938.36
10002	1	10/2/2011	£460.13
10002	2	10/2/2011	£1,540.66
10002	3	10/2/2011	£700.54
10002	4	10/2/2011	£628.16

Table 8.25 - The New Order Number Sequential Scheme

This scheme allows us to quickly identify how many orders a customer has generated since he or she became a client of Cafe Magnifico. Also, some companies like to generate order numbers that contain embedded information that appear in invoices.

For example, using the scheme above, we can generate and order number that looks like this:

```
ORD-10001-1-10.1.2011
```

This scheme tells the clerk that customer 10001 generated order 1 on October first 2011.

Getting back to our data dictionary, the design is fairly simple. It only stores the order date and the total amount of the order. A real example would include the total tax paid, the total discounts and the name or identifier of the sales person that generated the order.

Our mapping spreadsheet for order header information appears in Tables 8.26a and 8.26b.

Schema	Source Table	Source Column Name	Data Type
London	LondonOrderHeaderStg	Customer No	nvarchar(5)
London	LondonOrderHeaderStg	Order No	nvarchar(255)
London	LondonOrderHeaderStg	Order Date	datetime
London	LondonOrderHeaderStg	Order Total	money

Schema	Source Table	Source Column Name	Data Type
Torino	TorinoOrderStaging	Customer Name	nvarchar(255)
Torino	TorinoOrderStaging	Product	nvarchar(255)
Torino	TorinoOrderStaging	Quantity	float
Torino	TorinoOrderStaging	Total Price	money
Torino	TorinoOrderStaging	Discount	float
Torino	TorinoOrderStaging	Sales Price	money
Torino	TorinoOrderStaging	Order Date	datetime

Table 8.26a - Order Header Mapping Spreadsheet (source)

Schema	Target Table Name	Target Column Name	Target Data Type
IS2	Order Header	Customer No	nvarchar(5)
IS2	Order Header	Order No	nvarchar(12)
IS2	Order Header	Order Date	datetime
IS2	Order Header	Order Total	money

Schema	Target Table Name	Target Column Name	Target Data Type
IS2	Order Header	Customer No	nvarchar(5)
		Not applicable, goes to line item	
		Not applicable, goes to line item	
		Derived, sum of all line items	
		Not applicable, goes to line item	
		Not applicable, goes to line item	
IS2	Order Header	Order Date	datetime

Table 8.26b - Order Header Mapping Spreadsheet (target)

Notice that some of our entries in the spreadsheet are empty. This is because the source order information will be mapped to the order line table so we do not map them here as we are mapping the order header columns. (Also keep note of some of the data type conversions from source to target.)

Next is the data dictionary for our familiar identifier mapping table. This time we want to map new order numbers to old order numbers. Table 8.27 displays the data dictionary.

Logical Entity Name	Physical Table Name
Order ID Map	ORDER_ID_MAPPING_TBL

Logical Column Name	Physical Column Name	Data Type
Order No	**ORDER_NO**	nvarchar(12)
Old Order No	OLD_ORDER_NO	nvarchar(255)
Schema Name	SOURCE	nvarchar(255)

Table 8.27 - the Order Id Mapping Table Data Dictionary

As with customer and product we wish to track old order numbers against new generated order numbers when we load our ODS from the original source systems. The old order number column has a data type of nvarchar with a length of 255 just in case we load alpha numeric order numbers (as was the case in our London database).

Last but not least we look at the order line table.

Order Line Physical Model and DDL

Lastly, we prepare the data dictionary and mapping spreadsheet for the order line table. The data dictionary appears first in Table 8.28.

Logical Entity Name	Physical Table Name
Order Line	ORDER_LINE_TBL

Logical Column Name	Physical Column Name	Data Type
Customer No	**CUSTOMER_NO**	Integer
Order No	**ORDER_NO**	nvarchar(12)
Line Item	**ORDER_LINE_ITEM_NO**	smallint
Product No	PRODUCT_NO	nvarchar(9)
Quantity	LINE_ITEM_QTY	integer
Retail Price	LINE_ITEM_RETAIL_PRICE	money
Wholesale	LINE_ITEM_WHOLE_SALE_PRICE	money
Discount	LINE_ITEM_DISCOUNT_AMOUNT	float
Tax	LINE_ITEM_TAX_AMOUNT	money
Sub Total	LINE_ITEM_SUB_TOTAL_AMOUNT	money
Total Price	LINE_ITEM_TOTAL_AMOUNT	money

Table 8.28 - The Order Line Table Data Dictionary

Notice that the order line table contains a three column composite key made up of the CUSTOMER_NO, ORDER_NO and ORDER_LINE_ITEM columns. The remaining columns include the basic information you would expect in an order line item.

The DDL commands to create these tables and the primary to foreign key constraints appear below:

```
/********************/
/* ORDER_HEADER_TBL */
/********************/

CREATE TABLE ORDER_HEADER_TBL
(
CUSTOMER_NO              NVARCHAR(5)       NOT NULL,
ORDER_NO                 NVARCHAR(12)      NOT NULL,
ORDER_DATE               DATETIME,
ORDER_TOTAL_AMOUNT       MONEY
)
GO

/**************************/
/* Define the primary key */
/**************************/

ALTER TABLE ORDER_HEADER_TBL WITH NOCHECK
ADD CONSTRAINT PK_ORDER_HEADER_CUSTOMER_NO_ORDER_NO
      PRIMARY KEY CLUSTERED (CUSTOMER_NO,ORDER_NO)
WITH (FILLFACTOR = 75, ONLINE = ON, PAD_INDEX = ON);
GO

/************************************************************/
/* Define the foreign key between the order header table    */
/* and the customer table                                  */
/************************************************************/

ALTER TABLE ORDER_HEADER_TBL
WITH CHECK ADD
CONSTRAINT FK_ORDER_HEADER_TBL_TO_CUSTOMER_TBL
FOREIGN KEY(CUSTOMER_NO)
REFERENCES CUSTOMER_TBL (CUSTOMER_NO)
GO

/************************************************************/
/* Define the foreign key between the order header table    */
/* and the order id mapping table                           */
/************************************************************/

ALTER TABLE ORDER_HEADER_TBL
WITH CHECK ADD
CONSTRAINT FK_ORDER_HEADER_TBL_TO_ORDER_ID_MAPPING_TBL
FOREIGN KEY(ORDER_NO)
REFERENCES ORDER_ID_MAPPING_TBL (ORDER_NO)
GO
```

```
/************************/
/* ORDER_ID_MAPPING_TBL */
/************************/

CREATE TABLE ORDER_ID_MAPPING_TBL
(
ORDER_NO            NVARCHAR(12) NOT NULL,
OLD_ORDER_NO        NVARCHAR(255),
SOURCE              NVARCHAR(255)
)
GO

/*************************/
/* Define the primary key */
/*************************/

ALTER TABLE ORDER_ID_MAPPING_TBL WITH NOCHECK
ADD CONSTRAINT PK_ORDER_ID_MAPPING_ORDER_NO
      PRIMARY KEY CLUSTERED (ORDER_NO)
WITH (FILLFACTOR = 75, ONLINE = ON, PAD_INDEX = ON);
GO

/******************/
/* ORDER_LINE_TBL */
/******************/

CREATE TABLE ORDER_LINE_TBL
(
CUSTOMER_NO                 NVARCHAR(5)  NOT NULL,
ORDER_NO                    NVARCHAR(12) NOT NULL,
ORDER_LINE_ITEM_NO          SMALLINT     NOT NULL,
PRODUCT_NO                  NVARCHAR(9),
LINE_ITEM_QTY               INT,
LINE_ITEM_WHOLE_SALE_PRICE  MONEY,
LINE_ITEM_RETAIL_PRICE      MONEY,
LINE_ITEM_TAX_AMOUNT        MONEY,
LINE_ITEM_DISCOUNT_AMOUNT   MONEY,
LINE_ITEM_TOTAL_AMOUNT      MONEY,
LINE_ITEM_SUB_TOTAL_AMOUNT  MONEY
)
GO

/*************************/
/* Define the primary key */
/*************************/

ALTER TABLE ORDER_LINE_TBL WITH NOCHECK
ADD CONSTRAINT PK_ORDER_LINE_ORDER_NO
      PRIMARY KEY CLUSTERED (CUSTOMER_NO,ORDER_NO,ORDER_LINE_ITEM_NO)
WITH (FILLFACTOR = 75, ONLINE = ON, PAD_INDEX = ON);
GO
```

```
/************************************************************/
/* Define the foreign key between the order line table      */
/* and the order id mapping table                           */
/************************************************************/

ALTER TABLE ORDER_LINE_TBL
WITH CHECK ADD
CONSTRAINT FK_ORDER_LINE_TBL_TO_PRODUCT_TBL
FOREIGN KEY(PRODUCT_NO)
REFERENCES PRODUCT_TBL (PRODUCT_NO)
GO

/************************************************************/
/* Define the foreign key between the order line table      */
/* and the order id mapping table                           */
/************************************************************/

ALTER TABLE ORDER_LINE_TBL
WITH CHECK ADD
CONSTRAINT FK_ORDER_LINE_TBL_TO_ORDER_HEADER_TBL
FOREIGN KEY(CUSTOMER_NO,ORDER_NO)
REFERENCES ORDER_HEADER_TBL (CUSTOMER_NO,ORDER_NO)
GO
```

Last but not least is the mapping spreadsheet for order line attributes shown in Tables 8.29a and 8.29b.

Schema	Source Table	Source Column Name	Data Type
London	LondonOrderLineStg	Order No	nvarchar(255)
London	LondonOrderLineStg	Line Item	float
London	LondonOrderLineStg	Product No	nvarchar(255)
London	LondonOrderLineStg	Quantity	float
London	LondonOrderLineStg	Wholesale	money
London	LondonOrderLineStg	Retail	money
London	LondonOrderLineStg	Tax	money
London	LondonOrderLineStg	Sub Total	money
London	LondonOrderLineStg	Discount	float
London	LondonOrderLineStg	Total	money

Table 8.29a - The Order Line Mapping Spreadsheet (source)

Schema	Target Table Name	Target Column Name	Target Data Type
IS2	Order Line Item	Order No	nvarchar(12)
IS2	Order Line Item	Line Item	smallint
IS2	Order Line Item	Product No	nvarchar(9)
IS2	Order Line Item	Quantity	integer
IS2	Order Line Item	Wholesale	money
IS2	Order Line Item	Retail Price	money
IS2	Order Line Item	Tax	money
IS2	Order Line Item	Sub Total	money
IS2	Order Line Item	Discount	decimal(5,2)
IS2	Order Line Item	Total Price	money

Table 8.29b - The Order Line Mapping Spreadsheet (target)

Here is a tip for improving this mapping spreadsheet. I did not include the physical column names in the spreadsheet to save some space. In a real world situation, you would want to do this.

This concludes our generation of the physical data dictionaries, physical database model, mapping spreadsheet and DDL statements needed to create our ODS database.

Summary

As a reward for getting through reading all the tables and models, Figure 8.5 contains the final physical database model, showing all the subject areas.

Our design was simple so as not to cloud the purpose of this chapter. I wanted to show how all the design documents we generated during the schema integration process were an important set of tools used in the creation of the ODS. All of the conflict reports, ETL specifications and logical and physical models helped us create a database that pulls in data from several sources into one unified model.

We have two more chapters to go. Chapter 9 will show you how to create the actual ETL processes to load the data from our three source systems into our ODS. Chapter 10 will show a simple generic example on how to profile and cleanse data that comes into an ODS.

Chapters 9 and 10 assume you integrated the MySQL database into the ODS. Now would be a good time to try this exercise if you have not tried it already.

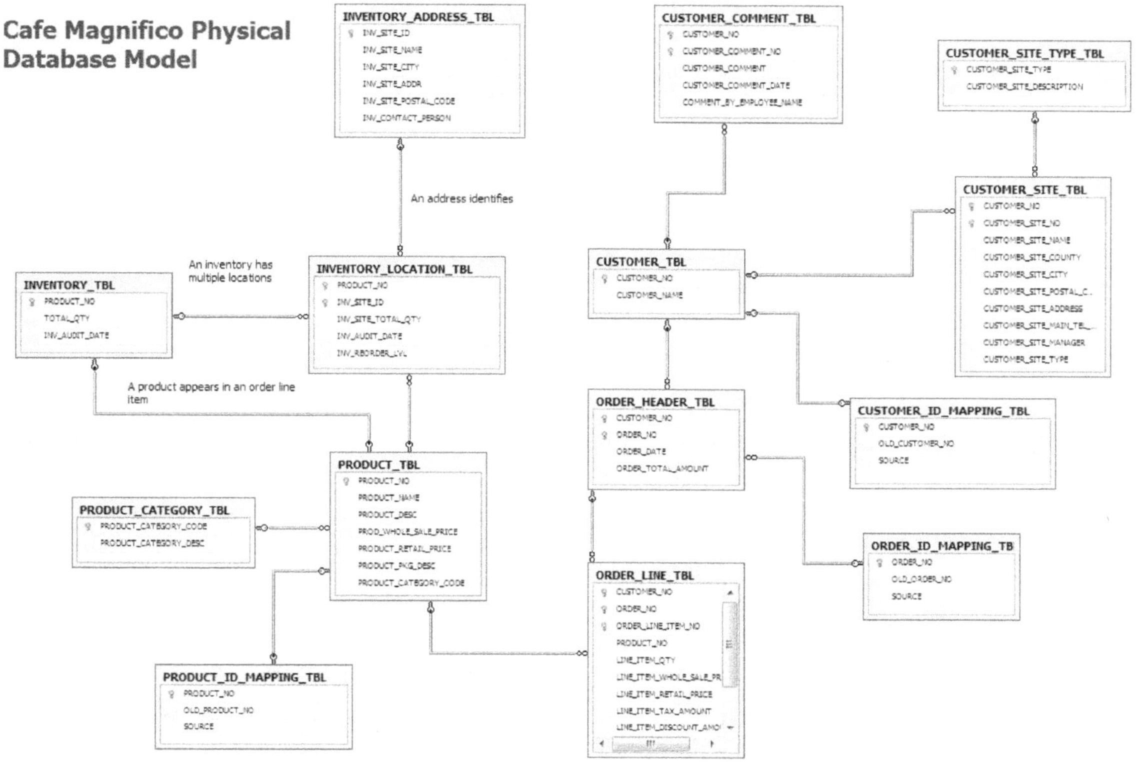

Figure 8.5 -The Final Cafe Magnifico Database Model

CHAPTER 9
Creating our ETL Processes with SSIS

Now that we have completed our schema integration analysis and created our ETL specifications we can roll up our sleeves and actually start to build the processes that extract the transactional data from our source databases and load it into our ODS.

I reference an extra database implemented with MySQL with the assumption that you have created this database and gone through all the proper steps identified in earlier chapters to integrate the data, identify the data conflicts and create the ETL specifications for the ETL processes. I did this for three reasons:

1. I wanted the reader to actually try to figure out the steps to add a new database on their own.
2. I wanted to increase the complexity of the integration process by adding an extra database to make this chapter a bit more interesting.
3. I wanted the reader to create their own SQL tasks and stored procedures.

(You can't let me have all the fun, can you?)

We will base our example discussion on Microsoft's SQL Server 2008 database management system and the ETL tool provided with SQL Server called SSIS (SQL Server Integration Services). You can use the process flows discussed in the chapter to create the ETL processes with other vendor tools such as Informatica or Data Flux.

We will create SSIS packages that:

- Stage the data from Excel, MS Access, and additional MySQL database and SQL2008 database
- Load all reference data like customer and product from the staging tables
- Load all tables in Interim Schema 1 (IS1)
- Load all tables in Interim Schema 2 (IS2)
- Load all tables in Interim Schema 3 (IS3) (additional schema you added as an extra source).

Figure 9.1 contains a typical screenshot showing the various tools, panels and features.

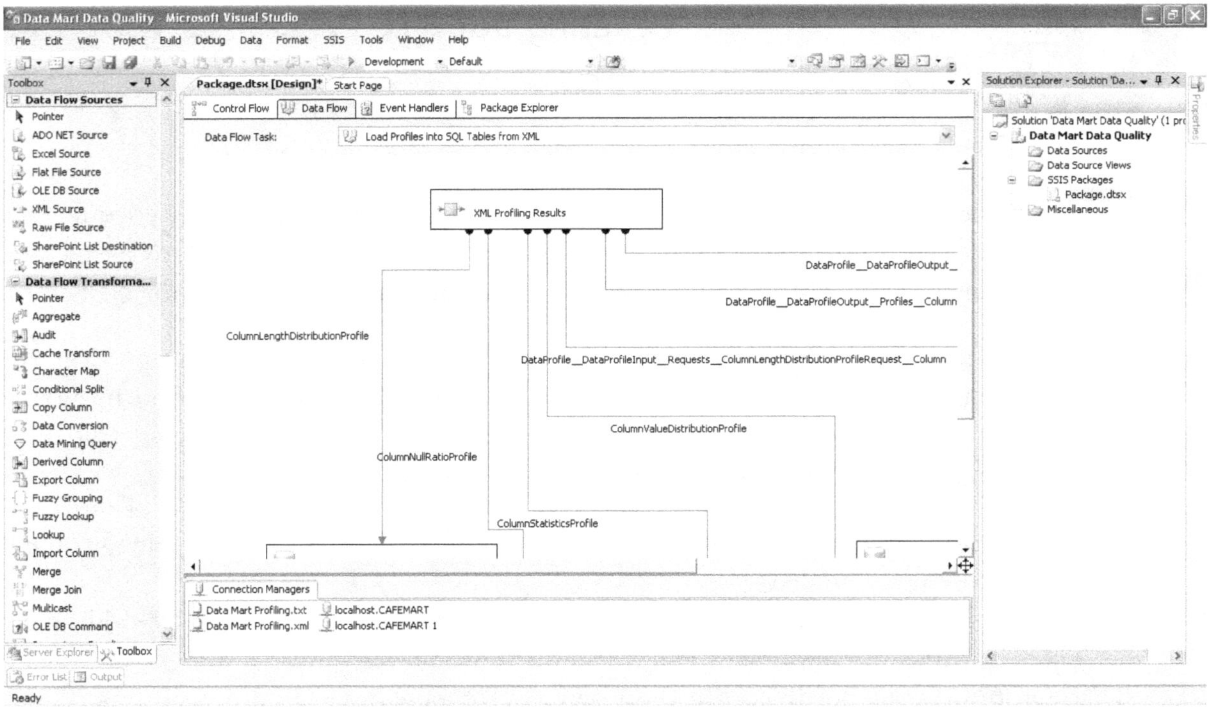

Figure 9.1 - SQL Server Integration Services Tools, Panels, and Features

The front end GUI contains several main panels and folders that allow you to select tasks, drag and drop tasks into the design window and create the flow that controls the sequence of ETL transformations.

The tool box on the left side contains all the low level tasks needed to perform control flow and data flow processes. Depending on which tab is selected, the contents of the tool box changes.

The main tabs include the Control Flow tab, the Data Flow tab and the Event Handler tab. The Control Flow tab allows you to define the process flow by dragging and dropping tasks into the design area (the large panel in middle of the screen) and connecting each task in the sequence your logic requires. The Data Flow tab allows you to enter more detailed data manipulation tasks such as sorting data, merging data streams and performing complex data processes such as profiling data or performing fuzzy matching to identify duplicate data items.

Lastly, the Event Handler tab allows you to create custom logic to handle more complex events such as error recovery if a task fails.

In conclusion, this is a graphical tool that presents developers with all the low level tasks to manage data manipulation, identification of source and target databases and a host of other ETL related tasks like defining the flow of execution of the ETL processes.

This chapter will have many screen shots so that you can follow along and then recreate the ETL packages on your own if you downloaded the evaluation copy of SQL Server 2008 R2 from the Microsoft web site.

Implementation Strategy

Our strategy will be simple; in order to create the complete ETL processes we will follow the specifications we created in earlier chapters. The steps we will follow are:

- Create a new SSIS project
- For each of the main ETL flows (staging, reference, IS1, IS2 and IS3) create a new package (Recall that IS3 would be created by you, the reader, as an exercise)
- For each package define a new connection to the database that holds the data
- Define all of the tasks as per the specifications we developed earlier.

Each of the sections in this chapter will follow the same basic structure. We will display screen shots of the flows, then present tables that shows the contents of each of the tasks. Each of the tasks can be implemented as a stored procedure or directly typed in SQL query statements or a pre-built task component provided by Microsoft. Let's start by creating a new project.

Simply go to the File menu and select File->New->Project. Select "Integration Services Project" and fill in the name a location of where you want the files stored. Notice that there are different types of project we can create.

The main types of tasks will be to pick "Execute SQL" tasks and fill in the SQL commands for each task. Below is a typical dialog box that allows us to create a SQL task. Just simply drag and drop the tasks from the toolbox into the design area. Double click on the task and the dialog box shown in Figure 9.2 appears.

You need to specify the server name, the log on credentials and the database to connect to. A push button exists that allows you to test the connection before you proceed. I highly recommend that you use this feature.

The second recurring connections we will use are the connections that allow us to connect to the various Microsoft Excel spreadsheet tabs, MS Access database, SQL Server database and MySQL database.

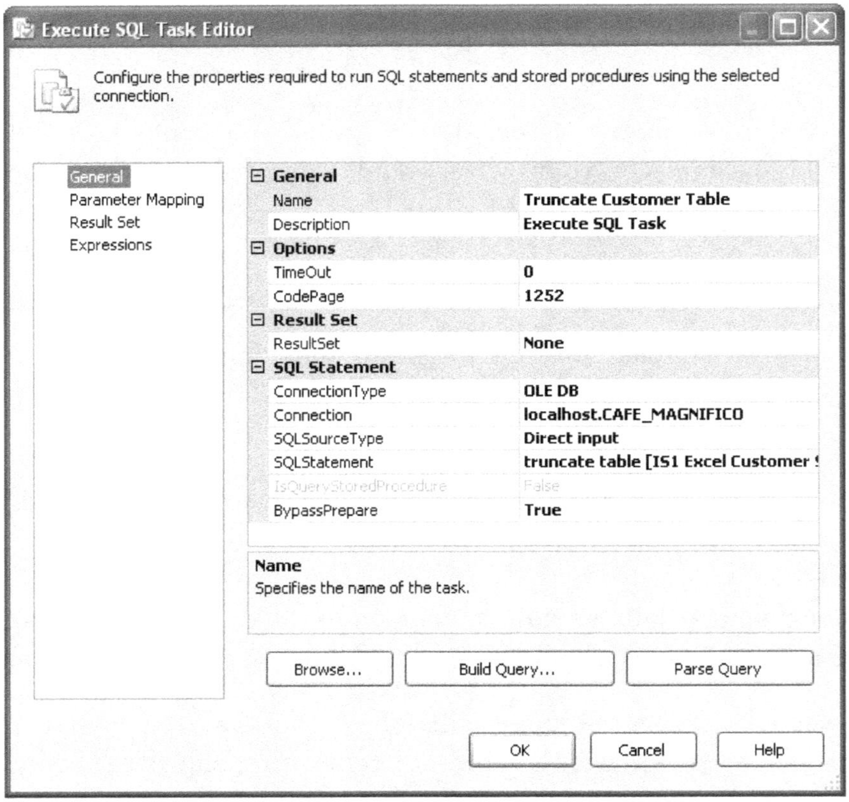

Figure 9.2 - Building a SQL Task

There are a few different ways to accomplish this. The easiest is to drag an Excel Source item from the Toolbox and drag and drop it into your design area. Double clicking on the source once it is in the design area produces the displayed in Figure 9.3.

The developer simply needs to identify the location of the spreadsheet and pick the tab in the spreadsheet that he or she wishes to connect to. Experiment a bit by creating a simple spreadsheet with a few tabs and then try to use the technique described above to establish a connection to each tab.

Clicking on the columns selection allows you to see the columns in the spreadsheet and clicking on "Error Output" allows you to specify how to handle errors in case the spreadsheet does not load properly.

That's pretty much it as far as establishing connections goes. One can establish connections to not only Excel spreadsheets but also to Oracle databases and other vendor products as long as you have the necessary OLEDB and ODBC connectors installed on your system.

You can even establish connections to SharePoint lists, download the lists and load them into SQL tables.

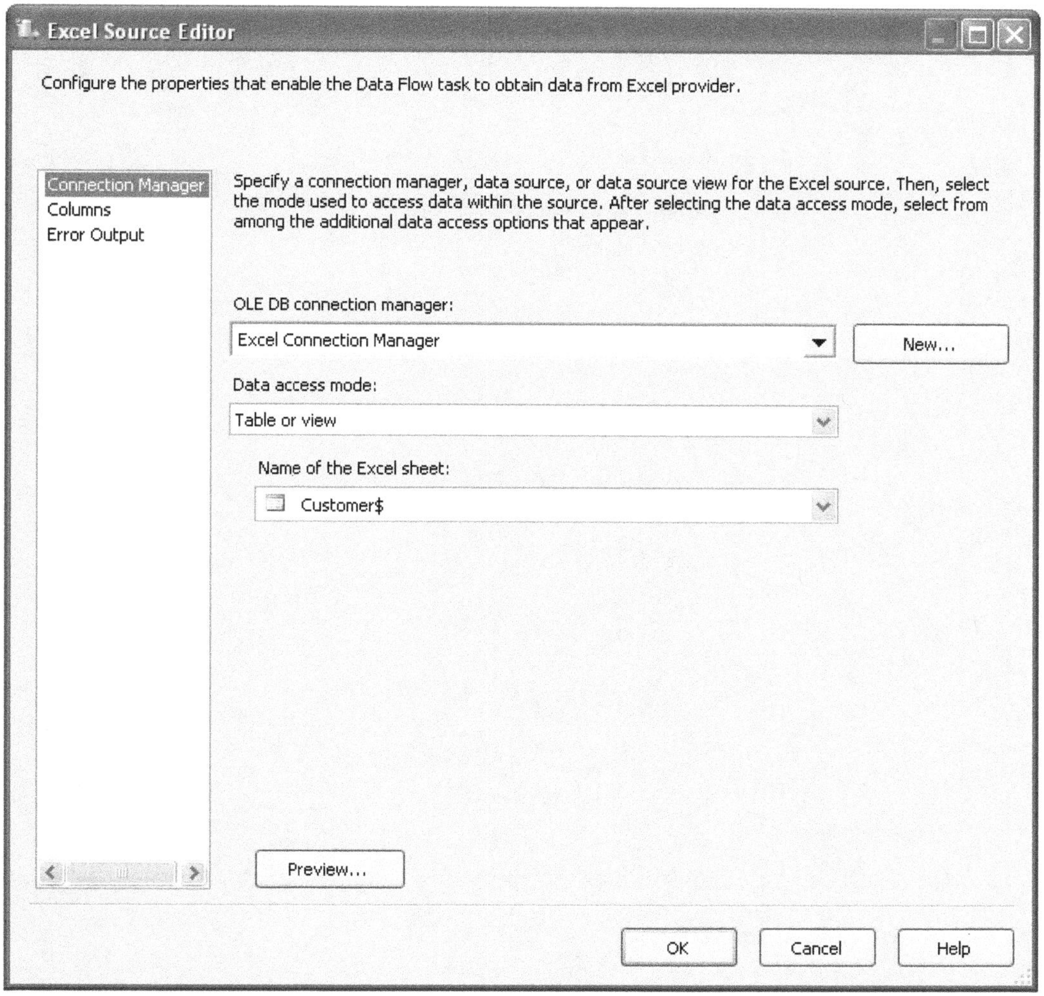

Figure 9.3 - Defining Excel Connections

Loading the Staging Tables

Now that we know how to create connections let's start by connecting to our IS1 database.

The dialog box to create connections appears in Figure 9.4. Dragging an "Execute SQL" task to the design area and double clicking on it will display the dialog box.

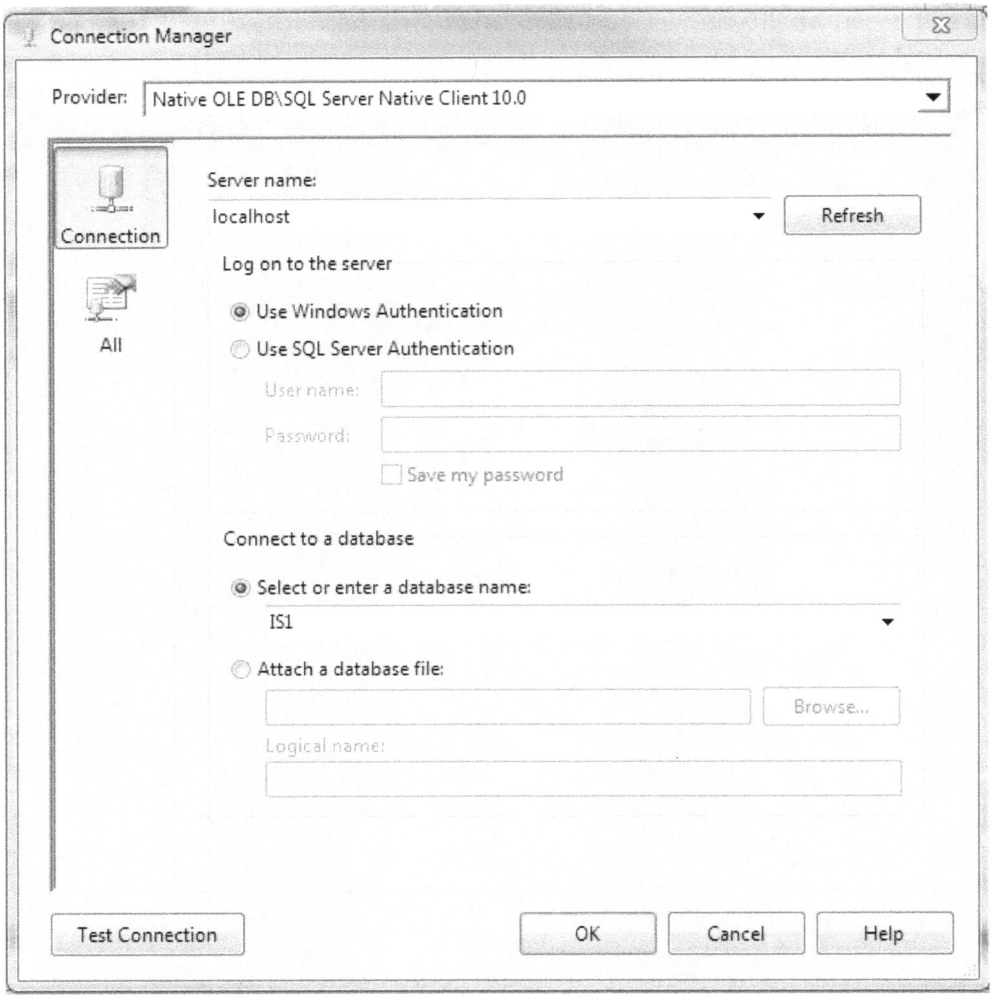

Figure 9.4 - Creating Database Connections

Connect to the IS1 database, enter the logon credentials and test the connection. Our goal is to now create the main package that loads the staging tables, the reference data and then the interim schema database.

The screen shot in Figure 9.5 shows part of this large package. We will describe each item that you need to create. These examples are a bit more detailed and refer to tables not discussed in the prior chapters. The idea is to show you how complex ETL processes can get that are required to load an ODS.

Notice that the screen fulfills the requirement that we create a process sequence diagram that defines the order of the flow. This tool provides one of the benefits of rapid application development in that it allows us to define the process flow while prototyping the actual code.

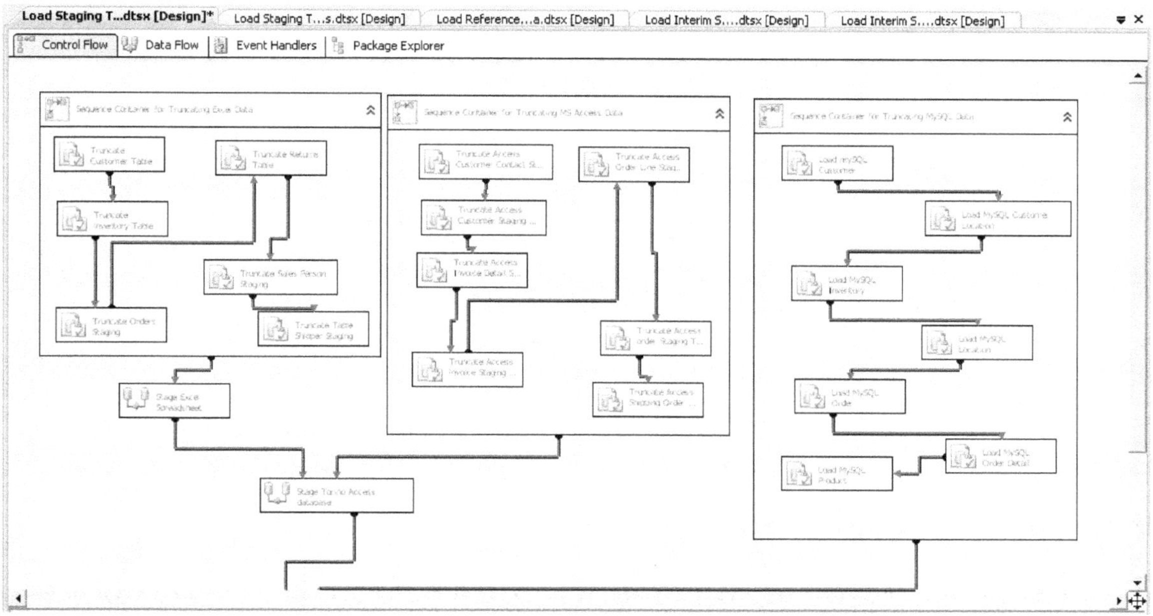

Figure 9.5 - Load Staging Tables Package

This package has several components:

- 3 sequence containers
- 2 data flow tasks (we can drill into these to see the individual data flows)
- 4 package tasks (packages can call other packages).

The next screen shot shows the remainder of the package. I told you this was a large one!

The screen shot above shows the data flow task called "Stage Torino Access database" that loads all the SQL Server 2008 staging tables with data from our Torino Access database. Notice that the control flow arrows from two of the sequence containers flow into this tasks. It is possible to specify not only sequential flows but also parallel flows.

Before I forget, sequence containers are special types of tasks that allow you to bundle related tasks together that perform a specific function. In this case we bundle all the tasks that truncate tables into a container so we can manage them better in case something goes wrong. There are also iterative containers that allow you to specify loops to perform tasks more than one time. (For example, setting up a loop to check for the availability of a file in a staging directory.)

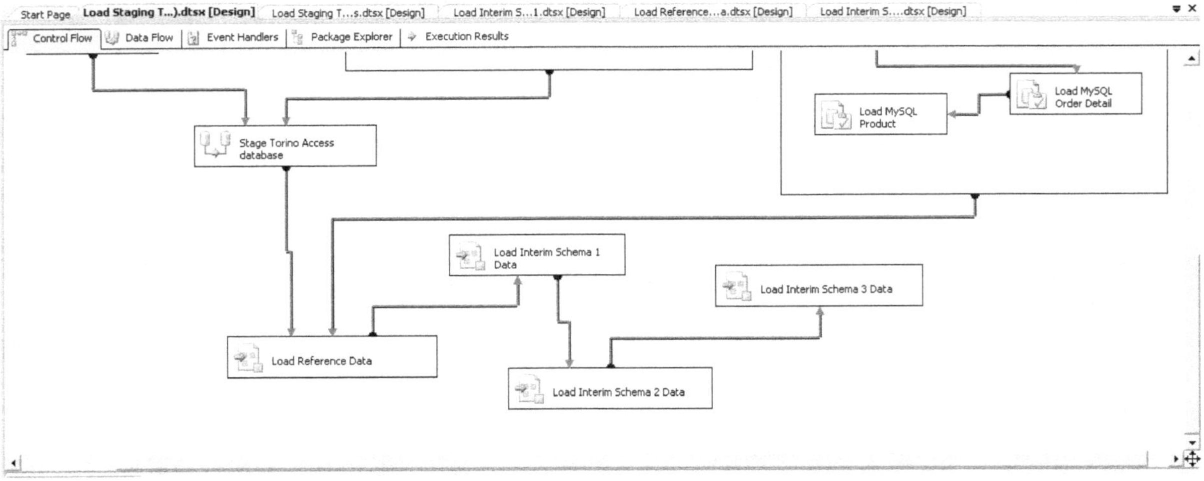

Figure 9.6 - Load Staging Tables Package (continued)

Let's conclude this section by identifying the contents of each individual task. We will do this by presenting a set of tables that identifies the contents for each sequence container and task. As far as the four packages, we will examine them in the subsequent sections in this chapter.

Table 9.1 identifies the tasks in the first sequence container in the package. The function of these tasks is to truncate all the staging tables that will store the raw data from the excel spreadsheets.

Task	Content
Truncate Customer Table	truncate table [IS1 Excel Customer Staging]
Truncate Inventory Table	truncate table [IS1 Excel Inventory Staging]
Truncate Orders Staging	truncate table [IS1 Excel Orders Staging]
Truncate Returns Table	truncate table [IS1 Excel Returns Staging]
Truncate Sales Person Staging	truncate table [IS1 Excel Sales Person Staging]
Truncate Table Shipper Staging	truncate table [IS1 Excel Shipper Staging]

Table 9.1 - Sequence Container for Truncating Excel Staging Tables

Use this table to create your first sequence container as you read along. Drag a sequence container from the Toolbox and drop it into the design areas. Rename the container by right clicking on it and select the "Rename" selection.

Now drag and drop six "Execute SQL" tasks into the next container. Connect each one to the other in sequence and rename each task as shown. You can connect tasks by clicking on them. A green arrow appears. Drag the arrow end from the task to the task you want to establish a connection to. Double click on each task and establish connections to the IS1 database as discussed earlier. Then, in the SQL Statement pull down list that appears to the right, click on the small three dot button so you can bring up the editor that allows you to enter the SQL statement you wish this task to execute. For this sequence container, the tasks are simple SQL truncate commands shown in the table above.

Table 9.2 contains the sequence container for the tasks that truncate the staging tables that will receive data from the Access database.

Task	Content
Truncate Access Customer Contact Staging	Truncate table [Access Customer Contact Staging]
Truncate Access Customer Staging Table	Truncate table [Access Customer Staging]
Truncate Access Invoice Detail Staging Table	Truncate table [Access Invoice Detail Staging]
Truncate Access Invoice Staging Table	Truncate table [Access Invoice Staging]
Truncate Access Order Line Staging Table	Truncate table [Access Order Line Staging]
Truncate Access Order Staging Table	Truncate table [Access Order Staging]
Truncate Access Shipping Order Staging Table	Truncate table [Access Shipping Order Staging]

Table 9.2 - Sequence Container for Truncating Access Staging Tables

Create this container by following the steps we discussed for the first container.

Lastly, we need to create a container for the tables that will store data from the new MySQL database that we added to make things a bit more complex. Here we will use a different approach. Instead of truncating the tables with a SQL command, we will use a stored procedure that not only truncates the table but also loads the data from the MySQL database.

Here is the code for the stored procedure that loads customer data from the MySQL table:

```
CREATEPROCEDURE [dbo].[usp_LoadMySQLCustomer]
AS
TRUNCATE TABLE CAFE_MAGNIFICO.dbo.MYSQL_CUSTOMER_STG ;

INSERT INTO CAFE_MAGNIFICO.dbo.MYSQL_CUSTOMER_STG
SELECT*
FROM OPENQUERY(MYSQLCOFFEE,'SELECT * FROM customer')
GO
```

The statement above creates the stored procedure. It contains the TRUNCATE command and then the INSERT command to insert rows into the staging table from the MySQL database. Notice that the command uses a system function called

OPENQUERY in the FROM clauses. This built in system function contains the name of the linked server together with the SQL statement that retrieves the rows from the MySQL table.

If you are following along, try and create the rest of the stored procedure that truncates tables using the example above as your guide.

Let's create the last sequence container below in your package by using the information in the Table 9.3.

Task	Content
Load MySQL Customer	EXEC usp_LoadMySQLCustomer
Load MySQL Customer Location	EXEC usp_LoadMySQLCustomerLocation
Load MySQL Inventory	EXEC usp_LoadMySQLInventory
Load MySQL Location	EXEC usp_LoadMySQLLocation
Load MySQL Order	EXEC usp_LoadMySQLOrder
Load MySQL Order Detail	EXEC usp_LoadMySQLOrderDetail
Load MySQL Product	EXEC usp_LoadMySQLProduct

Table 9.3 - Sequence Container for Truncating and Loading MySQL Data

Next, we examine that data flow task that actually allows us to load the staging tables from Excel. Drag a data flow task on the design area, rename it and connect it to the first sequence container. Now double click on it and create pairs of connections as shown in Figure 9.7.

For each pair, drag an Excel source connection and then an OLE DB destination connection onto the design area. Connect each pair as shown, rename and fill in the information for each connection as described in earlier sections of this chapter.

Double click on each of the connections and supply the requested information. You will be asked to supply parameters like where the Microsoft Excel spreadsheet files are and the name of the target database and table. If the table does not exist there is a feature that creates it for you. It suggests a default DDL statement which you can accept or modify as required.

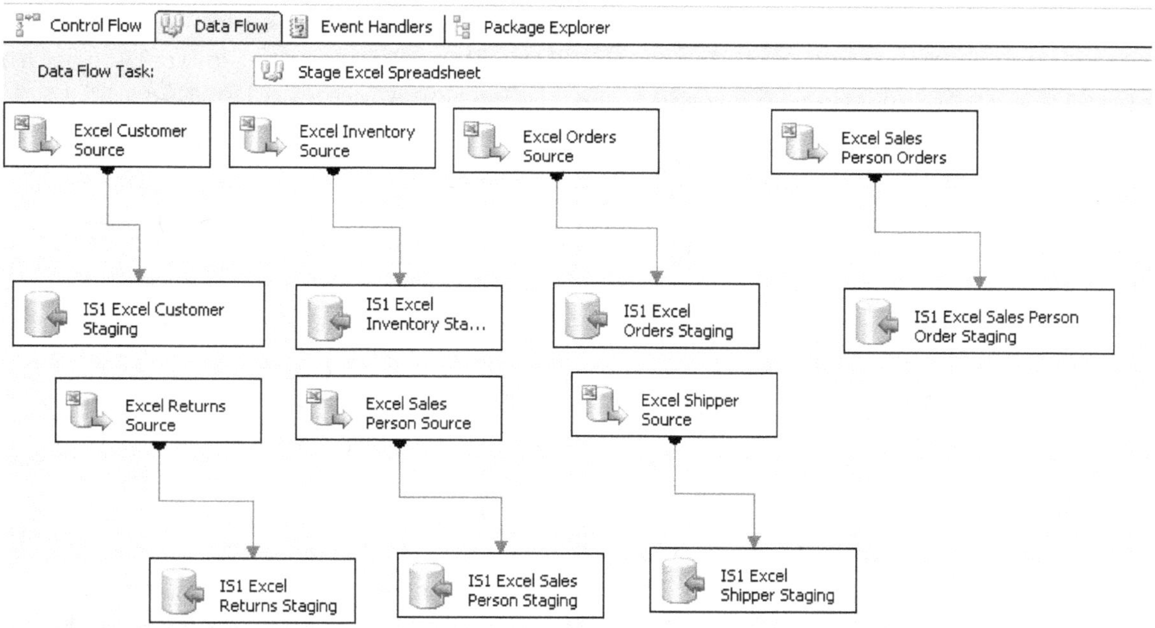

Figure 9.7 - Excel Source to Target Connections

Table 9.4 describes each connection you need to create on this data flow control task for the Excel spreadsheets.

Task	Content
Excel Customer Source	This is the connection to the individual spreadsheet tab.
Excel Inventory Source	This is the connection to the individual spreadsheet tab.
Excel Orders Source	This is the connection to the individual spreadsheet tab.
Excel Sales Person Orders	This is the connection to the individual spreadsheet tab.
Excel Returns Source	This is the connection to the individual spreadsheet tab.
Excel Sales Person Source	This is the connection to the individual spreadsheet tab.
Excel Shipper Source	This is the connection to the individual spreadsheet tab.
IS1 Excel Customer Staging	This is the connection to the target SQL staging table.
IS1 Excel Inventory Staging	This is the connection to the target SQL staging table.
IS1 Excel Orders Staging	This is the connection to the target SQL staging table.
IS1 Excel Sales Person Staging	This is the connection to the target SQL staging table.
IS1 Excel Returns Staging	This is the connection to the target SQL staging table.
IS1 Excel Sales Person staging	This is the connection to the target SQL staging table.
IS1 Shipper Staging	This is the connection to the target SQL staging table.

Table 9.4 - Connections for Excel to Staging Data Flow

As stated earlier, drag and drop the required connections and supply the necessary parameters via the supplied dialog boxes. Table 9.5 describes the source Access and target OLE DB connections you need to create for the staging tables that will receive the data from Access.

Task	Content
Access Customer Table	This is the connection of the source MS Access table.
Access Customer Contact Table	This is the connection of the source MS Access table.
Access Invoice Table	This is the connection of the source MS Access table.
Access Invoice Detail Table	This is the connection of the source MS Access table.
Access Order Table	This is the connection of the source MS Access table.
Access Order Line Table	This is the connection of the source MS Access table.
Access Shipping Order Table	This is the connection of the source MS Access table.
Access Customer Staging	This is the connection for the target SQL staging table.
Access Customer Contact Staging	This is the connection for the target SQL staging table.
Access Invoice Staging	This is the connection for the target SQL staging table.
Access Invoice Detail Staging	This is the connection for the target SQL staging table.
Access Order Staging	This is the connection for the target SQL staging table.
Access Order Line Staging	This is the connection for the target SQL staging table.
Access Shipping Order Staging	This is the connection for the target SQL staging table.

Table 9.5 - Connections for Access to Staging Data Flow

As with the connections we created for the Excel spreadsheet tabs, we can use this table to create the connection pairs to load the Access tables into the SQL Server tables.

Create these connections as shown in Figure 9.8.

These source to target connection pairs are created in the same way as the ones we created for the Excel spreadsheets. Simply drag and drop each connection from the Toolbox, connect the source and target pairs as shown and rename each connection as per the table above. Double click on each connection so as to fill in the dialog box with connectivity information as described earlier.

After creating these connections go back to the flow control tab and connect this data flow task to the data flow task that loaded the Excel spreadsheet.

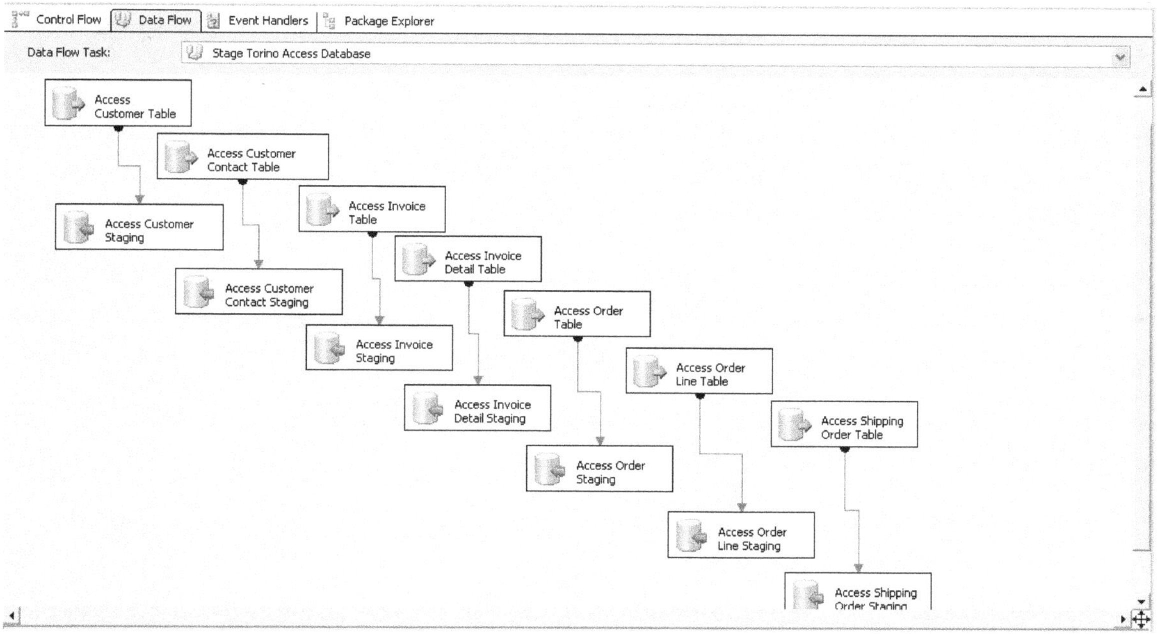

Figure 9.8 - Access Source to Target Connections

Last but not least we need to drag and drop the four packages that will load the reference data and the IS1, IS2 and IS3 databases. For now just drag and drop the four package tasks onto the design area and rename and connect them to the Access tasks as shown in diagram 13.7. We will create these packages in the next sections. Use Table 9.6 as your guide.

Load Reference Data	This is the package that holds all the tasks and flows to load reference data.
Load Interim Schema 1 Data	This is the package that holds all the tasks and flows to load the IS1 schema.
Load Interim Schema 2 Data	This is the package that holds all the tasks and flows to load the IS2 schema.
Load Interim Schema 3 Data	This is the package that holds all the tasks and flows to load the IS3 schema.

Table 9.6 - Package Descriptions for Loading Reference and IS1, IS2 and IS3 Databases

Next, we will define the package for loading most of our reference data. The process will be easy to follow and will be the same as the one we used in this chapter.

Loading the Reference Tables

Now that all of the transactional data is loaded into staging tables, we need to address our reference data. By reference data we mean data that rarely changes like product information, customer name and address, shippers, vendors and sales person information.

We want to merge and load this first into our target ODS database so that the new keys we assign to each of the rows in the reference tables will be available when we load transactional data like orders and invoices.

Our next package will deal with our reference data and is fairly large. Fortunately for us, we covered the mechanics behind the creation of source and target connections, sequence containers and basic tasks that execute SQL commands or stored procedures.

Let's start by looking at the overall control flow for this package. Figure 9.9 and Figure 9.10 will be your guide for creating this package.

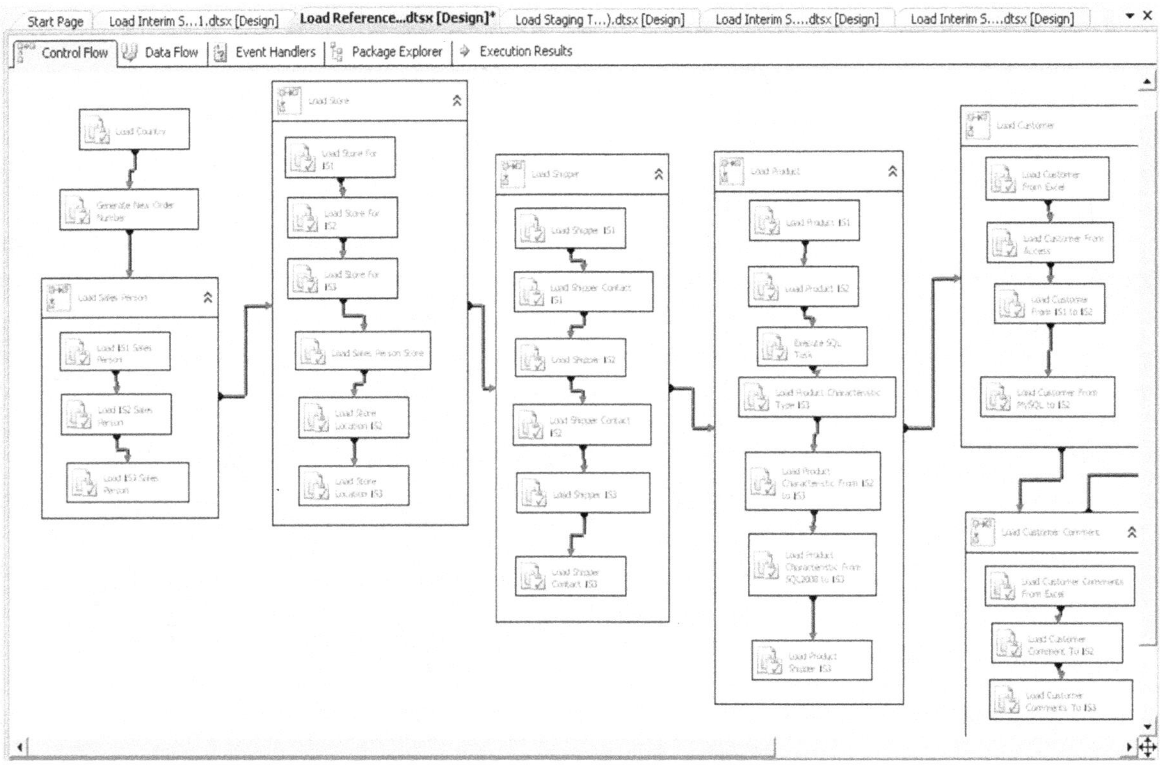

Figure 9.9 - Load Reference Tables Package

I split the package into two screen shots as it is a fairly large package. Both screen shots overlap a bit. You should first add the two basic tasks and then the nine sequence containers as described earlier in the chapter by dragging and dropping the tasks from the toolbox into the design area. Then rename each object as per the tables that follow and connect them as per these two screen shots. Once you have the basic flow designed you can complete each task by double clicking on it and supplying the connectivity information and the SQL queries in the dialog boxes for each task.

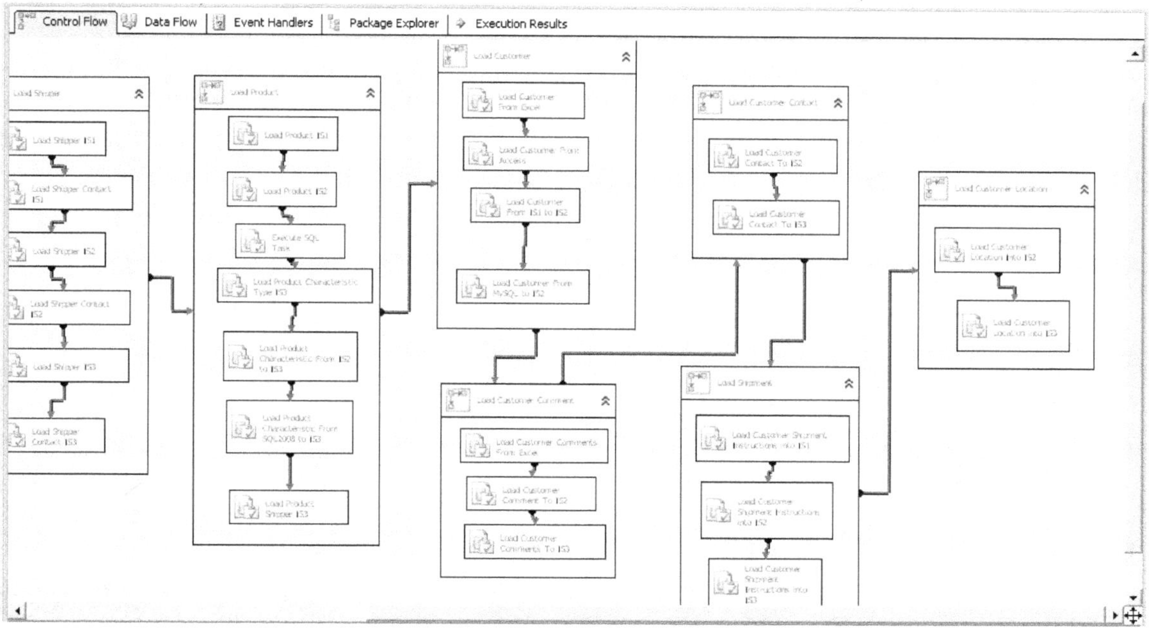

Figure 9.10 - Load Reference Tables Package (continued)

As can be seen there are two simple "Execute SQL" tasks and nine sequential container tasks. Each sequential container contains two or more basic "Execute SQL" tasks. The connection of one container to the next defines the flow we wish to execute.

The first task loads ISO country code tables from each of the three schemas. The stored procedure that is called for this task appears below:

```
/********************************/
/* Load Country Reference tables */
/********************************/
CREATE PROCEDURE [dbo].[usp_LoadCountryCodes]
AS
TRUNCATE TABLE IS2.dbo.COUNTRY_IS2;

INSERT INTO IS2.dbo.COUNTRY_IS2
SELECT * FROM IS1.dbo.COUNTRY_IS1;

TRUNCATE TABLE IS3.dbo.COUNTRY_IS3;

INSERT INTO IS3.dbo.COUNTRY_IS3
SELECT * FROM IS2.dbo.COUNTRY_IS2;

GO
```

We simply load each table from the related table in the prior schema. This logic will be implemented in most of the stored procedures that load the tables from schema to schema. The complexity comes in when we merge each prior table with the related table from one of the source databases.

In this case the tables contain the ISO country codes and names that we will use in the address tables. There are plenty of sources on the web where you can obtain these codes for free. Just perform a search on ISO country codes. There are two types: three character ISO codes and two character ISO codes. The schema for this table appears below:

```
CREATE TABLE COUNTRY_IS1(
      COUNTRY_KEY          int           NOT NULL,
      COUNTRY_ISO_CODE     varchar(3)    NOT NULL,
      COUNTRY_NAME         varchar(256)NOT NULL,
      SYS_CREATE_DATE      datetime      NOT NULL,
      SYS_MODIFY_DATE      datetime      NULL
)ON [PRIMARY]
GO
```

I included columns to show when the row is inserted and also when the row is modified for tracking purposes (SYS_CREATE_DATE and SYS_MODIFY_DATE). Below are the tables that identify the commands that go into each task for each of the sequence containers and tasks. The commands required to load the reference data are shown in Table 9.7.

Task	Content
Load Country	EXEC usp_LoadCountryCodes
Generate New Order Number	EXEC usp_GenerateNewOrderNumbers

Table 9.7 - Load Reference Data Individual Tasks

If you are following along, use the previous example as a guide and create the stored procedures.

Next is the first container that loads the sales person reference data into each of the three databases that represent the three integrated schema. This can be seen in Table 9.8.

Task	Content
Load IS1 Sales Person	EXEC usp_LoadSalesPersonForIS1
Load IS2 Sales Person	EXEC usp_LoadSalesPersonForIS2
Load IS3 Sales Person	EXEC usp_LoadSalesPersonForIS3

Table 9.8 - Sequence Container for Loading Sales Persons

Basically, as there are no other sales person tables you load the table in the first interim schema to the related table in the second interim schema and so on. You do this as you want the key information to be available as you integrate each of the subsequent schemas.

Next is the sequence container that contains the tasks to load store information, store location information and lastly link sales persons to their respective stores. This information is shown in Table 9.9.

Task	Content
Load Store For IS1	EXEC usp_LoadStoresForIS1
Load Store For IS2	EXEC usp_LoadStoresForIS2
Load Store For IS3	EXEC usp_LoadStoresForIS3
Load Sales Person Store	EXEC usp_LoadSalesPersonStores
Load Store Location IS2	EXEC usp_LoadStoreLocationIS2
Load Store Location IS3	EXEC usp_LoadStoreLocationIS3

Table 9.9 - Sequence Container for Loading Stores

As stores refer to sales persons, we loaded the sales person reference tables in each of the interim schema first.

Table 9.8 identifies the tasks for loading shipper and shipper contact information. Recall that a shipper can have one or more related contact records.

Task	Content
Load Shipper IS1	EXEC usp_LoadShipperIS1
Load Shipper Shipper Contact IS1	EXEC usp_LoadShipperContactIS1
Load Shipper IS2	EXEC usp_LoadShipperIS2
Load Shipper Contact IS2	EXEC usp_LoadShipperContactIS2
Load Shipper IS3	EXEC usp_LoadShipperIS3
Load Shipper Contact IS3	EXEC usp_LoadShipperContactIS3

Table 9.10 - Sequence Container for Loading Shippers

Let's take a peek at one of the stored procedures so you can use it as a guide to create the remaining stored procedures:

```
/*************************************************************/
/*                SHIPPER REFERENCE DATA                      */
/*************************************************************/

CREATE PROCEDURE [dbo].[usp_LoadShipperIS1]
AS
TRUNCATE TABLE IS1.dbo.SHIPPER_IS1;

/*********************/
/* ETL IS1 REF - 2.1 */
/*********************/

INSERT INTO IS1.dbo.SHIPPER_IS1
SELECT DISTINCT
      [Shipper Identifier],
      'Acme Shippers',
      'ACCESS'
FROM CAFE_MAGNIFICO.[dbo].[Access Shipping Order Staging]
ORDERBY
[Shipper Identifier];

/***************************/
/* ETL IS1 REF - 2.2 - 2.3 */
/***************************/
INSERT INTO IS1.dbo.SHIPPER_IS1
SELECT DISTINCT
      CONVERT(integer,[Shipper Number])AS SHIPPER_NO,
      CONVERT(VARCHAR(256),[Shipper Name])As SHIPPER_NAME,
      'EXCEL'
FROM CAFE_MAGNIFICO.dbo.[IS1 Excel Shipper Staging];

GO
```

Notice that what appears to be a simple task, that is, execute a stored procedure, hides a lot of complexity. The stored procedure above truncates the SHIPPER_IS1 table so as to make sure we do not insert duplicate rows.

Next, it inserts rows from the Access database and then rows from the Excel spreadsheet staging table. Recall that we loaded the staging tables directly from the Access database and the Excel spreadsheet tabs.

Next we turn our attention to the sequence container that loads the product reference tables. We need to load the product information, the related product characteristics information and the product shipper information. Table 9.11 shows the tasks we need to implement in our package.

As before, if you have not inserted this container and the related tasks. do so at this time by dragging and dropping each item from the Toolbox. Once this is accomplished, rename each object as per the table above, link the tasks in the container and identify the connections and EXEC statements for each task.

Task	Content
Load Product IS1	EXEC usp_LoadProductIS1
Load Product IS2	EXEC usp_LoadProductIS2
Load Product IS3	EXEC usp_LoadProductIS3
Load Product Characteristic Type IS3	EXEC usp_LoadProductCharacteristicTypeIS3
Load Product Characteristic From IS2 To IS3	EXEC usp_LoadProdCharFromIS2ToIS3
Load Product Characteristics From SQL 2008 to IS3	EXEC usp_LoadProdCharFromSQL2008_IS3
Load Product Shipper	EXEC usp_LoadProductShipperIS3

Table 9.11 - Sequence Container for Loading Products

Next we create the container and tasks for the customer related information. This can be seen in Table 9.12.

Task	Content
Load Customer From Excel	EXEC usp_LoadCustomerIS1FromExcel
Load Customer From Access	EXEC usp_LoadCustomerIS1FromAccess
Load Customer From IS1 to IS2	EXEC usp_LoadCustomerFromIS1ToIS2
Load Customer From MySQL to IS2	EXEC dbo.usp_LoadCustomerFromMySQLToIS2

Table 9.12 - Sequence Container for loading Customers

Notice that I try to make the names of the stored procedures as descriptive as possible. Also notice that we load customer data from Excel and Access into IS1. Then we load from IS1 to IS2 and finally we load IS2 with customer data from MYSQL. We do not load IS3 customer data as we need to restructure the customer tables so that they take advantage of the new address and location schema we derived for IS3 (separate the customer address attributes into a new table). Create this container and the related tasks as per the techniques we used for the other containers. We also need to load comments associated for the customers. Use Table 9.13 as your guide.

Task	Content
Load Customer Comments From Excel	EXEC usp_LoadCustomerCommentIS1FromExcel
Load Customer Comment To IS2	EXEC usp_LoadCustomerCommentIS2FromIS1
Load Customer Comment to IS3	EXEC usp_LoadCustomerCommentIS3FromIS2

Table 9.13 - Sequence Container for Loading Customer Comments

Lastly we need to load customer contact information. This is a small sequence container with only two tasks and is shown in Table 9.14.

Task	Content
Load Customer Contact To IS2	EXEC usp_LoadCustomerContactIS2FromIS1
Load Customer Contact To IS3	EXEC usp_LoadCustomerContactIS3FromIS2

Table 9.14 - Sequence Container for Loading Customer Contacts

Note: you need not attempt to create all the packages, tasks and stored procedures I describe. Maybe pick a few of the interesting ones and start with a small subset. Your solution may be different than mine.

Next we need to create the sequence container that holds the tasks for loading shipment data. As you create these containers and tasks, don't forget to connect them as per the screen shots. The required stored procedures are shown in Table 9.15.

Task	Content
Load Customer Shipment Instructions into IS1	EXEC usp_LoadCustomerShipmentInstructionIS1
Load Customer Shipment Instructions into IS2	EXEC usp_LoadCustomerShipmentIntructionIS2
Load Shipment Instructions Into IS3	EXEC usp_LoadCustomerShipmentInstructionIS3

Table 9.15 - Container for Loading Shipment Data

Last but not least is the container for loading customer location and address data. Implement this container and the related tasks and connect to the other containers as per the earlier screen shots. The required stored procedures are shown in Table 9.16.

Task	Content
Load Customer Location Into IS2	EXEC usp_LoadCustomerLocationIS2
Load Customer Location Into IS3	EXEC usp_LoadCustomerLocationIS3

Table 9.16 - Container for Loading Customer Locations

As a reminder, use the specifications created in Chapter 8 as your guide to the data transformation ETL required by each stored procedure.

I hope you agree that this was fairly simple. We followed a cookbook approach and created each of the containers, one at a time so as to implement the desired ETL flow. We used TSQL (Transact-SQL, a Microsoft SQL Server SQL and control language syntax) stored procedures to keep things simple in the tasks. The TSQL logic was based on the ETL specifications created in Chapter 8.

The logic in the stored procedures could have been implemented with pure SSIS tasks. We could have completely eliminated the need for stored procedures and used the various tasks that come in the toolbox to accomplish the same logic. Tasks exist to sort data, merge multiple streams of data into one stream and also perform data type conversion.

Figure 9.11 shows an alternate approach to loading shipper data using pure SSIS tasks.

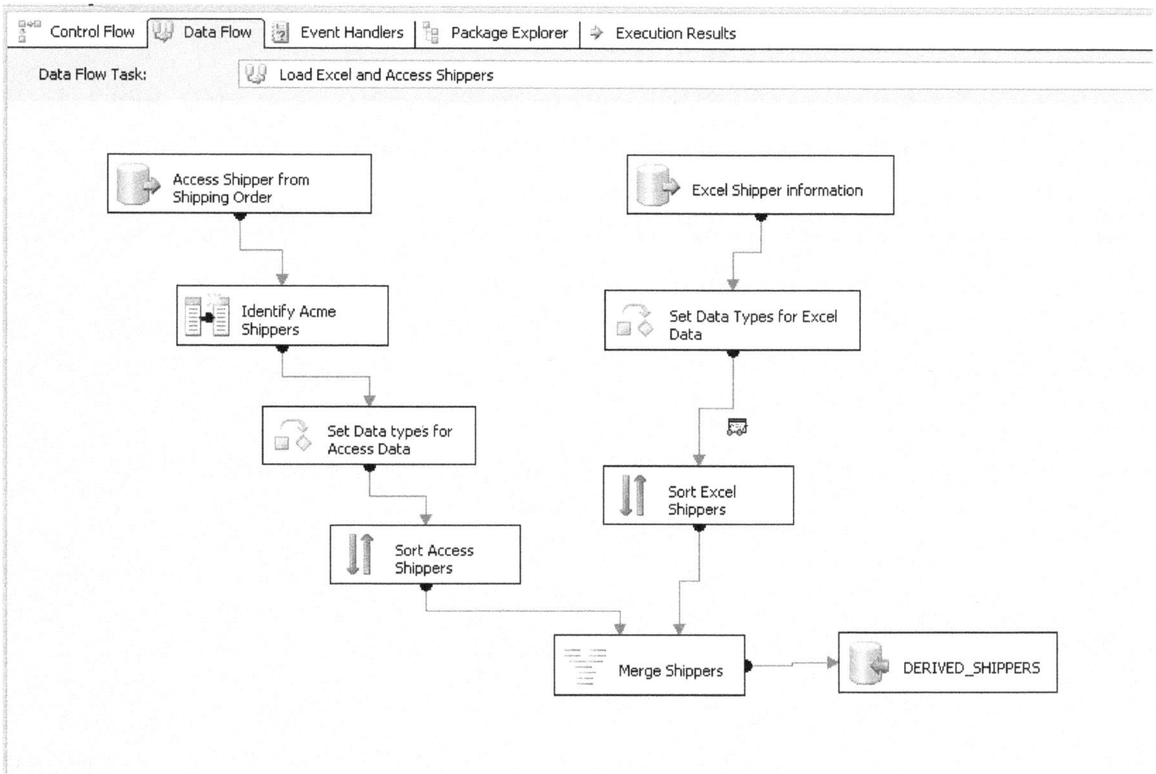

Figure 9.11 - Load IS1 Schema

We begin as usual by defining our connections to the Access and Excel staging tables in our SQL 2008 database. We then drag and drop a derived column task and create a variable that contains the string “Acme Shippers”. We connect the derived column task to the Access source so we can pick the shipper number and shipper name which is now “Acme Shippers”. Recall we have only one shipper for this company. We then drag and drop a data conversion task and connect it to the derived column task. We want to make sure that the data types of the two columns are set to the same corresponding data types for the Excel flow appearing to the right.

Next we sort the output and connect it to a merge task. The Excel flow on the right uses the same logic. We create the Excel staging table connection and then make sure that the data types of the shipper number and name columns are the same as the ones we selected for the Access data. We sort the outputs of the Excel data and then connect it as the right side of the merge tasks. The two streams are then merged and directed to a new output table called DERIVED_SHIPPERS_EXAMPLE.

So, as we can see, there are a lot more steps then the SQL stored procedure. My suggestion is to pick the easiest technique and reserve the more complicated approaches only when required.

Now that we have created the ETL packages to stage the source data and load our reference tables, we can turn our attention to the transactional data.

Loading Integrated Schema 1 (IS1)

Next on the agenda is to create the package that loads the transactional order and invoice tables from the staging tables into IS1. We also load shipment orders, inventory data and return data. By the way, you create your package by right clicking on SSIS Packages in the Solution Explorer window and selecting "New Package".

Use the screen shot displayed in Figure 9.12 as a guide to create your package.

Not a hard package to design and create. There are two sequence containers and three tasks. All are interconnected sequentially. The first sequence container contains the tasks to load order header and order line information into IS1 from the staging tables. We also load some order comments from the Excel spreadsheets.

The second sequence container loads the invoice header and invoice details from the Microsoft Access database. Lastly, the three individual tasks that load shipment orders, inventory data from the Excel spreadsheet tab and returns from the Excel spreadsheet tasks. I did not put them in sequence containers as I considered them stand alone tasks. I guess we could always put them in a sequence container called "miscellaneous".

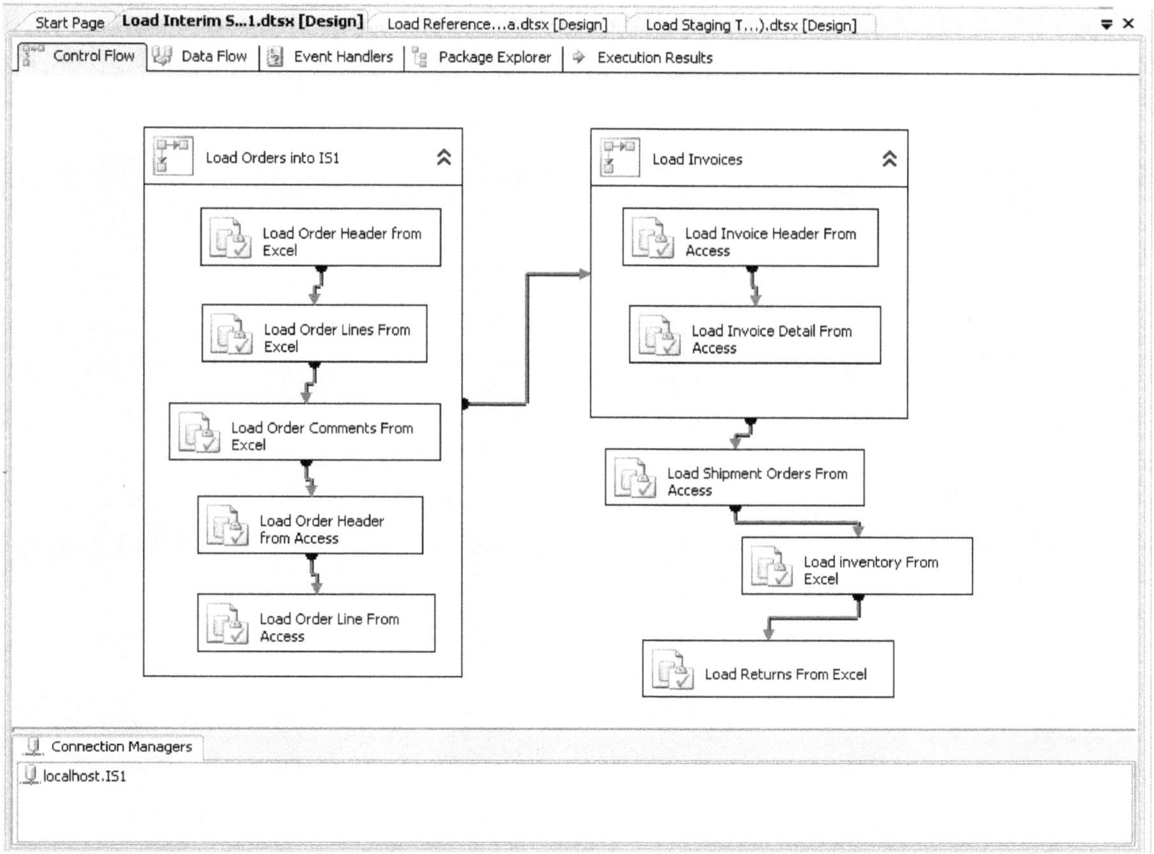

Figure 9.12 - Load IS1 Schema

Next, refer to Table 9.17 together with the screen print for this package to build your own package and stored procedures.

Task	Content
Load Order Header From Excel	EXEC usp_LoadOrderHeaderIS1
Load Order Lines From Excel	EXEC usp_LoadOrderLineIS1FromExcel
Load Order Comments From Excel	EXEC usp_LoadOrderCommentIS1FromExcel
Load Order Header From Access	EXEC usp_LoadOrderHeaderIS1FromAccess
Load Order Line From Access	EXEC usp_LoadOrderLineIS1FromAccess

Table 9.17 - Container for Loading Order Data

As usual, drag and drop the sequence container task first, rename it as per above and then drag and drop the five Execute SQL tasks into the sequence container. Rename each of the tasks and connect them as per the order in the table. Refer to the screen shot in Figure 9.12 if necessary.

Lastly, for each task define connectivity information and enter the EXEC statement for each stored procedure by double clicking on the task to bring up the dialog box that allows you to complete the task.

Table 9.18 shows the commands required for the invoice header and detail ETL tasks.

Task	Content
Load Invoice Header From Access	EXEC usp_LoadInvoiceHeaderFromAccess
Load Invoice Detail From Access	EXEC usp_LoadInvoiceDetailFromAccess

Table 9.18 - Container for Loading Invoice Data

By the way, here's a hint. You might want to create all the packages, flows and tasks first. Then create connections and stubs for the stored procedures. That is, stored procedures without any logic inside. Maybe just some insert statements that log the progress of the steps in some sort of log table. You can then add the logic as you refer back to the ETL specifications in Chapter 8.

Next perform the same steps for the Invoice container and the individual tasks shown in Table 9.19.

Task	Content
Load Shipment Orders from Access	EXEC usp_LoadShipmentOrderFromAccessIS1
Load Inventory From Excel	EXEC usp_LoadInventoryFromExcelIS1
Load Returns From Excel	EXEC usp_LoadReturnsFromExcelIS1

Table 9.19 - Container for Loading Shipment Orders, Inventory & Returns

This completes all of the packages and tasks for staging and loading IS1. Remember that we need to refer back to Chapter 8 for the required ETL logic for any data transformations, data enrichment or data type conversions.

Loading Integrated Schema 2 (IS2)

We are making progress. Let's continue with the package that loads IS2. IS2 will merge the Excel and Access data with data from the MySQL database. As a reminder, earlier chapters did not discuss this database. I am leaving this as an exercise for you, to introduce this database into the integration process and develop your own set of ETL tasks to load the data into the target ODS.

Use the screen shot in Figure 9.13 as your guide.

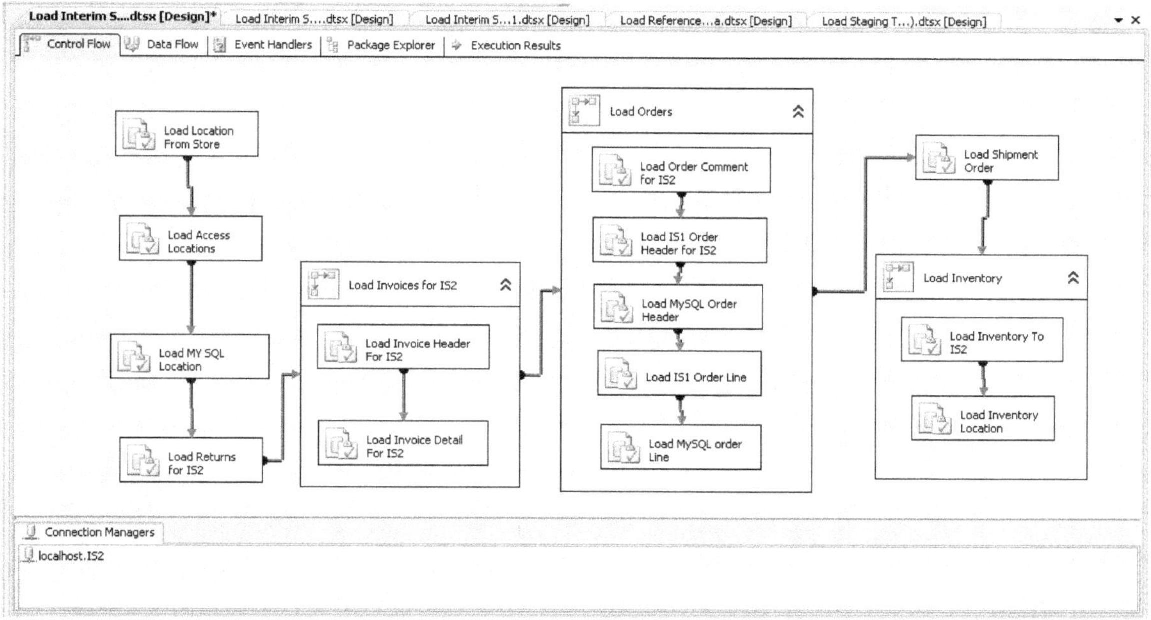

Figure 9.13 - Load IS2 Schema

We can see four standalone tasks, executed in sequence, that are connected to two sequence containers. The first sequence container loads invoice header and detail from IS1 to IS2. The second container loads order information from IS1 and also order information from the MySQL database. Next is a task to load the shipment order data from IS1 to IS2 and last but not least we see a sequence container that loads the inventory data from IS1 to IS2.

Table 9.20 identifies the stored procedures that need to go in the stand alone tasks.

Task	Content
Load Location From Store	EXEC usp_LoadLocationFromStoreIS2
Load Access Locations	EXEC usp_LoadIS2Location
Load My SQL Location	EXEC usp_LoadLocationFromMySQLToIS2
Load Returns For IS2	EXEC usp_LoadReturnsIS2

Table 9.20 - Stand Alone Tasks

Start with the first four standalone tasks and drag them into the design area. Connect them as per the screen shot and then drag and drop the two empty sequence containers. Connect the four tasks and two sequence containers and then rename them as required.

Next, drag and drop the individual task that will load the shipment orders and final sequence container for loading inventory data into IS2.

Now drag and drop the two tasks into the invoice sequence container. Rename as defined in Table 9.21 and complete each task by specifying the connectivity information and the EXEC statements for the stored procedures that will do the job. Don't forget to connect the tasks.

Task	Content
Load Invoice Header For IS2	EXEC usp_LoadInvoiceHeaderIS2
Load Invoice Detail For IS2	EXEC usp_LoadInvoicedetailIS2

Table 9.21 - Container for Loading Invoice Data

Next, do the same for the tasks in the order sequence container as per the specifications in Table 9.22.

Task	Content
Load Order Comment For IS2	EXEC usp_LoadOrderCommentIS2
Load IS1 Order Header for IS2	EXEC usp_LoadOrderHeaderFromIS1ToIS2
Load MySQL Order Header	EXEC usp_LoadOrderHeaderFromMySQLToIS2
Load IS1 Order Line	EXEC usp_LoadOrderLineFromIS1ToIS2
Load MySQL Order Line	EXEC usp_LoadOrderLineFromMySQLToIS2

Table 9.22 - Container for Loading Order Data

Notice how this sequence container handles all of the order data. It is good practice to use sequence containers for each of the business subject areas. You can even start your package with only sequence containers so you can layout your process flow.

Now complete the individual task that will load shipment orders from IS1 to IS2: Use Table 9.23 as your guide.

Task	Content
Load Shipment Order	EXEC usp_LoadShipmentOrderIS2

Table 9.23 - Task for Loading Shipment Orders

The Shipment Order table is only in the MySQL database. Refer to the model shown in Chapter 5 as a reference.

Last but not least complete the tasks in the inventory sequence container. Use Table 9.24 as your guide.

Task	Content
Load Inventory To IS2	EXEC usp_LoadInventoryIS2
Load inventory Location	EXEC usp_LoadInventoryLocationIS2

Table 9.24 - Container for Loading Inventory Data

By now you should know that the required logic for these stored procedures is in Chapter 8 but a little reminder never hurts. Also, for the stored procedures that manipulate the MySQL tables you should have created your own ETL specifications.

Don't forget to make sure everything is connected as per the original screen shot at the beginning of the section.

Loading Integrated Schema 3 (IS3)

One more package to go! This last package loads all the tables from IS2 and merges the SQL Server 2008 data into IS3. Below is the screen shot of the completed package.

As a reminder, notice that it doubles as a data flow or process dependency diagram that shows the sequence of execution of the ETL process. SSIS is also a good tool for prototyping the process flow. As we design and code we can check our assumptions of which table to load first and what steps can be executed in parallel.

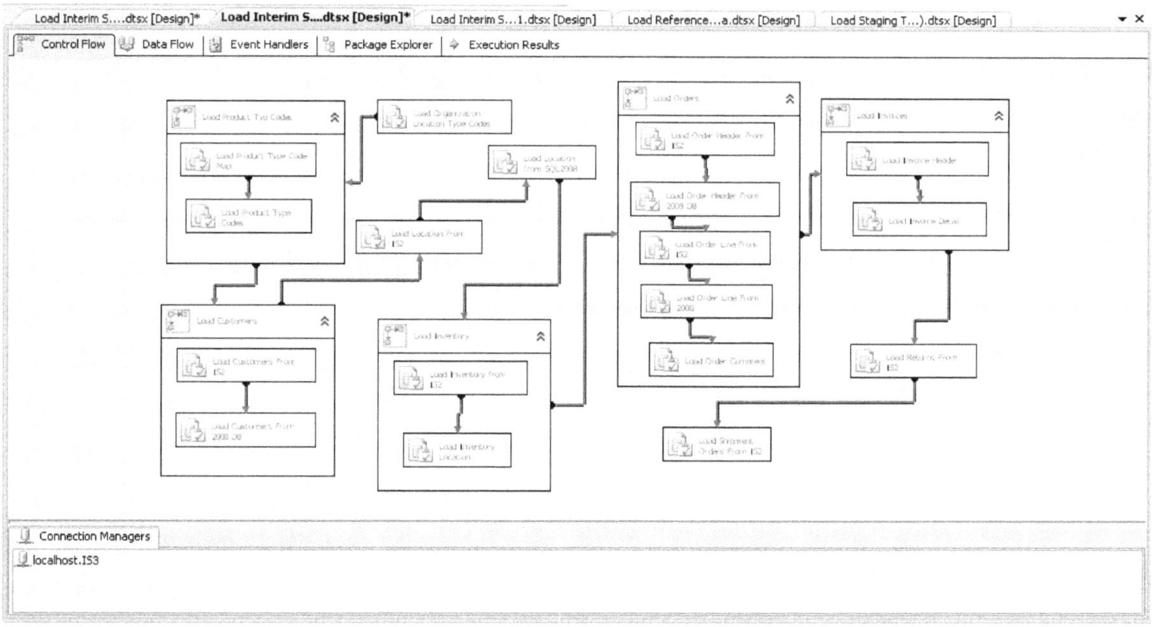

Figure 9.14 - Load IS3 Schema

Let's take inventory of the objects we need for this last package. As can be seen we have five sequence containers and five tasks. The order of execution is as follows:

- Load Location Type Codes – a task.
- Load Product Type Codes – a sequence container with two tasks.
- Load Customers – a sequence container with two tasks.
- Load Locations from IS2 – a task.
- Load Locations from SQL2008 – a task.
- Load Orders – a sequence container with five tasks.
- Load Invoices – a sequence container with two tasks.
- Load Returns – a task.
- Load Shipment Orders – a task.

As per the technique we used in the prior sections, drag and drop these objects from the toolbox and connect them in the sequence shown. Rename the objects as per the names used in the screen shot and connect them in the order described above. Then drag and drop the Execute SQL tasks in the containers, rename them and connect them in the sequence described in the tables below.

Lastly, for each of the tasks, complete the connectivity and query strings by double clicking on each task and bringing up the dialog box that allows you to complete each task.

Below is the last set of tables that contain the details behind each of the tasks in the package. Also, make sure you created a connection to the IS3 database as this is what you will use.

Task	Content
Load Organization Type Codes	EXEC usp_LoadOrgLocTypecodeIS3

Table 9.25 - Standalone Task for Loading Organization Type Codes

This task will load the organization location type code table with the following codes:

```
CODE  DESCRIPTION
1     Customer Location
2     Inventory Physical Location
3     Shipper Location
4     Store location
```

Table 9.26 shows the two stored procedures required to load product type codes.

Task	Content
Load product Type Code Map	EXEC usp_LoadProductToTypeCodeMapIS3
Load Product Type Codes	EXEC usp_LoadProductTypeCodeIS3

Table 9.26 - Container for Loading Product Type Codes

A hint for these stored procedures, make sure to include the TRUNCATE TABLE command and then the individual INSERT statements to load the codes and descriptions.

Make up some product type codes, for example:

1 - Chocolates

2 - Espresso

3 - Cookies

4 - Coffee Maker

The two tasks above will generate a map that links products to type codes and then generates the product type code table by taking distinct values of each product type. Now we need to load customers into the last integrated schema.

Task	Content
Load Customers From IS2	EXEC usp_LoadCustomerFromIS2ToIS3
Load Customers From 2008 DB	EXEC usp_LoadCustomerFrom2008ToIS3

Table 9.27 - Container for Loading Customer Data

The two tasks described in Table 9.27 for this container load the customer data from IS2 to IS3 and from the SQL 2008 database (our 4th source of transactional data) into the IS3 database.

Next we need to load the location information. The required stored procedures are identified in Table 9.28.

Task	Content
Load Location From IS2	EXEC usp_LoadLocationIS3
Load Location From SQL 2008	usp_LoadLocationIS3FromSQL2008

Table 9.28 - Stand Alone Tasks to Load Location Information

These next two tasks load the location data from IS2 to IS3 and from the SQL 2008 database (our 4th source of transactional data) into the IS3 database. Another reminder, in order to code these stored procedures you need:

- The specifications you developed on your own as an exercise.
- The example stored procedures developed in this chapter as a guide.
- The data models from Chapter 8.

The stored procedures you need to create are identified in Table 9.29.

Task	Content
Load Inventory From IS2	EXEC usp_LoadInventoryIS2ToIS3
Load Inventory Location	EXEC usp_LoadInventoryLocationIS2ToIS3

Table 9.29 - Container for Loading Inventory Data

The two tasks in this container load the inventory data from IS2 into the IS3 database.

We are almost finished. Order Header and Order Line and Order comments are next.

Task	Content
Load Order Header From IS2	EXEC usp_LoadOrderHeaderIS2ToIS3
Load Order Header From 2008 DB	EXEC usp_LoadOrderHeader2008ToIS3
Load Order Line From IS2	EXEC usp_LoadOrderLineIS2ToIS3
Load Order Line From 2008	EXEC usp_LoadOrderLine2008ToIS3
Load Order Comment	EXEC usp_LoadOrderCommentIS3

Table 9.30 - Container for Loading Order Data

The five tasks identified in Table 9.30 need to be created in the sequence container that loads the order data in IS3. These sets of tables have a lot of data transformations so make sure you refer to the specifications in Chapter 8 in order to create your own ETL logic and code.

Last but not least are the invoice returns and shipments. Table 9.31 shows the two tasks and stored procedures you need to create to load this data.

Task	Content
Load Invoice Header	EXEC usp_LoadInvoiceHeaderIS3
Load Invoice Detail	EXEC usp_LoadInvoiceDetailIS3

Table 9.31 - Container for Loading Invoice Data

And finally, returns and shipments. The tasks and stored procedures required to load this data are identified in Table 9.32.

Task	Content
Load Returns From IS2	EXEC usp_LoadReturnsIS3
Load Shipment Orders From IS2	EXEC usp_LoadShipmentOrderIS3

Table 9.32 - Standalone Tasks to Load Returns and Shipment Orders

The last two tasks that need to be created appear in the table above. As there are no return or shipment orders in the fourth source database, we simply need to copy over the tables from the IS2 schema into IS3. These stored procedures are simple to code. Just include a TRUNCATE TABLE statement and an INSERT/SELECT statement for each respective stored procedure.

This completes the loading of our third and final interim schema which will be our target ODS database. We loaded one schema at a time so that we could see the transformations that need to occur to resolve the conflicts we identified earlier.

As an exercise, see if you can now optimize the logic by eliminating IS1 and IS2 and use temporary tables to accomplish the data flow steps. That is, the tables that appeared in IS1 and IS2 are implemented in the stored procedures as temporary tables to control the transformations at each step.

Also, see if you can enhance the stored procedures by adding error trapping code and log tables so that each step of the transformation is logged together with a timestamp. This provides a valuable tool for debugging and also controlling any data problems that might pop up during the loads.

Now that all of our packages are created and tested, we need to deploy the packages to SQL Server so that they can work together and so that we can schedule them to run at specified times.

Deploying the Completed Packages

Now that we have created and tested all of our packages we need to present them to SQL Server so we can schedule them to execute as desired. This process is called "deployment" and is easily accomplished with a deployment tool that comes with SQL Server SSIS.

The first step is to enable this tool. By right clicking on the package name in the Solution Explorer, we select the Properties selection in the menu that appears so as to display the window shown in Figure 9.15.

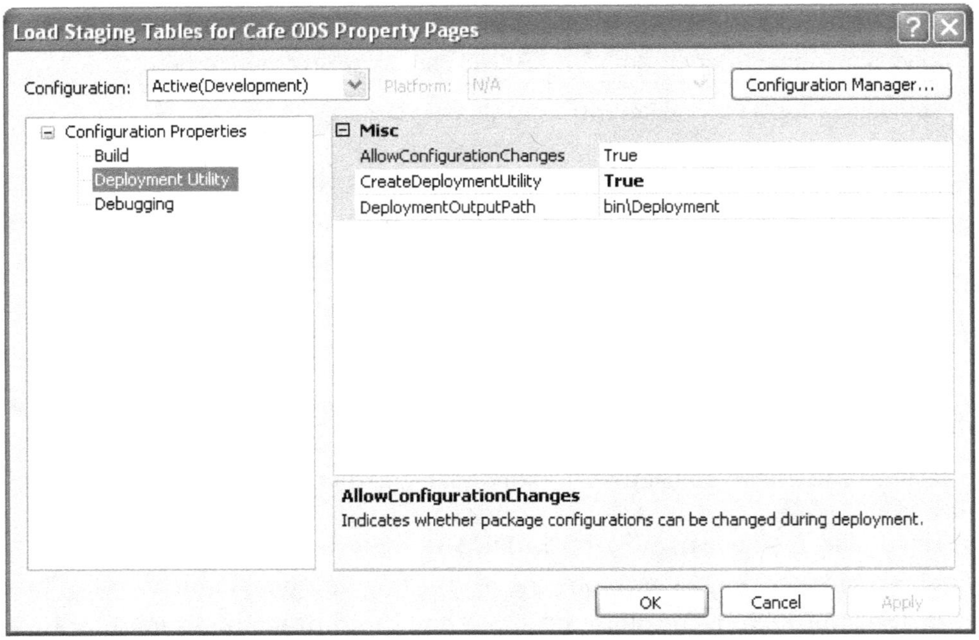

Figure 9.15 - Enabling Deployment

Clicking on the "Deployment Utility" selection we are presented with a panel that contains miscellaneous parameters that enable deployment. We set the "CreateDeploymentUtility" parameter to TRUE and keep the default "DeploymentOutputPath setting.

We click the OK button and the deployment utility is created in the BIN sub directory off your own main project directory.

The utility is called:

```
ODS.SSISDeploymenManifest
```

We right click on the file and select "Deploy" so as to start up the Deployment Wizard Utility shown in the next screen.

We will now describe each step of the wizard by navigating from screen to screen. An introductory screen appears and we can select not to display it next time by clicking on the "Do not show this page again" checkbox.

Now press the "Next" push button on the introductory screen for the next wizard. This is shown in Figure 9.16.

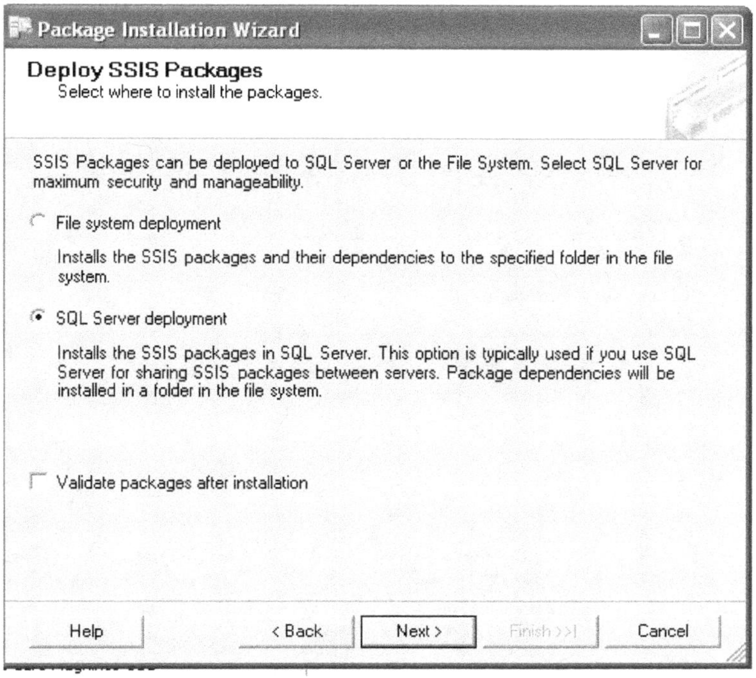

Figure 9.16 - Deploying the Packages

This page allows us to select how we deploy the package. We can deploy it to a directory in the file system of our computer or deploy it to SQL Server. We pick the SQL Server deployment option. We can also optionally select to validate the packages after installation by clicking the checkbox labeled "Validate packages after installation".

Once the necessary selections are made click on the "Next" push button to proceed to the next step.

This page of the wizard allows us to specify the target server for our deployment. We can either deploy to the same server or computer that we created the SSIS packages on or to a different server which might be a dedicated SSIS server. In our case we deploy to the local computer and select "Use Windows Authentication" as the security credentials.

Click on the small push button with the three dots (...) so as to identify the location that the package will be stored in within the SSIS server. In this case the packages are stored in the MSDB database (this is a system database created by SQL Server when it is first installed on your server or laptop).

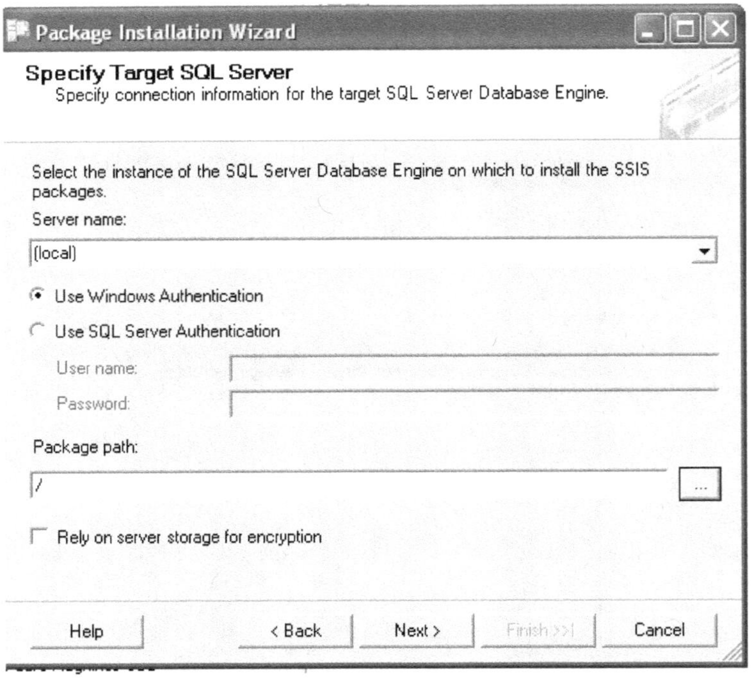

Figure 9.17 - Deploying the Packages, specify target server

Simply accept the default that is shown, click OK and then click on the "Next" push button on this page to proceed to the next step. See Figure 9.18.

This next step allows us to specify the file location where the SSIS package dependencies are stored. For details behind this step refer to the SQL Server SSIS documentation. For now, simply accept the default path. Click on the "Next" push button to continue to the next step.

We have now completed all the steps so all that is left is to confirm the installation. Click next to continue. A final screen appears that lists all of our options. See Figure 9.19. Click finish to deploy the solution.

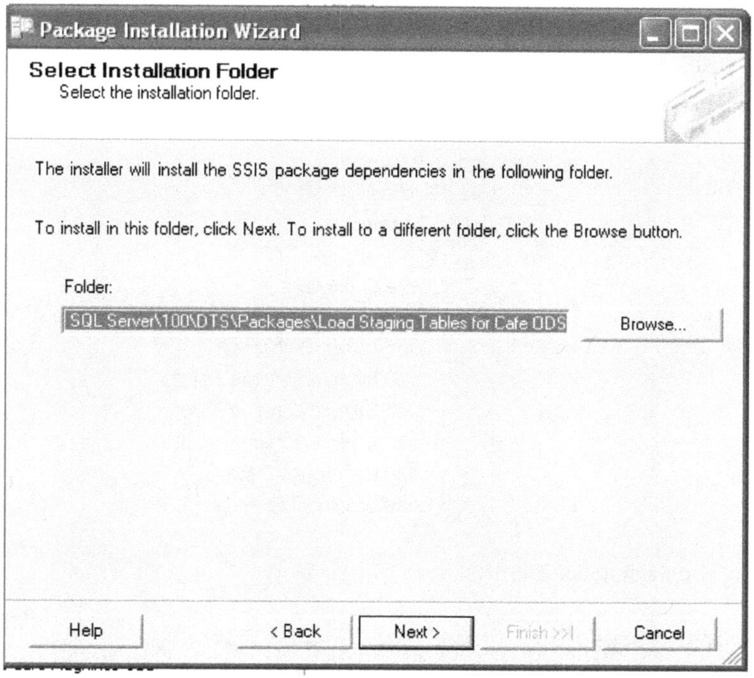

Figure 9.18 - Deploying the Packages – select Installation Folder

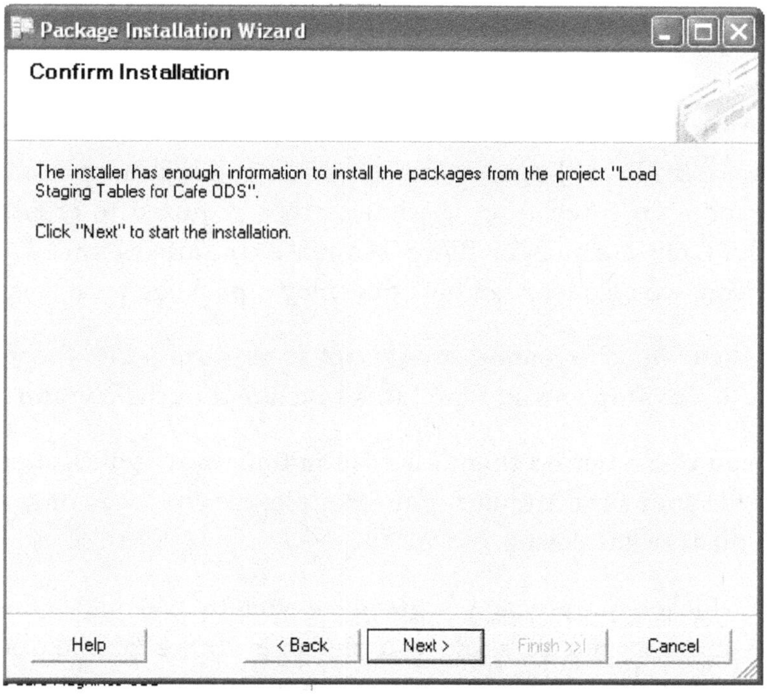

Figure 9.19–Deploying the Packages - Confirming the Installation

Review the options and click "Finish" to deploy. After a few seconds the wizard is finished and the package is deployed. The next screen shot shows all of our packages deployed to the SQL server MSDB database.

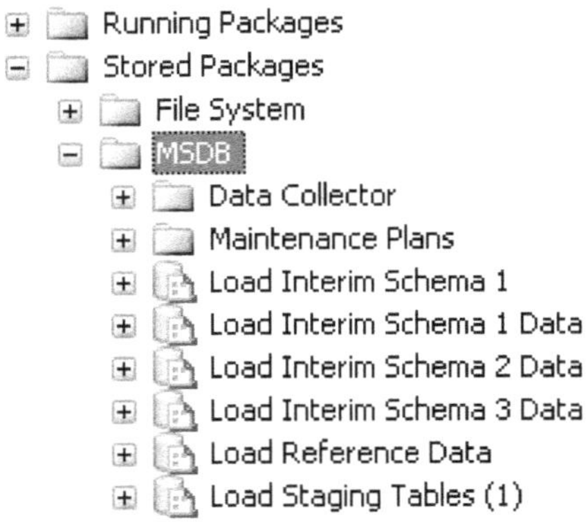

Figure 9.20–Deploying the Packages – MSDB View

Our package is now deployed!

We can schedule the package to run as a SQL Server Agent job. Please refer to your SQL Server documentation for the steps required to schedule the deployed package as a schedule job.

Summary

We have now created all of the packages required to load our Café Magnifico ODS. This chapter served as a tutorial on the basic steps required to create packages that contain various ETL objects such as flows, sequence containers, tasks and connections. As part of the lesson, we also learned how to deploy a package once it is completed.

I realize that I asked you, the reader, to attempt to perform a lot of steps and coding as exercises using a few examples and templates I included in the chapter.

Do not worry if you could not do them all. You might want to pick a smaller subset of tables and tasks for your first attempt. For example, maybe focus only on the customer related tables in all four databases.

The key goal of this chapter was to introduce you to one of the many ETL tools available on the market and to show you the importance of the specifications and models we created in earlier exercises.

In this chapter we will perform some data quality profiling checks on the order fact table. Typically, we would perform data profiling on all the tables in the ODS that feed our data mart. As space is limited in this chapter, I will pick a simple example to illustrate the main tools that are provided with the SQL Server 2008 architecture.

Let's take a look at where we are first from an architectural perspective. Figure 10.1 below shows the completed architecture.

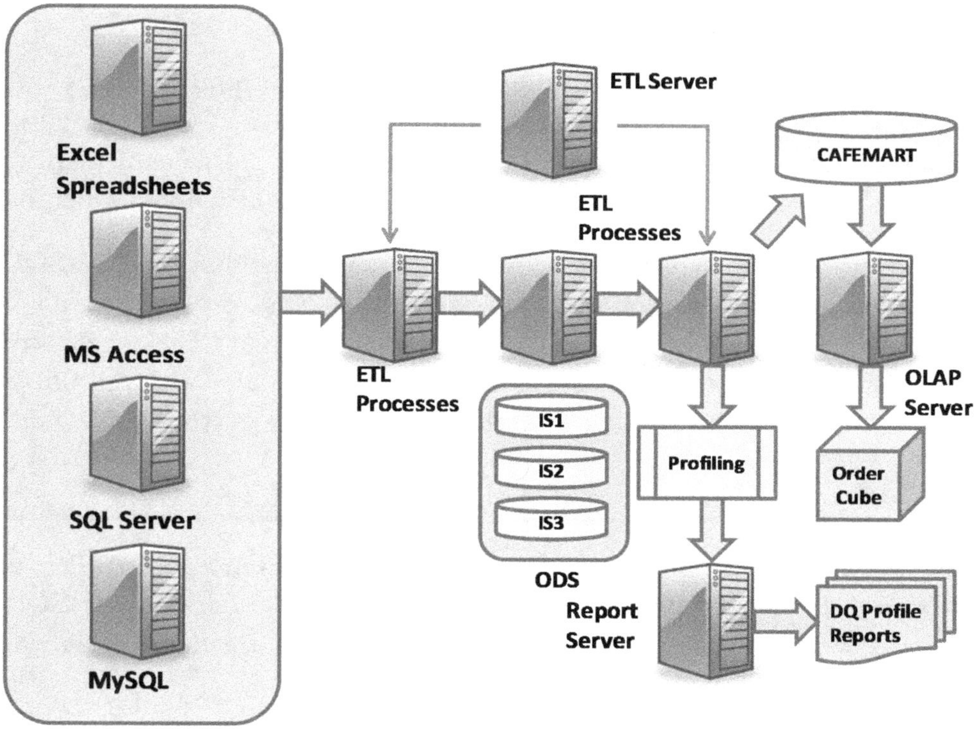

Figure 10.1 - Completed Cafe Magnifico Data Mart

The flow begins at the left. Recall that, we created all of the ETL packages based on our conflict resolution analysis and mapping specifications. We loaded all the IS schemas. Our ODS is the IS3 schema.

We will use some of the data quality profiling tasks that are included in the data flow toolbox to check the quality of the data we loaded into the data mart. In an actual production architecture we would want to profile data in at least two points in the data flow:

- Perform data profiling from staging tables to ODS
- Perform data profiling from ODS to Data Mart.

If bad data is identified, we would add an extra layer of data cleansing processes that are controlled by the various SSIS tasks.

What we will do in this chapter is collect the profile statistics generated by the SSIS tasks and load them into some relational tables. The profiling tasks store the profile statistics in an XML file so we will have to design a package that generates the statistics, creates the XML files, reads the XML files and loads the statistics into the relational tables.

Additionally we will take a look at another important data quality task called Fuzzy matching. This task allows us to identify duplicate data, for example matching customer names from different sources (or the same table) so we can identify names that are almost identical: IBM versus I.B.M. or International Business Machines.

Once the data is loaded in the tables we will create a simple SSRS (SQL Server Reporting Services) model so that we can generate a web report that displays the statistics as a report loaded on the SQL Server report server. These tasks represent the data quality life cycle that one needs to introduce into an ODS and data mart or data warehouse architecture in order to make sure users are getting quality data.

Data Profiling

By now you will have noticed that everything we do with SQL Server SSIS requires a connection to a data source or target database. Luckily, if you are new to SQL Server, SSIS has many wizards that are available to help you get through the various tasks required to create an ETL process.

We will begin by dragging and dropping a Data Profiling task from the Control Flow toolbox. We double click on the tasks so as to bring up the wizard shown in Figure 10.2.

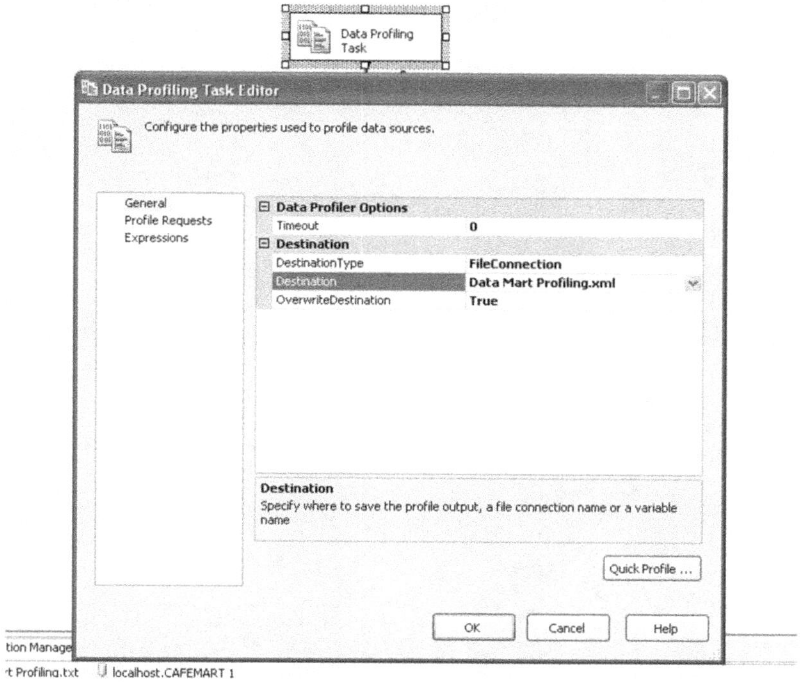

Figure 10.2 - Creating the Data Profiling Task

We accept all of the default parameters except for the Destination parameter. Here we supply a simple name for the XML file that will get generated by the task once it is executed. I called it Data Mart Profiling.xml. Click the Quick Profile button so we can select the profiling tasks we wish to perform. A pop up window appears and is displayed in Figure 10.3.

Place a check box next to the tasks you want to perform. In this case I picked:

- Column Null Ratio Profile
- Column Statistics Profile
- Column Value Distribution Profile
- Column Length Distribution Profile
- Column Pattern Profile.

We will see what each of these means shortly but you can guess by the names what statistics are produced. Click OK and run the task. SSIS provides a simple tool to view the profiling statistics generated. It is accessed by clicking on the Tool item in the menu bar and selecting the Data Viewer item.

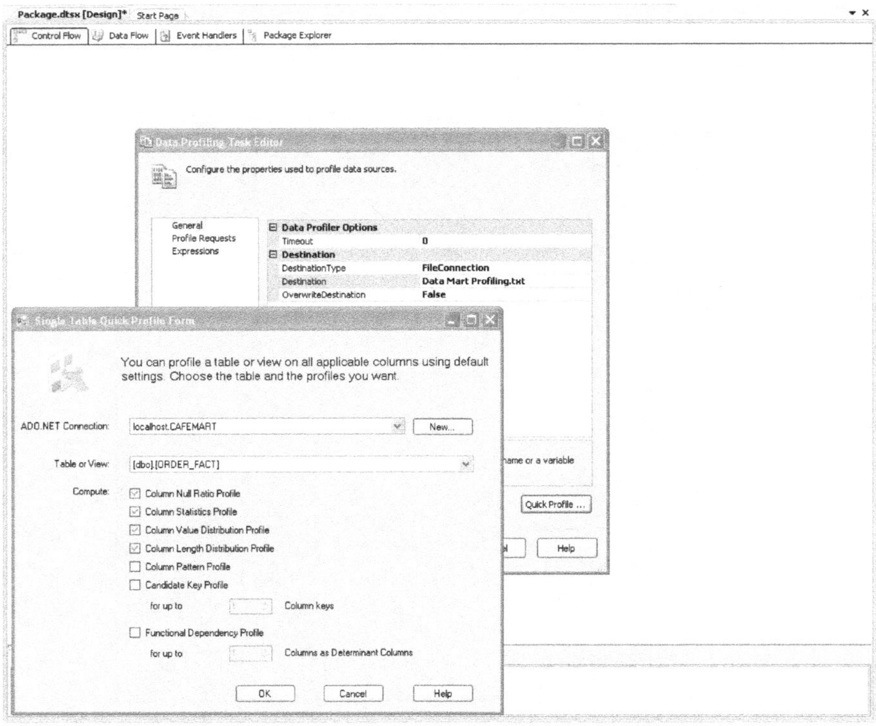

Figure 10.3 - Picking the Profiling Tasks

Figure 10.4 below shows the resulting window for this tool. Go to Open and browse to the location of the XML file that was specified.

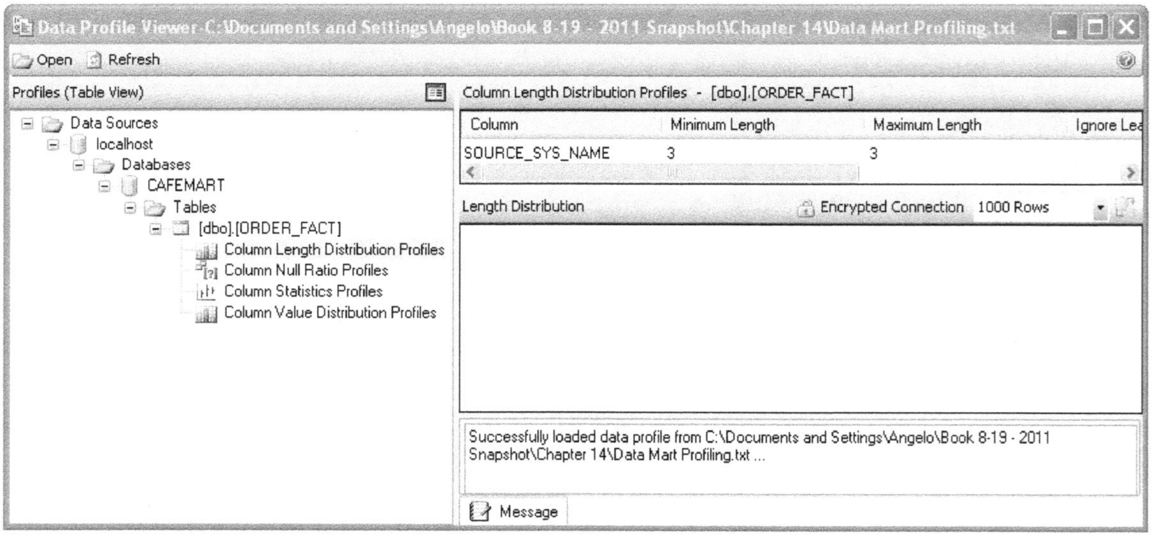

Figure 10.4 - Browsing the Profiling Statistics XML File

Double click on the Column Null Ratio Profiles. A nice graphical scorecard is generated and is shown in Figure 10.5.

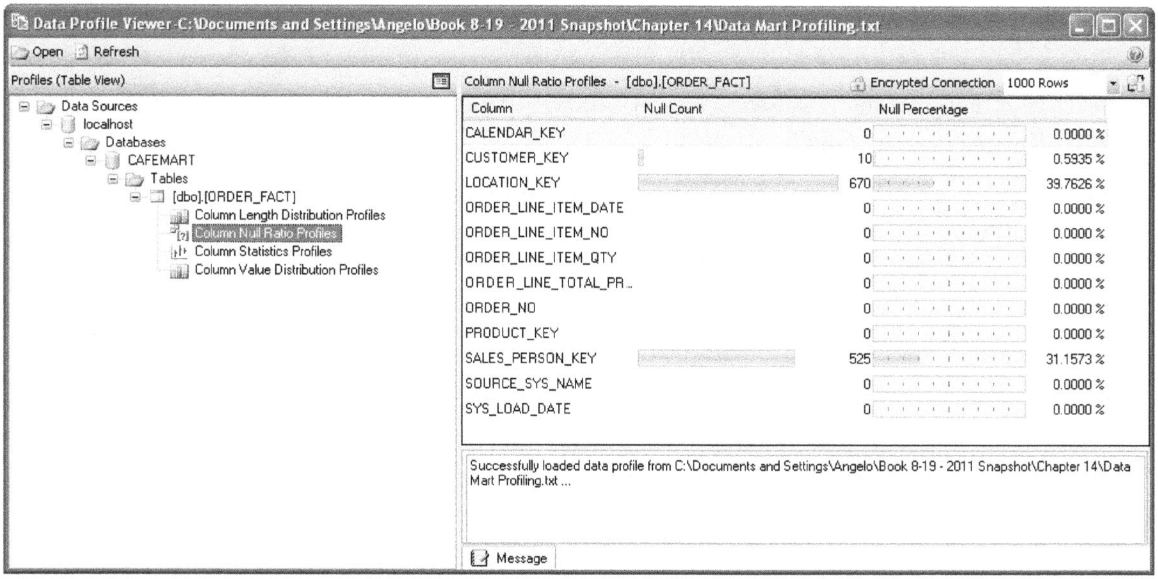

Figure 10.5 - The Column NULL Ratio Profile Scorecard

This was a pretty neat little scorecard. Let's look at some of the others. Click on Column Statistics profile to generate the scorecard shown in Figure 10.6.

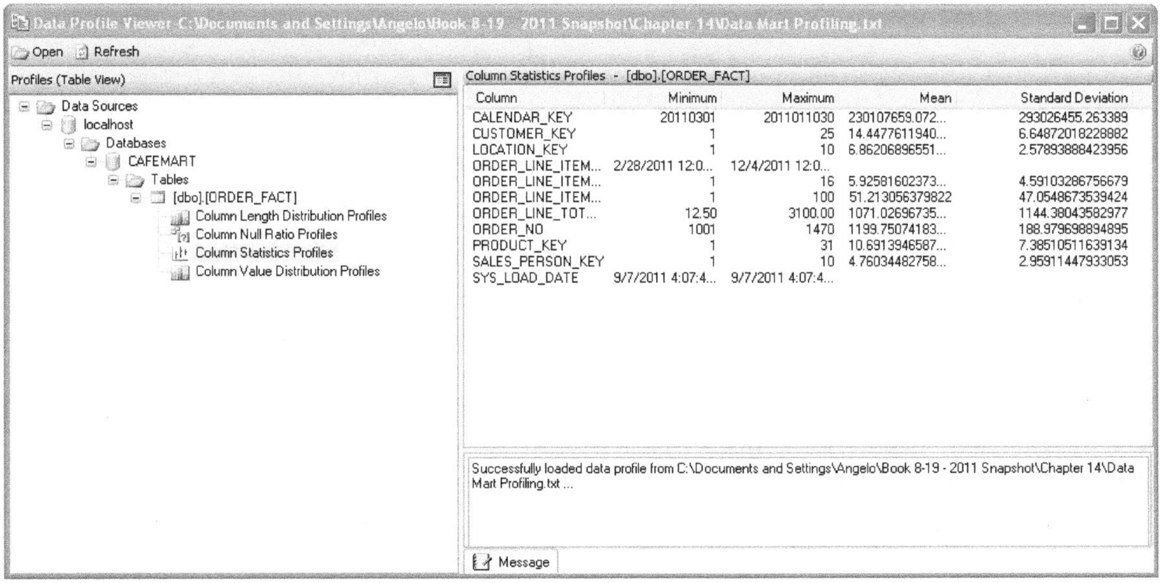

Figure 10.6 - The Column Statistics Profile Scorecard

Another nice scorecard. This time we see the maximum and minimum values of the columns in the report together with some statistical parameters such as Mean and Standard Deviation. These may or may not be interesting depending on the data you want to profile.

Lastly, let's click on the Column Value Distribution Profiles selection. The scorecard shown in Figure 10.7 appears.

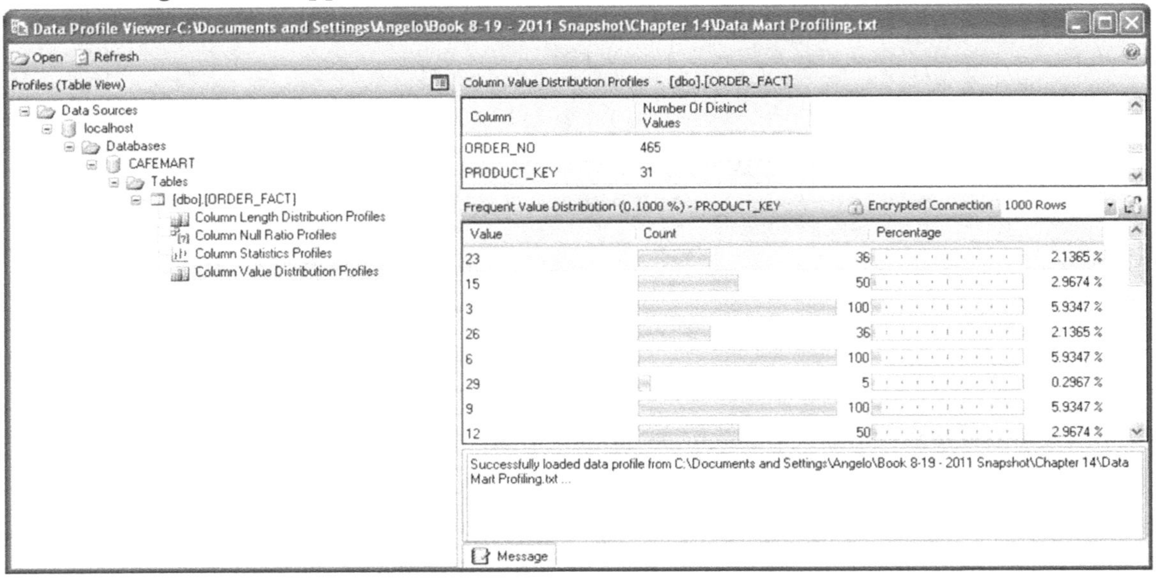

Figure 10.7 - Column Value Distribution Profiles

This scorecard displays the count and percentage distribution values for the contents of each row column. For example, in the scorecard above we see that the 31 value of the PRODUCT_KEY above appears 31 times. Sadly we need to now execute a query to see what the actual product name for key 31 is.

A better approach for profiling the data from a fact table might be to join the fact table keys to the actual dimensions so we can see names like product and customer as opposed to keys.

Recall that this data profiling task, once executed, generates an XML file. This is all fine and good for very general purposes. The utility above reads this XML file so as to produce the scorecards we just viewed with the SSIS tool.

A snapshot of part of this file is shown in Figure 10.8.

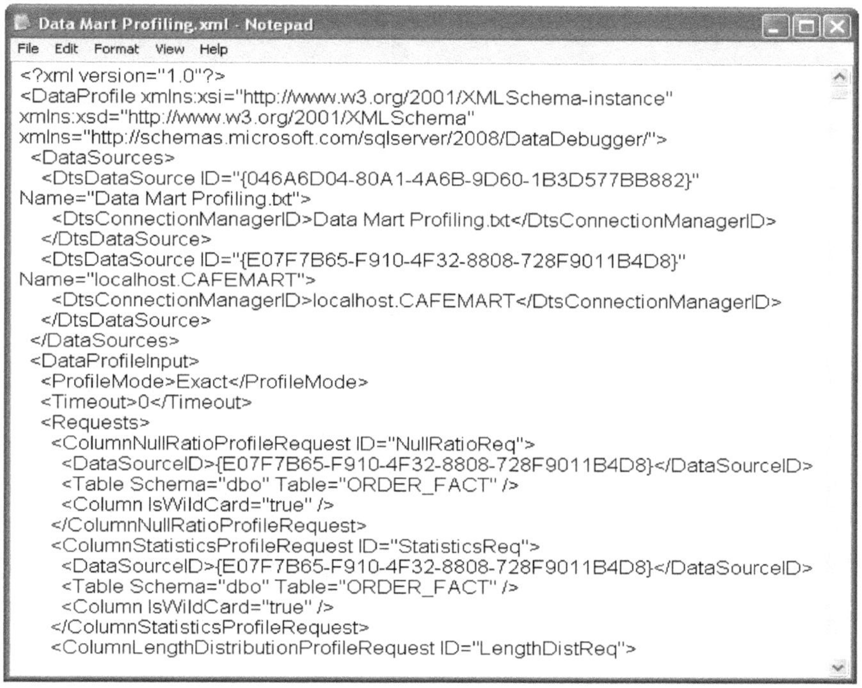


```
<?xml version="1.0"?>
<DataProfile xmlns:xsi="http://www.w3.org/2001/XMLSchema-instance"
xmlns:xsd="http://www.w3.org/2001/XMLSchema"
xmlns="http://schemas.microsoft.com/sqlserver/2008/DataDebugger/">
 <DataSources>
  <DtsDataSource ID="{046A6D04-80A1-4A6B-9D60-1B3D577BB882}"
Name="Data Mart Profiling.txt">
   <DtsConnectionManagerID>Data Mart Profiling.txt</DtsConnectionManagerID>
  </DtsDataSource>
  <DtsDataSource ID="{E07F7B65-F910-4F32-8808-728F9011B4D8}"
Name="localhost.CAFEMART">
   <DtsConnectionManagerID>localhost.CAFEMART</DtsConnectionManagerID>
  </DtsDataSource>
 </DataSources>
 <DataProfileInput>
  <ProfileMode>Exact</ProfileMode>
  <Timeout>0</Timeout>
  <Requests>
   <ColumnNullRatioProfileRequest ID="NullRatioReq">
    <DataSourceID>{E07F7B65-F910-4F32-8808-728F9011B4D8}</DataSourceID>
    <Table Schema="dbo" Table="ORDER_FACT" />
    <Column IsWildCard="true" />
   </ColumnNullRatioProfileRequest>
   <ColumnStatisticsProfileRequest ID="StatisticsReq">
    <DataSourceID>{E07F7B65-F910-4F32-8808-728F9011B4D8}</DataSourceID>
    <Table Schema="dbo" Table="ORDER_FACT" />
    <Column IsWildCard="true" />
   </ColumnStatisticsProfileRequest>
   <ColumnLengthDistributionProfileRequest ID="LengthDistReq">
```

Figure 10.8 - XML File Generated by the Data Profiling Task

I don't know about you but this is rather cryptic and I would not look forward to parsing this out so as to create some web reports. The viewing tool we just examined is nice but you need to have SSIS loaded so you can look at the profiling data.

A good approach for making this profiling data available to the data stewards would be to somehow load it into a set of relational database and then create some web reports that query the tables so that the statistics can be made available on a web server. This way, data stewards need only go to a web site and select the reports that are of interest to them without pouring through XML files.

Fortunately for us SSIS has a task that allows us to read the XML data, parse it into the sections that contain statistics for each profile we select and then route the data into a set of relational tables. This is real easy to do!

First, let's drag and drop a new data flow task to the control flow design area and rename it to "Load Profiles into SQL tables from XML". Double click on this task to drill into the data flow design area.

Once in the data flow design area, drag an XML task to the design area and open it up. The window in Figure 10.9 appears.

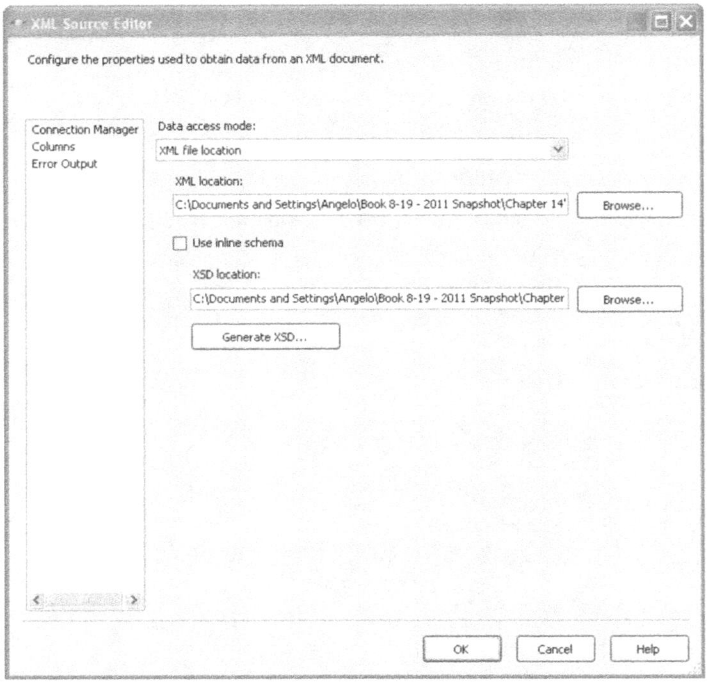

Figure 10.9 - Configuring the XML Task

All we need to do is to select the location of the XML file and generate an XSD file. Click the Browse button to find the location of the file in your files system. Next, click on the Generate XSD file.

By the way, an XSD file is an XML Schema Definition file. It describes the structure of an XML file.

Once this is accomplished, click on the Columns entry in the list box to the left of the window to view the structure of the file. Leave Output name to DtsDataSource for now. We can generate all the outputs we want in the next steps. This particular selection will output the names of the data source for the XML file.

This step is shown in Figure 10.10.

Click OK to finish this step of the configuration. We now want to connect this source to multiple destinations so that we can store the various outputs of the XML file in separate relational tables.

Let's drag an OLE DB Destination item from the toolbox and drop it on the design pane. Connect it to the XML Profiling Results. The arrow should point from the XML Profiling Results source to this OLE DB destination.

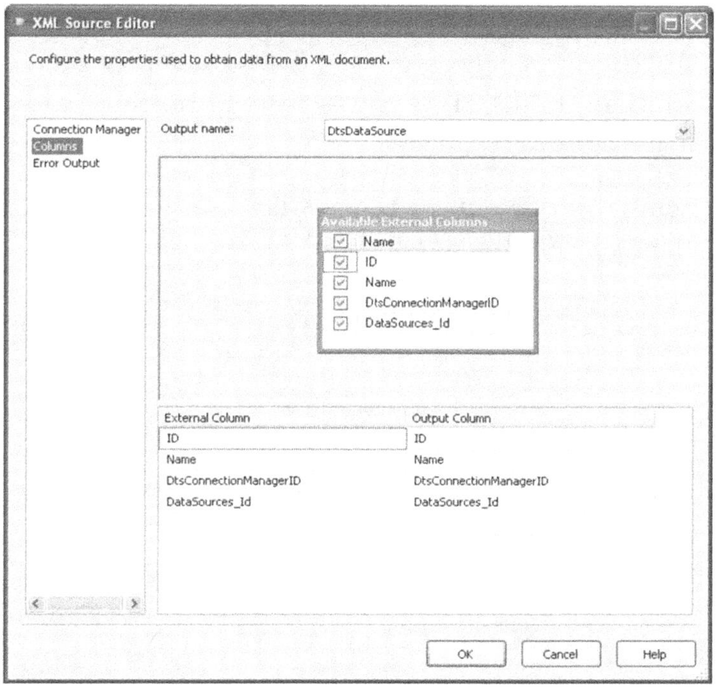

Figure 10.10 - Configuring the XML Source

Double click on it after making the connection. Figure 10.11 appears. This is where we get to pick the XML outputs we want to extract and load into a relational table.

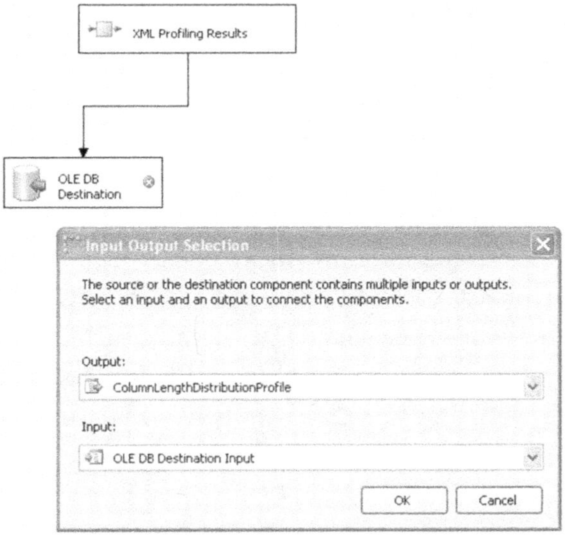

Figure 10.11 - Selecting the XML Outputs for the Relational Table

Notice that the Input Output Selection dialog box is telling us there are multiple outputs. The XSD file that was generated was used to identify this fact. Each output is dedicated to one of the profile tasks we selected. In this case let us select the ColumnLength DistributionProfileOutput.

Next, we want to configure our output table. Click OK and the OLE DB Destination Editor appears as shown in Figure 10.12.

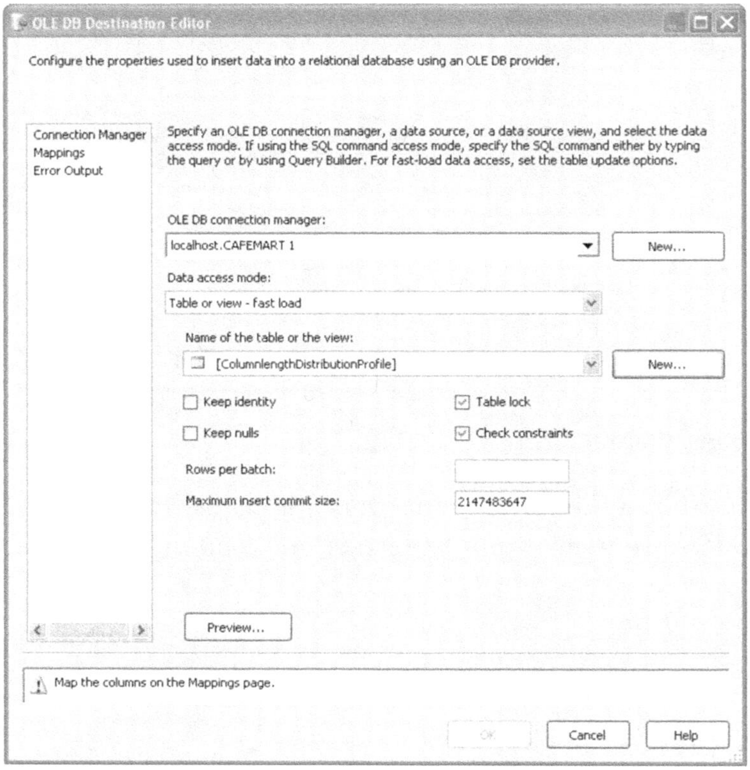

Figure 10.12 - The OLE DB Destination Editor

We are already familiar with this window as we configured other relational destination tables before. Select localhost.CAFEMART 1 as the connection manager. Next, click on the New button so as to configure the DDL command that will connect the table. Accept the default of ColumnLengthDistributionProfile so as to keep things simple. This name matches the name of the XML output. The results are shown in Figure 10.13.

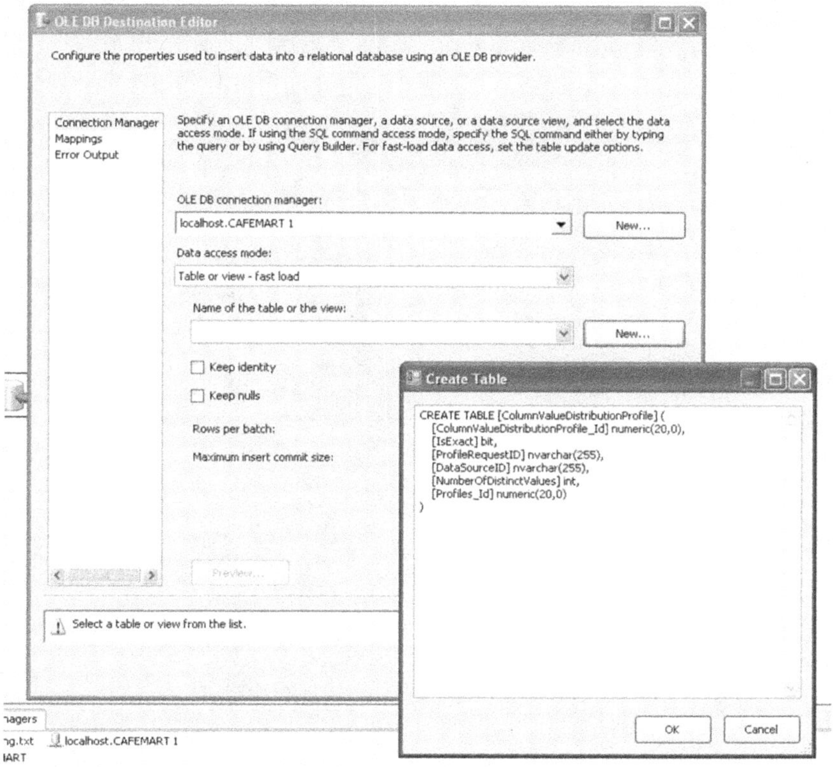

Figure 10.13 - Displaying the Table DDL that was Generated

Click on the Mappings selection so as to view how SSIS mapped the XML output columns to the new table. This is shown in Figure 10.14.

This is a basic one to one mapping from the XML columns to the relational table columns. This is what we want.

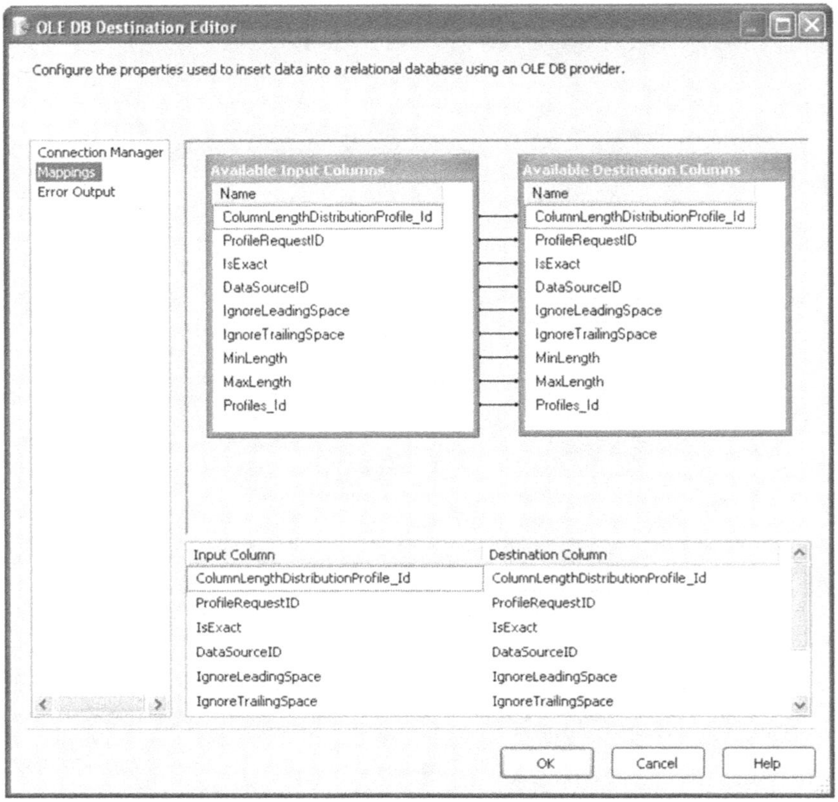

Figure 10.14 - XML to Table Output Mapping

Try out another output on your own using the steps we just followed. I added a few more outputs. The results are shown in Figure10.15.

My advice if you are new to this is to add one output at a time. That is, pick one XML output, connect it to an OLE DB output object and configure. Also remember that after the table is generated you need to add an EXECUTE SQL tasks in the control pane design area so that the output tables are truncated each time statistics are run. If you want to keep old statistics so you can generate histograms of the data as loads occur, add a timestamp column to the table and also a derived column to the flows so you can view statistics by date.

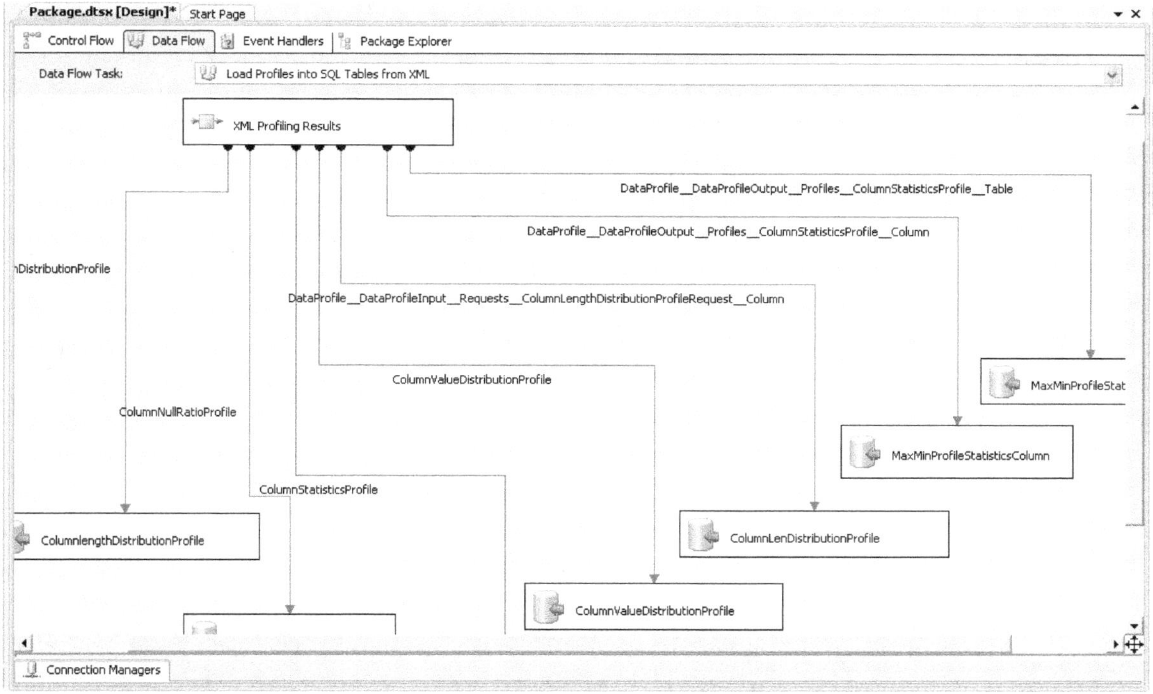

Figure 10.15 - Design Pane After Adding More XML Outputs

Fuzzy Matching

The next data quality process we look at that's available with SSIS is called fuzzy matching. In plain English, it is a process that tries to match strings like names that are not spelled exactly the same but point to the same business object.

Let's take a simple example. Let us assume we are pulling in data related to customers from two different sources. Our goal is to identify any duplicate names. If we have the name IBM in one source record and the name I.B.M. in a second source record we are pretty sure they are the same name. Fuzzy matching uses specialized algorithms to match the strings and assign them a score.

The higher the score the higher the certainty that the objects point to the same name. Once these scores are assigned we can write more logic to pick one name and use it as the master.

Let's see how to implement fuzzy matching inside the SSIS task we are building. Drag a new data flow control task onto the design pane in the control flow tab. Name it something like "Fuzzy Lookup Test" (or use your own name). Double click on the tasks to drill into the data flow design pane. The resulting screen appears as shown in Figure 10.16.

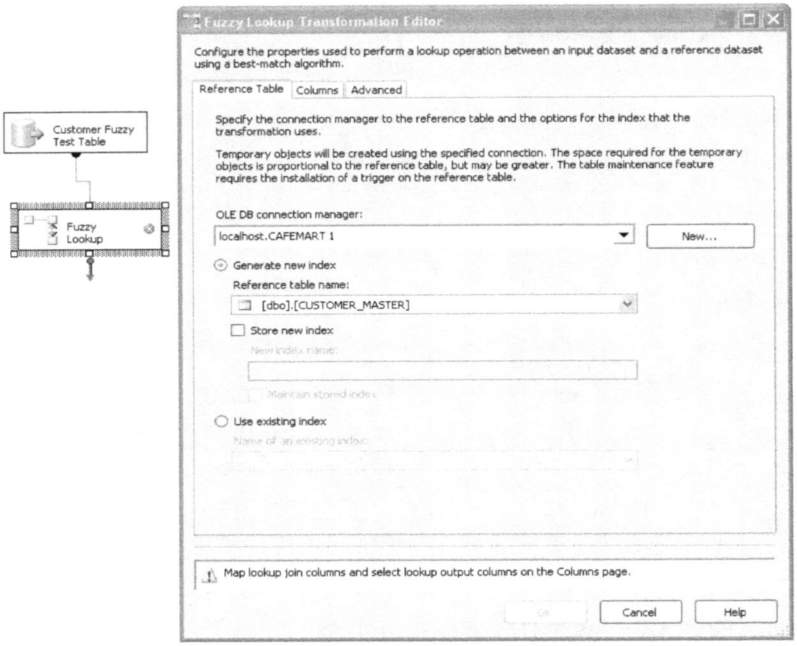

Figure 10.16 - The Fuzzy Lookup Transformation Editor

As usual, we need to define a connection. We already have a connection to the data mart called localhost.CAFEMART 1 so let us use that. We could create a new connection if necessary.

We also need to pick a reference table. A reference table is a table that holds the master copies of data. Let's assume our data stewards agree on names for all the customers and these were loaded into a table called CUSTOMER_REFERENCE. It is a simple table that has only a primary surrogate key and a customer name.

Select this table from the Reference table name list box and click on the Columns tab in the window. A new tab appears as shown in Figure 10.17.

Since we only want to match on customer name we select the CUSTOMER_NAME field on the left hand side and drag it to the CUSTOMER_NAME field on the right hand side of the model. We select all the columns on the left hand side by clicking the Pass Through checkboxes as we want to generate a full customer record. We accept the assigned output alias for the duplicate column name of CUSTOMER(1) as seen in the screen shot.

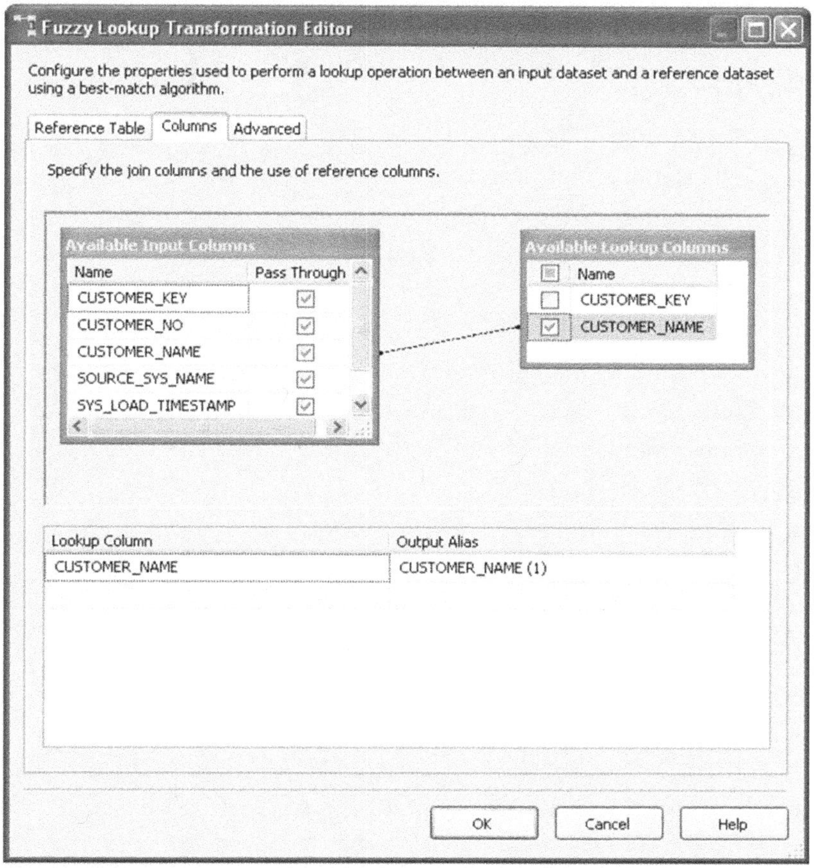

Figure 10.17 - Fuzzy Lookup Transformation Editor - Matching Columns

We could make further fine tuning by adjusting the similarity threshold or specify additional delimiters to look for in case they are not in the default delimiter list. This can be done in the Advanced tab shown in Figure 10.18.

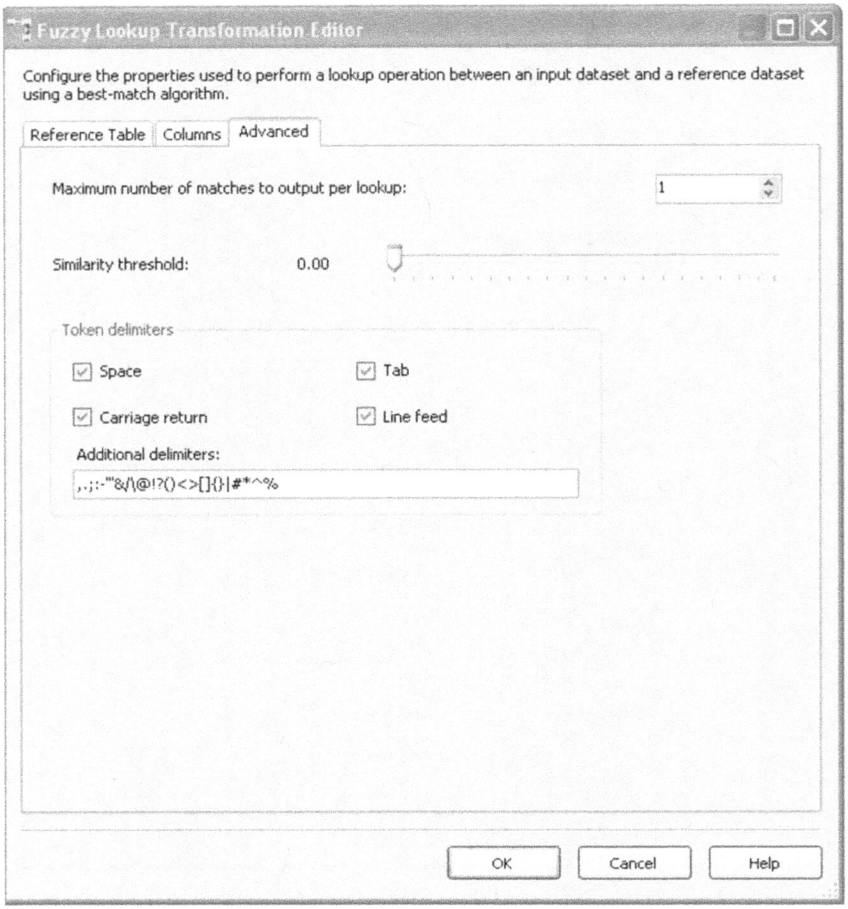

Figure 10.18 - Advanced Fuzzy Matching Settings

Try adjusting these on your own after you have successfully created and tested the fuzzy matching test to see how the output changes. Last but not least we want to check the mapping of the input columns to the output columns. Click on the Mappings selection to view the mapping specification. This can be seen in Figure 10.19.

Notice three new columns are added:

- _Similarity
- _Confidence
- _Similarity_CUSTOMER_NAME.

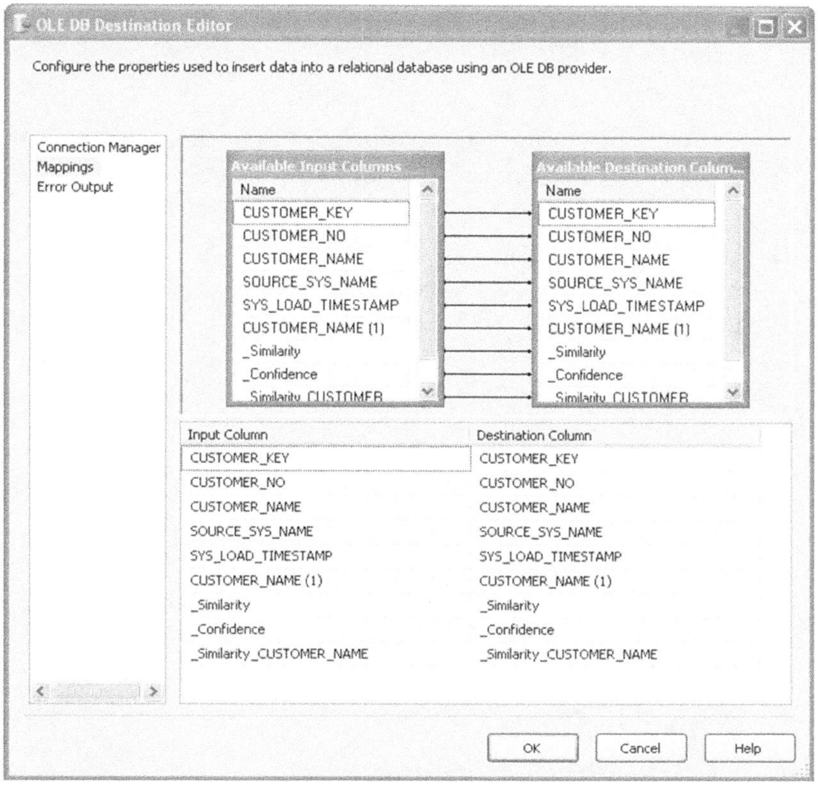

Figure 10.19 - Fuzzy Matching Mappings

These three columns will hold the fuzzy matching columns we are interested in. In a real world case we would also include address information so we can make sure that company names that are spelled differently but are located in the same location are actually the same company!

We now want to complete a flow by creating a destination table that will hold the results. Let's drag and drop an OLE DB Destination task form the toolbox onto the design area. Configure the destination by naming it "CustomerFuzzyMatchResults" and entering the connectivity information as shown in Figure 10.20.

Click new and accept the DDL that was created. If we properly name the connection, the name the table uses is the name of the connection. At this stage the table is created. Click on the Mappings tab to review and make sure the columns were mapped properly and click the OK button once you are done.

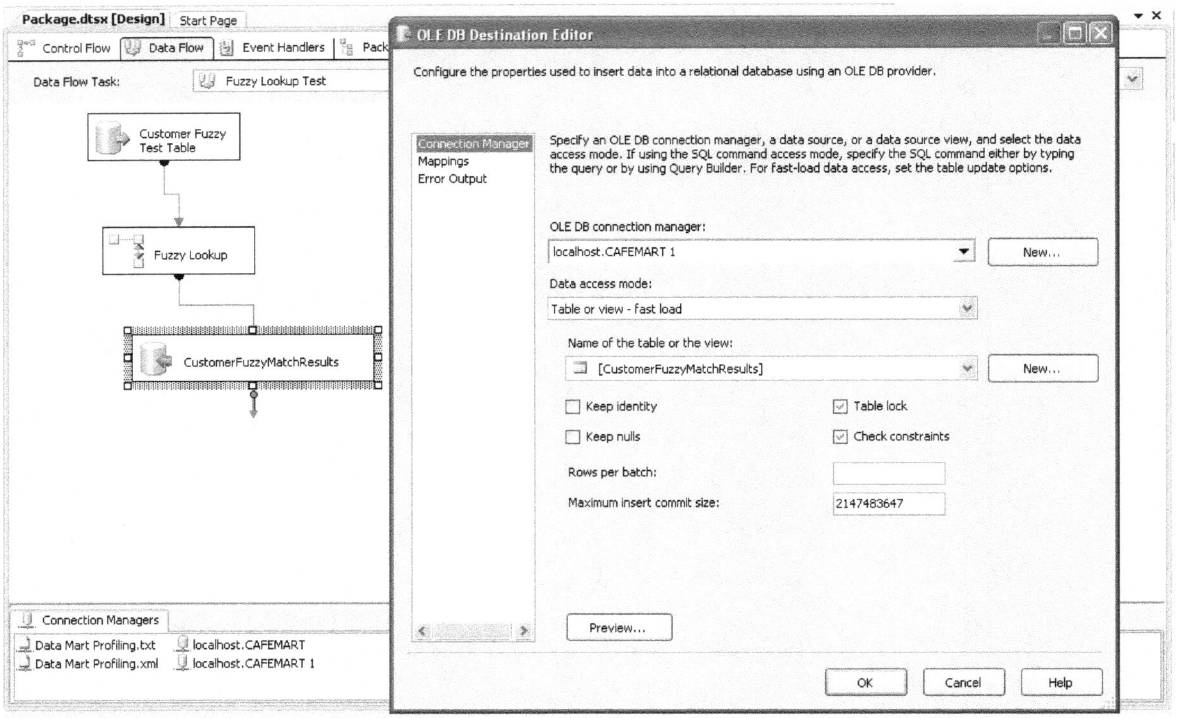

Figure 10.20 - Creating the Table to Hold Fuzzy Matching Results

Below is the DDL used to create the table:

```
CREATETABLE [dbo].[CustomerFuzzyMatchResults](
      [CUSTOMER_KEY]                    [int]           NULL,
      [CUSTOMER_NO]                     [varchar](12)   NULL,
      [CUSTOMER_NAME]                   [varchar](256)  NULL,
      [SOURCE_SYS_NAME]                 [varchar](3)    NULL,
      [SYS_LOAD_TIMESTAMP]              [datetime]      NULL,
      [CUSTOMER_NAME (1)]               [varchar](256)  NULL,
      [_Similarity]                     [real]          NULL,
      [_Confidence]                     [real]          NULL,
      [_Similarity_CUSTOMER_NAME]       [real]          NULL
)ON [PRIMARY]
GO
```

Figure 10.21 shows the completed data flow.

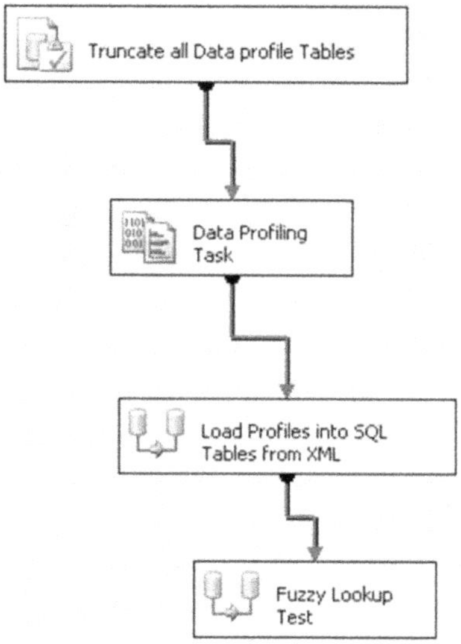

Figure 10.21 - The Completed Fuzzy Matching Data Flow

I went ahead and added more destinations for most of the outputs generated by the fuzzy matching tasks. The resulting data flow container looks like the one shown in Figure 10.22.

I also forgot to mention that we need a task that truncates all of the tables that hold the statistics each time the data flow is run. In the control panel, add an Execute SQL tasks and after specifying the proper connection parameters add the following TSQL code in the editor:

```
truncatetable dbo.ColumnLenDistributionProfile
go

truncatetable dbo.ColumnlengthDistributionProfile
go

truncatetable dbo.ColumnNullRatioProfile
go

truncatetable dbo.MaxMinColumnStatisticsProfile
go

truncatetable dbo.ColumnValueDistributionProfile
go

truncatetable dbo.DataProfiles
go
```

```
truncatetable dbo.CustomerFuzzyMatchResults
go

truncatetable dbo.MaxMinProfileStatisticsTable
go

truncatetable dbo.MaxMinProfileStatisticsColumn
go

truncatetable dbo.DataSources
go

truncatetable dbo.DTSDataSources
go

truncatetable dbo.ValueDistributionItem
go
```

Notice that we can generate quite a few statistics table. We will need to understand the underlying schema so we can create reports that join tables to each other so we can display the names of the tables, the associated columns and the associated statistics we want to report on. We will see how to do this later. Figure 10.22 shows the final version of the fuzzy matching data flow after we added several more output profiling statistics flows.

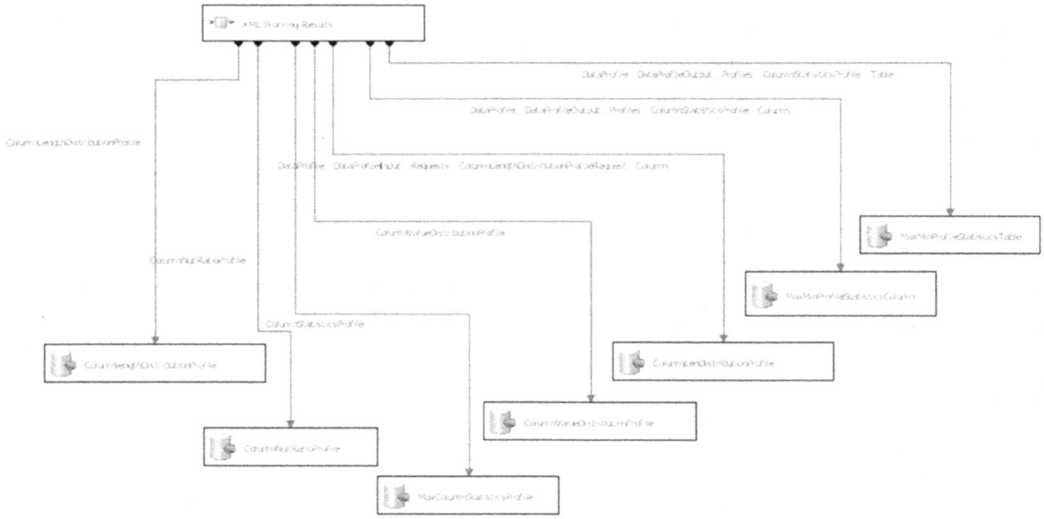

Figure 10.22 - The Final Version of the Fuzzy Matching Data Flow Package

As a check, Figure 10.23 shows the final version of the fuzzy matching control flow.

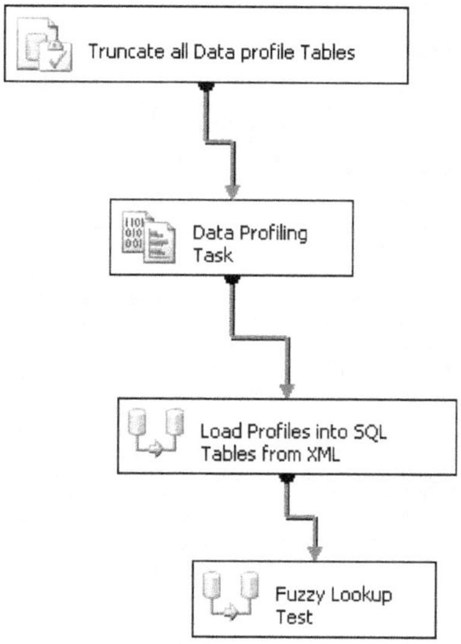

Figure 10.23 - The Final Version of the Fuzzy Matching Control Flow

If you have been following along, we now can see the logic of the flow:

- Truncate all profile tables
- Generate profile statistics
- Load statistics from XML file to relational tables
- Perform Fuzzy Matching.

Now the fuzzy matching exercise we did was just a demo that we set up. In real life, assume that after we profiled the data we suspected some duplicate customer names because the results were not what we expected. We could set up a fuzzy matching test to confirm our results and then write some logic to select the name we want to act as the unique name in the data mart.

Our goal though, at this stage, is to create some nice web reports that will allow our data stewards to see the results of the profiling process. For this we need to understand the data model of the physical tables we generated. In other words, we want to identify primary and foreign keys so we can join meta data to statistics and create reports that make sense.

Figure 10.24 shows an example for one of the statistics tables.

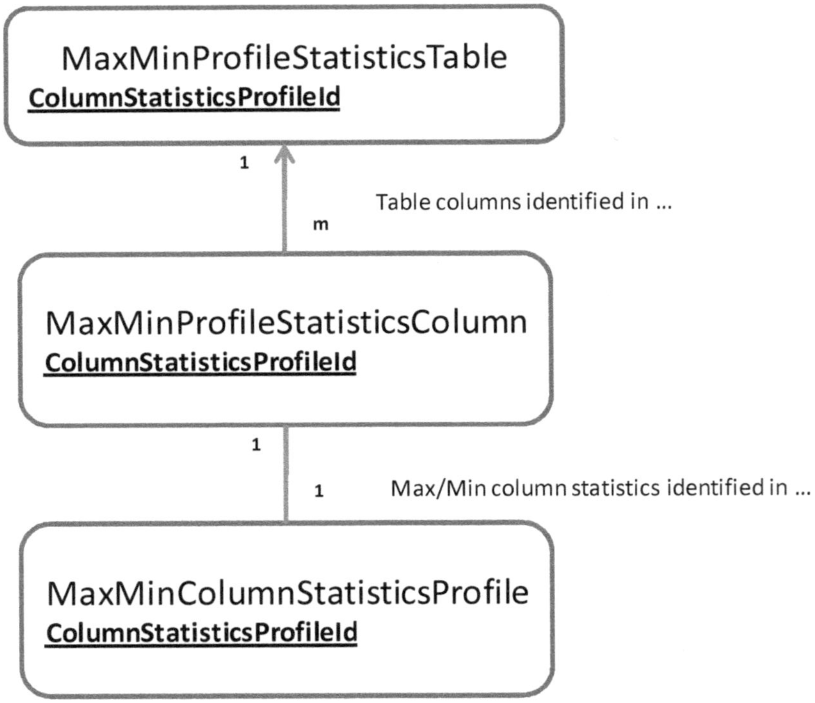

Figure 10.24 - Logical Model for Max/Min Profile Statistics

One of the sets of statistics we generated was for maximum and minimum values for columns in a table. We would like to understand how to join the tables that contain:

- Table names
- Column names
- Statistics generated from a profile test.

The main column that is used for joining tables is the ColumnStatisticsProfileId. Notice that our data model shows the following relationships:

- A table can have multiple columns
- A column has one set of statistics.

Therefore we want to generate a report that joins the tables. One approach is to create a SQL view. We can then use it over and over to generate our web report. It could be based on the query used in the CREATE VIEW statement shown in Figure 10.25.

```
SQLQuery1.sql...\
CREATE VIEW MAX_MIN_COLUMN_STATSTICS_VIEW
AS
SELECT
    A.[Schema]      AS DB_SCHEMA,
    A.[Table]       AS TBL_NAME,
    B.[Name]        AS [COL_NAME],
    C.MinValue      AS MIN_VALUE,
    C.MaxValue      AS MAX_VALUE,
    C.Mean          AS MEAN,
    C.StdDev        AS STD_DEV

FROM
    dbo.MaxMinProfileStatisticsTable A
    JOIN dbo.MaxMinProfileStatisticsColumn B
          ON A.ColumnStatisticsProfile_Id = B.ColumnStatisticsProfile_Id
    JOIN dbo.MaxMinColumnStatisticsProfile C
          ON B.ColumnStatisticsProfile_Id = C.ColumnStatisticsProfile_Id
GO
```

Figure 10.25 - A SQL View to Display MAX/MIN Profile Statistics

We could create these types of views for each of the different profile statistics outputs available in SSIS. We could then create web reports and scorecards that use this data so as to present it to our data stewards. As data profiling is executed on a scheduled basis the data stewards can monitor the progress and make sure that any new data cleansing logic applied via SSIS is actually improving the data quality.

Let's see how we can use SQL Server Reporting services to create a small reporting model that can be used as the basis of creating these types of reports.

We will also look at how we can create these types of reports as standalone reporting projects.

Creating a Data Quality Report Model

Now that our profiling statistics are loaded into relational tables, we are ready to see how to create reporting models and reports for this data. A reporting model is a layer of meta data that is presented to the report designer. He or she can use this layer to create web reports that are loaded on to SQL Server Reporting Services server. A report is a smaller meta data layer that can be used to generate a stand-alone report. We will examine both approaches in this section.

Let's begin with creating a reporting model. Create a new project as we did before but this time select the Reporting Model selection and pick a location to store the files that are generated. We will be using more wizards that will facilitate our task.

As usual, we need to start by creating a data source. Right click on Data Sources in the Solution Explorer tree and select Add New Data Source. The wizard introductory panel appears. Just click the NEXT push button to get to the next screen.

The familiar data source panel appears in Figure 10.26.

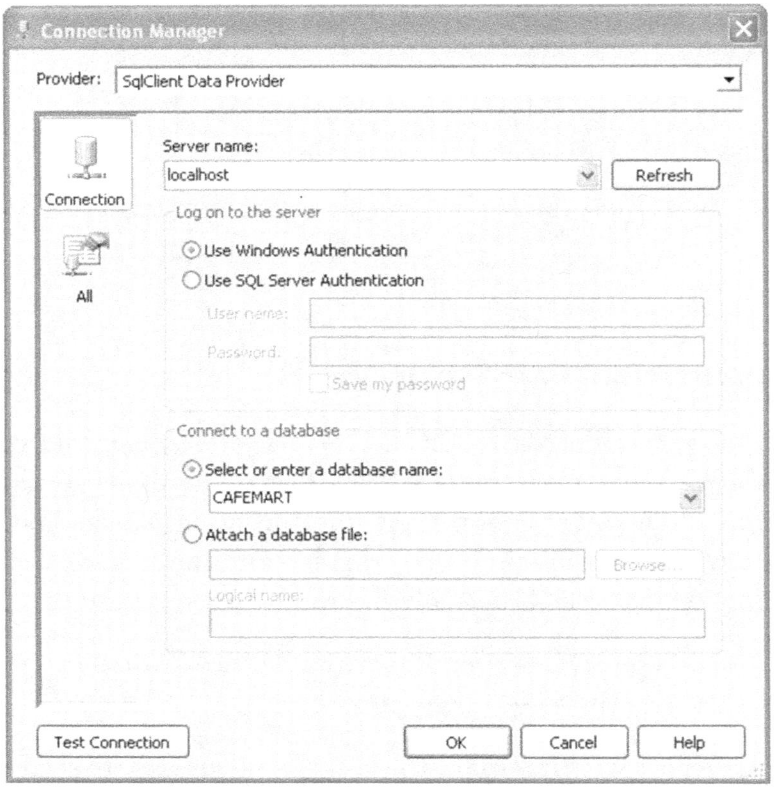

Figure 10.26 - The Data Source Connection Manager

In the second panel, enter localhost as the server name, use Windows Authentication as the logon credentials and select CAFEMART as the source database. This is where all the profiling statistics tables are although we could have created a dedicated database to store the statistics. (Don't forget to test the connection before exiting this dialog box.)

Click on OK and the Completing the Wizard panel appears in Figure 10.27.

The completed connection string that will be used is displayed. Click on the Finish Button to confirm the connection. Remember we could always use the Back button in case we made a mistake.

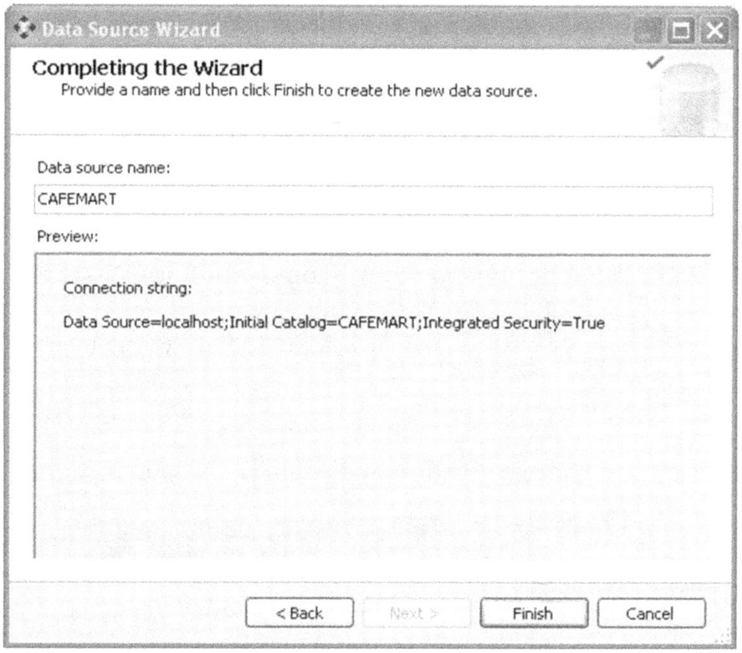

Figure 10.27 - Completing the Data Source Wizard Screen

Now that we have a connection we need to specify the data source. Right click on Data Sources and click Add New Source. The next wizard appears and is shown in Figure 10.28.

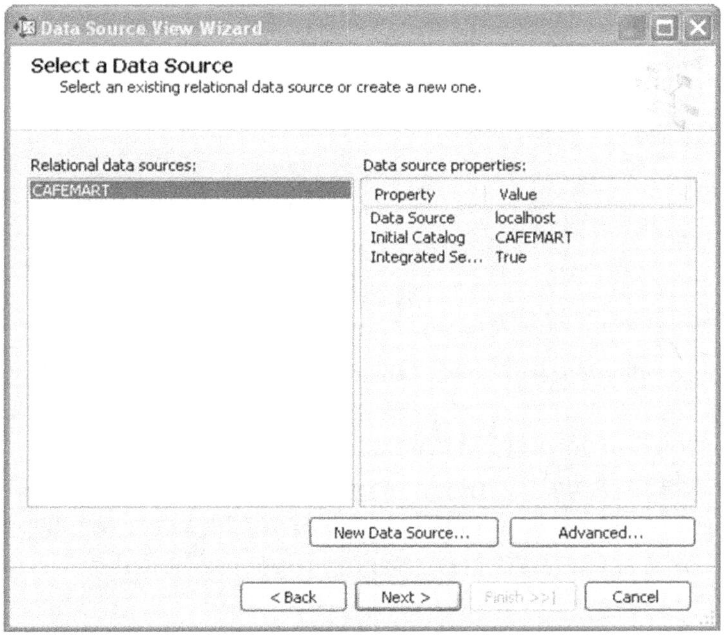

Figure 10.28 - Selecting a Data Source

As usual, the introductory page appears. Click the NEXT push button to bypass it. The panel in Figure 10.28 appears.

Our data source is already there so pick CAFEMART where our profiling statistics tables are. Click Next so we can pick the tables we wish to use in the model. The table select lists are shown in Figure 10.29.

We want to create a small model based on only one set of statistics so select:

```
MaxMinProfileStatisticsTable
MaxMinProfileStatisticsColumn
MaxMinProfileStatisticsProfile
```

Select items by clicking on them and then clicking on the > arrow push button.

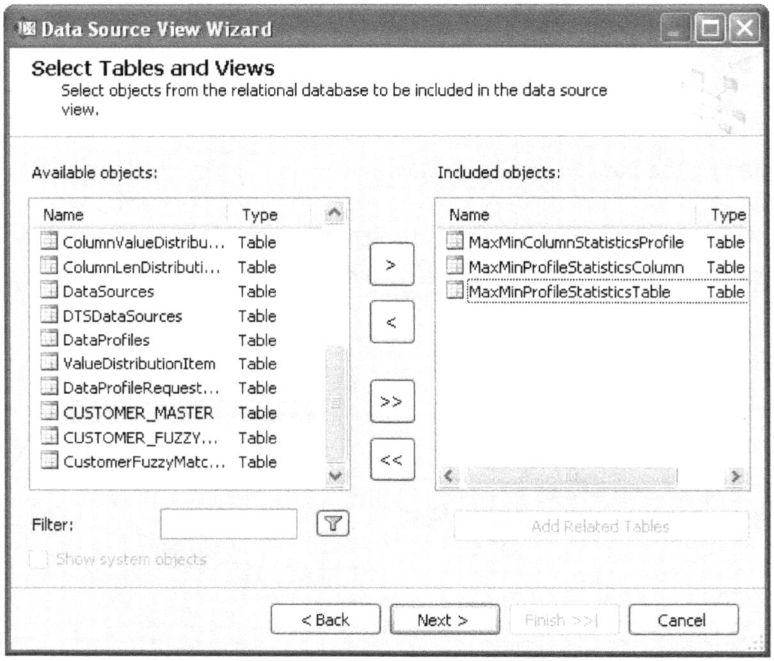

Figure 10.29 - Data Source View Wizard - Select Tables and Views

Click the Next button to complete the wizard. The final panel in the wizard appears in Figure 10.30. We are only half way through. Now we need to create the actual model, and yes, we will do this with another wizard. Right click on Report Models in the Solution Explorer and select Add New Report Model. The introductory screen appears again so click the NEXT push button to bypass it.

We now need to select a data source view for the model so we pick the view we just created. This is accomplished in the next wizard panel shown in Figure 10.31.

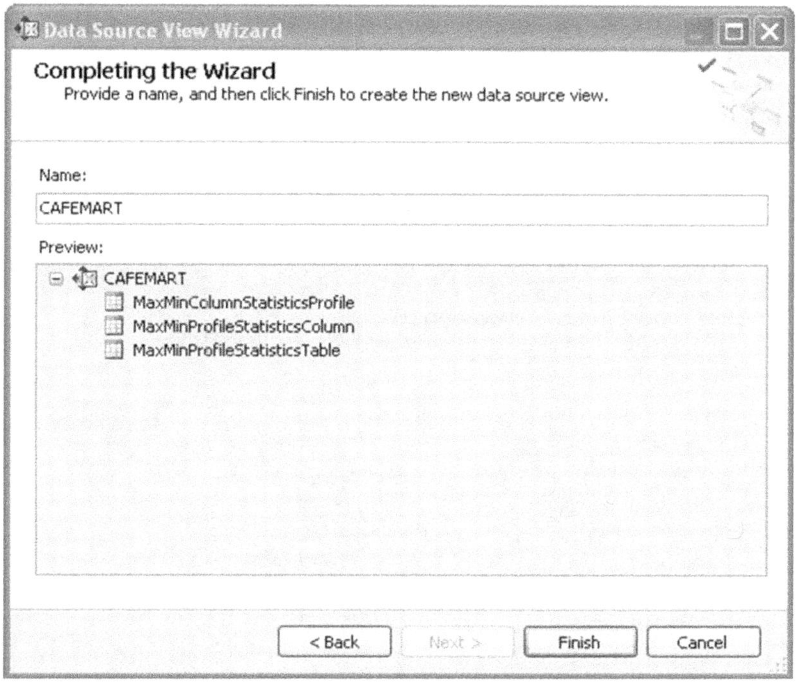

Figure 10.30 - Completing the Wizard

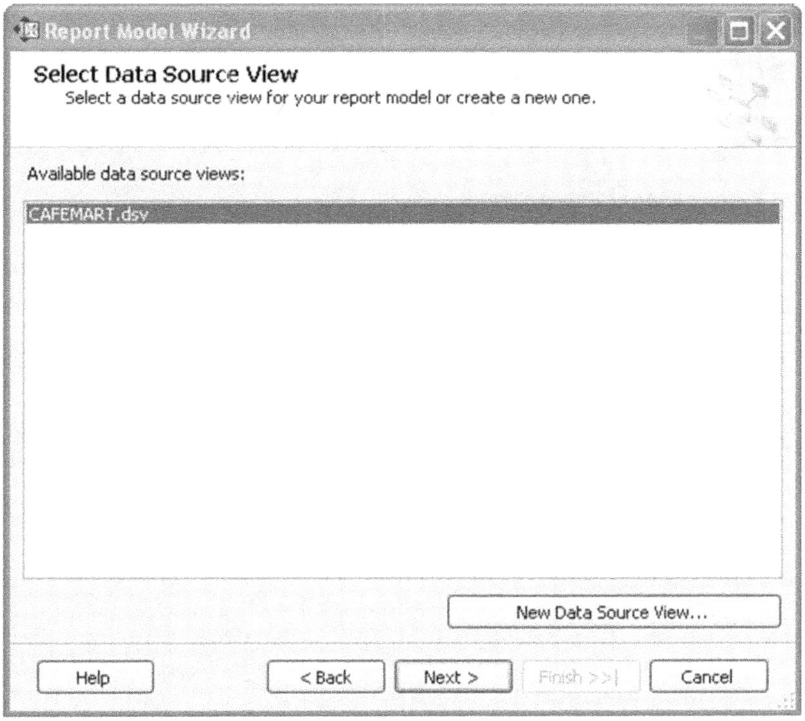

Figure 10.31 - Selecting the Data Source View for the Model

The next step requires us to select the model generation rules. Just accept all of the default rules the wizard selected for us by clicking on the NEXT button so as to take us to the next step (If you wish more detail on this topic refer to the Microsoft documentation).

The next panel is displayed in Figure 10.32.

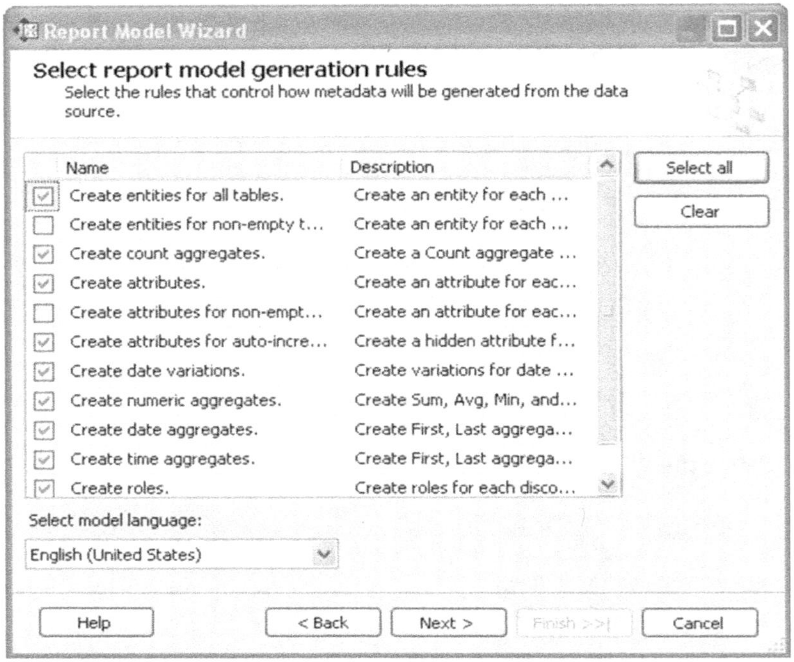

Figure 10.32 - Select Report Model Generation Rules

Next, we want to make sure that we have all the latest statistics for our model so we need to select a method to collect the statistics. The panel in Figure 10.33 allows us to select from two methods:

- Update Model statistics before generating
- Use current model statistics stored in the data source view.

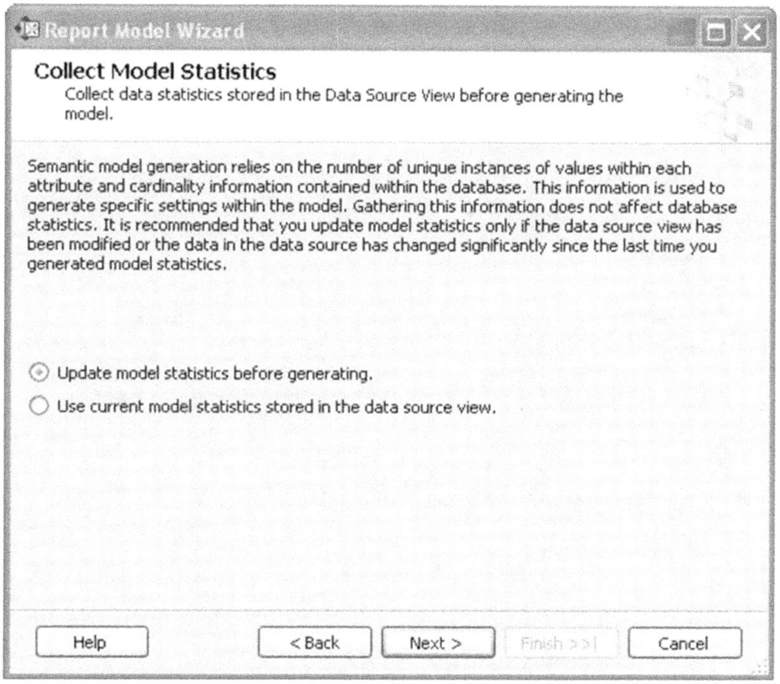

Figure 10.33 - Collecting Model Statistics

At this stage simply select the first choice. Click next to begin completing the wizard.

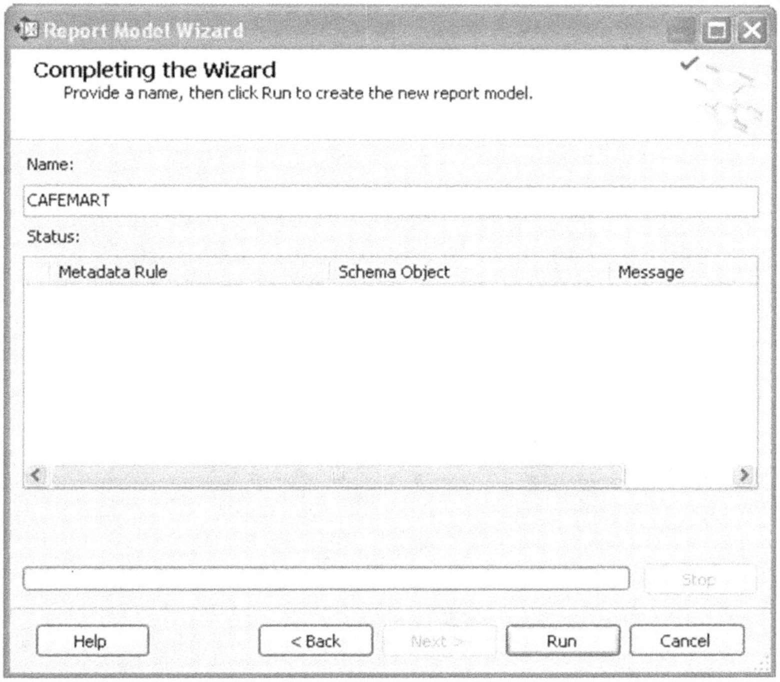

Figure 10.34 - Completing the Wizard

Click in the Run button to start the process. You should you see the results shown in Figure 10.35.

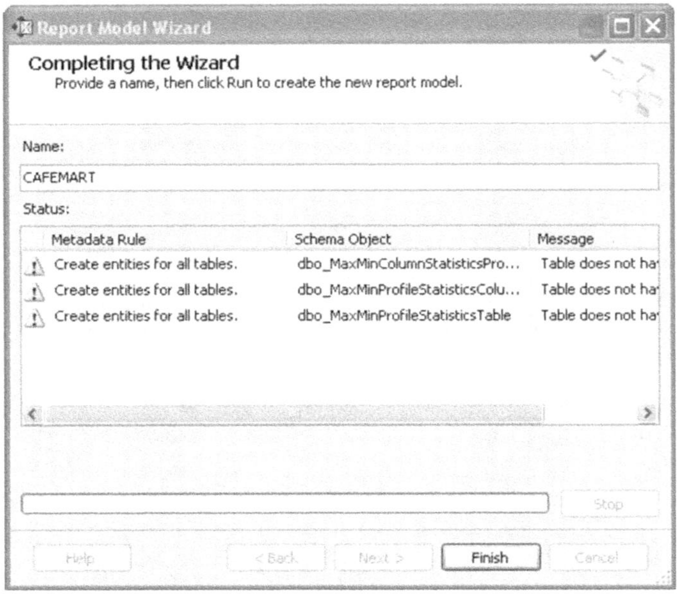

Figure 10.35 - The Completed Wizard

Some minor warnings appeared. These were generated because I failed to create primary and foreign keys to establish relations between the tables. We will define these in the next steps. Click Finish and our model appears in Figure 10.36.

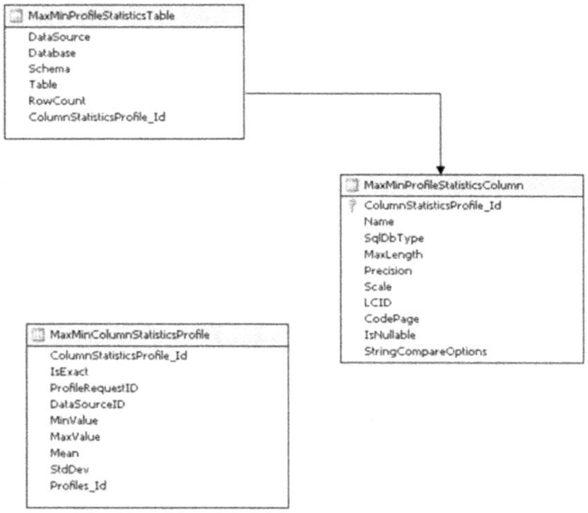

Figure 10.36 - Our generated MAX/MIN Profile Model

I already created the first relationships. Let's work through the second relationship between MaxMinProfileStatistics table and the MaxMinProfileStatisticsColumn table so you can see how it is done. Right click anywhere on the design panel and select New Relationships, Figure 10.37 appears.

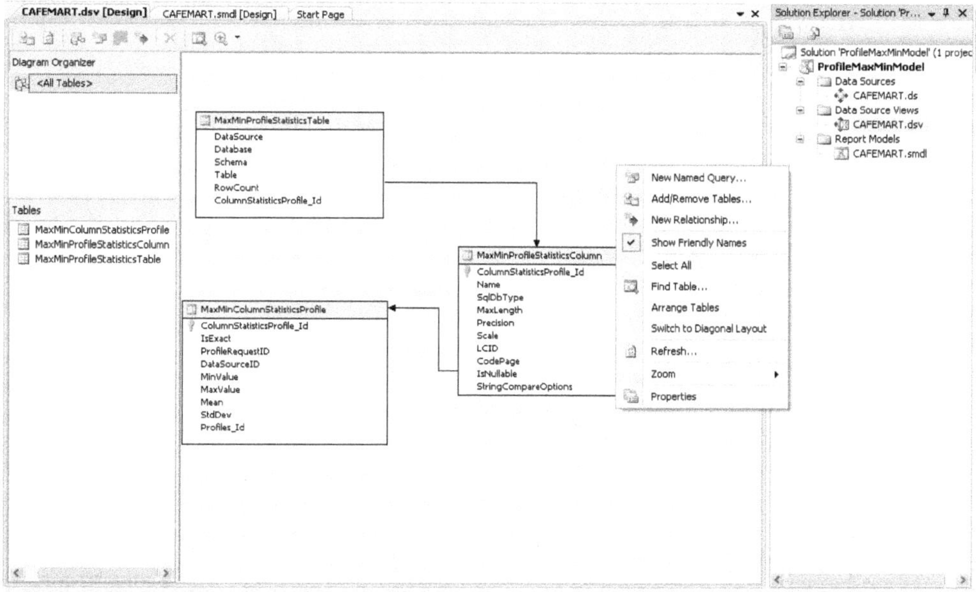

Figure 10.37 - Creating Relationships

Select New Relationship and the panel in Figure 10.38 appears on the GUI.

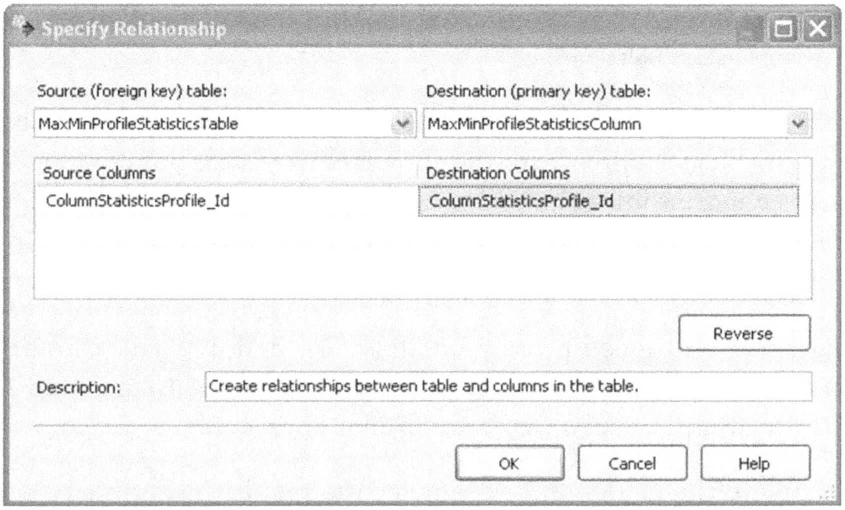

Figure 10.38 - Defining Relationships

Two list boxes are displayed that let you confirm the columns to establish the relationship on. For source columns we select ColumnStatisicsProfile_Id and we select the same column in the Destinations Columns list. Click OK to accept the relationship.

Now we need to do the same for the relationships between the MaxMinProfileStatisticsColumn and the MaxMinColumnStatisticsProfile table. This will be a one-to-one relationship.

Figure 10.39 below shows the same panel that we use to define this relationship.

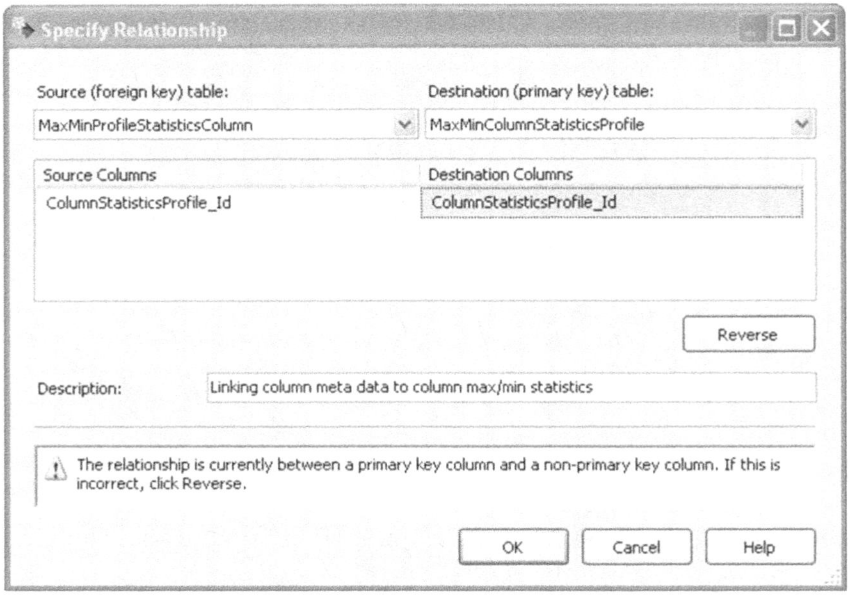

Figure 10.39 - Creating the Last Relationship

In this scenario that we just completed the exercise was simple as we had only three tables to work with. It does illustrate the importance of creating a model beforehand if we have several or more tables that we want to base the model on. Understanding the relationships is key because if we get them wrong, the reports produced from the model will yield incorrect results.

You can bypass the relationship creation tasks by defining the primary/foreign key constraints in the database using SQL Server Enterprise Manager and the necessary DDL commands to create the primary and foreign keys.

Click OK to complete the model and we can see the results in Figure 10.40.

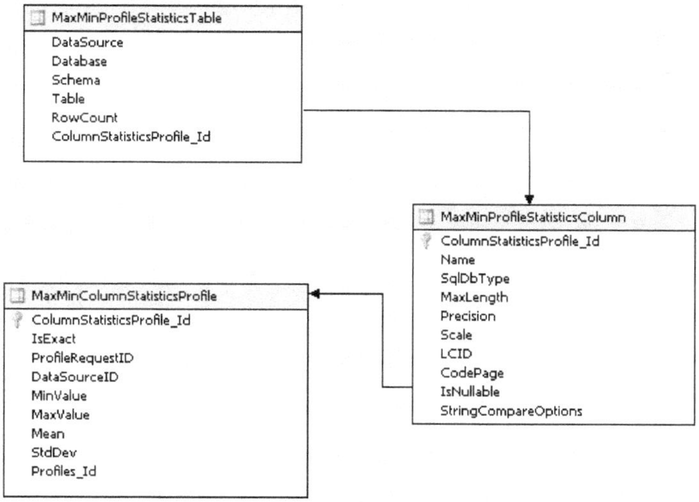

Figure 10.40 - The Completed MAX/MIN Profile Reporting Model

Now that the model is complete, we have only one step left to perform. We need to deploy the model to the report server. On the menu bar, click on build and then select Deploy Solution. The screen in Figure 10.41 appears.

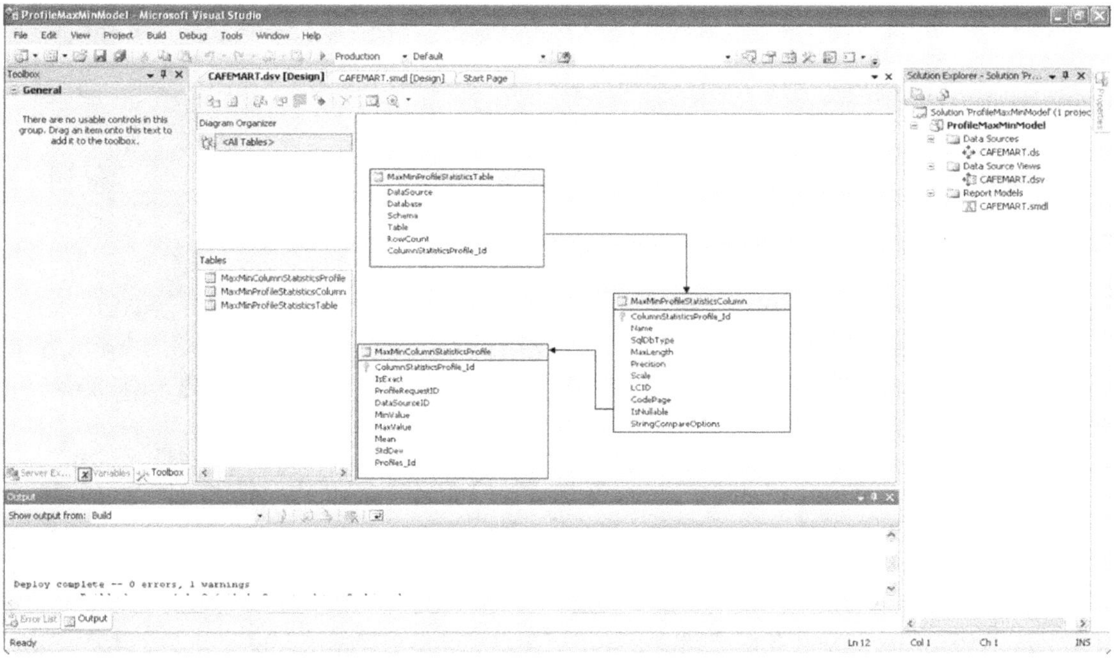

Figure 10.41 - Deploying the Reporting Model

Everything went as planned. No errors appeared so let's go to the web server and see if the model is present. Simply navigate to the Reports page on your computer and from the home page select Models.

Figure 10.42 appears and shows that we were successful in deploying the model.

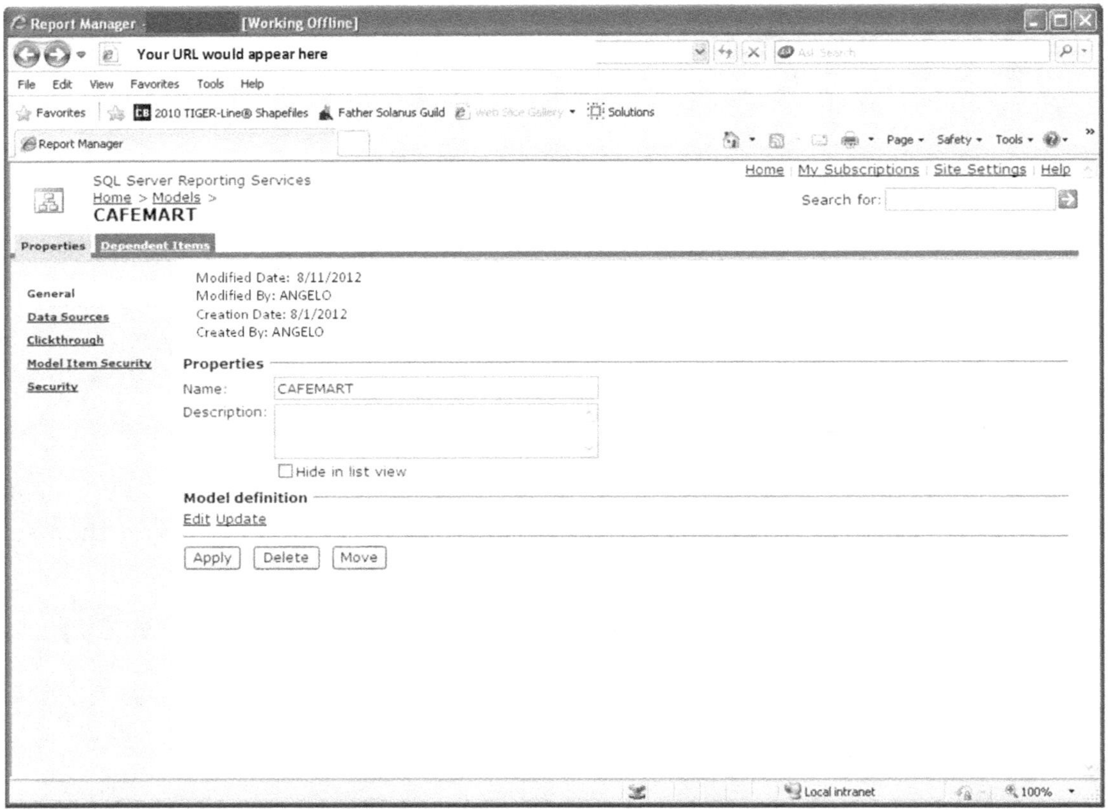

Figure 10.42 - Model Successfully deployed to the Web Server

By the way, I am assuming that if you loaded SQL Server 2008 R2 to your computer, you also installed the SSRS Report Server. You should install it if you have not. Just accept all default connections and make sure it starts automatically as a service on your system.

We could now create a report from this model by going to the home page of the report server and selecting new reports. A tool called Report Builder would appear and we could select this model or any model you created as the basis of the reports.

We will show you a different approach in the next section so that we cover all the main types of projects you can create with the various utilities that come with SQL Server.

Creating a Data Quality Report

Let's create a very basic report based on the query we defined earlier in the chapter that was used to create one of the profile output views. Create a new project with the BIDS tool (SQL Server Business Intelligence Developer). This time select Report Server project, give it a name, identify the location where you want to store the files and the Report Wizard introductory panel appears. Click the NEXT push button to bypass it.

The connection property panel shown in Figure 10.43 appears. Enter localhost as the server name and pick CAFEMART (or whatever you called your own database if you are following along) as the database to connect to.

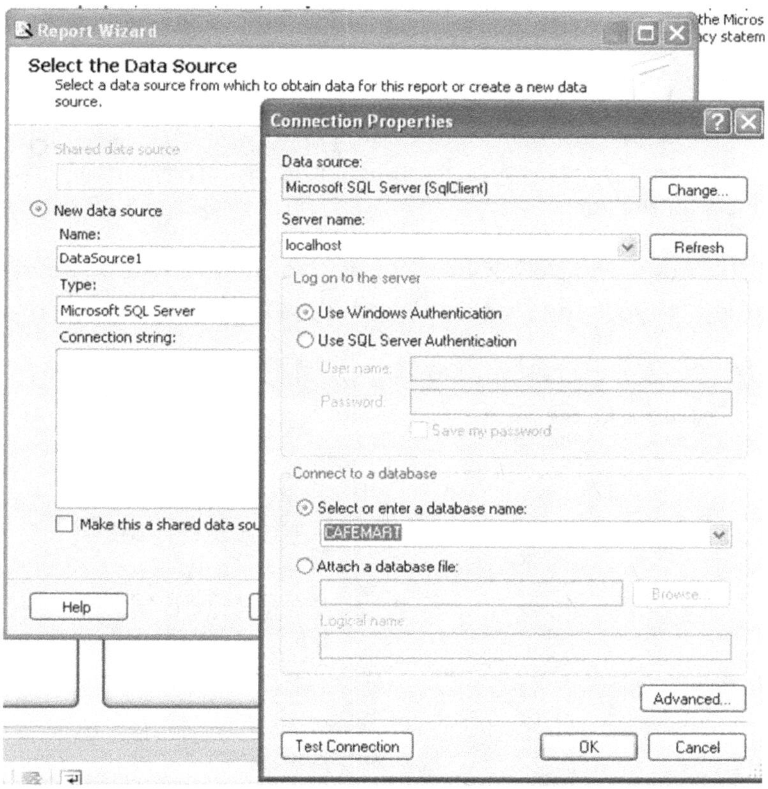

Figure 10.43 - Filling in Connection Properties

Once we are finished, click OK and we can proceed to create the query that will be used for the report. The Report Builder wizard presents us with some choices. We could either build the query manually or else cut and paste an existing query into the query edit windows. Let's choose the easiest route. Figure 10.44 shows the wizard after we cut and pasted the query use to create the view that we discussed earlier.

Figure 10.44 - The Query for the Report

Copy and paste the query and click next so we can choose the type of report. Another panel appears called "Select the Report Type". This is shown in Figure 10.45.

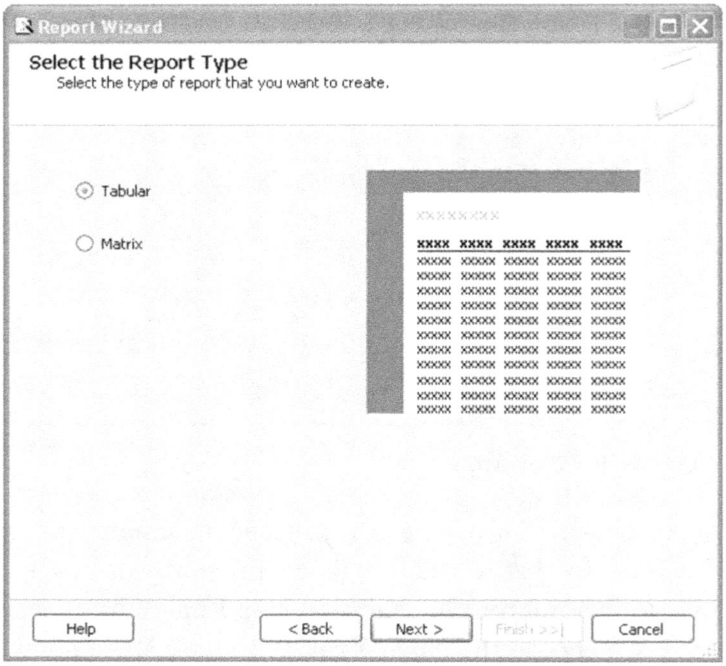

Figure 10.45 - Choosing the Report Type

As can be seen, we have two choices, tabular or matrix. We choose tabular. Click next so we can choose the columns we want in the report. A panel called "Design the Table" appears. This can be seen in Figure 10.46.

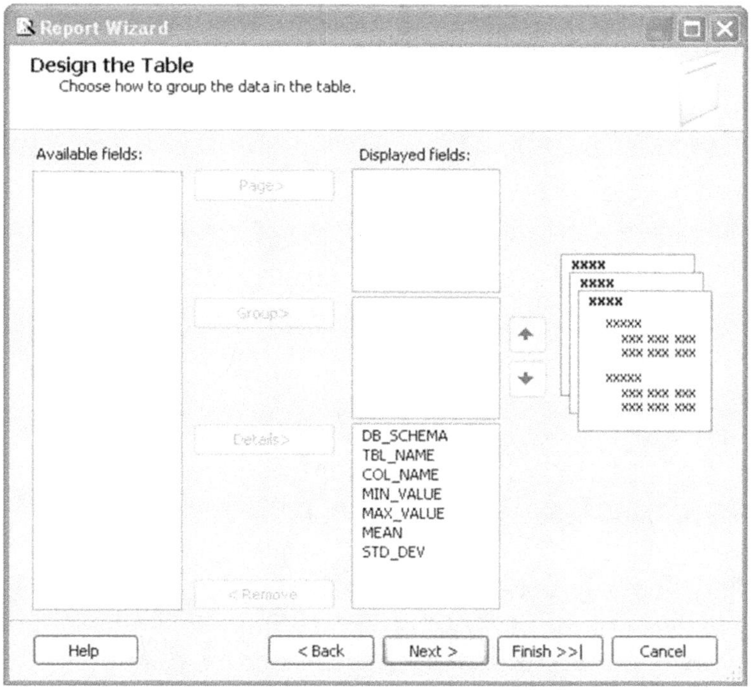

Figure 10.46 - Choosing the Report Columns

Highlight all the columns and click the Details button so they are used only as details. Click next and the "Choose Table Style" panel. This is shown in Figure 10.46. Now click the NEXT push button so as to display the "Choose the Table Style" panel. This can be seen in Figure 10.47.

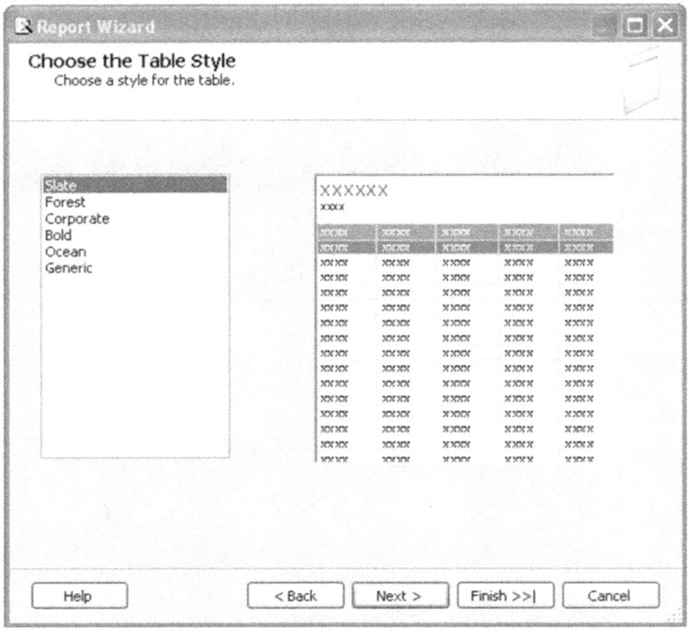

Figure 10.47 - Choosing the Table Style

Choose any style you wish, I picked Slate. Click the Next button and the wizard displays all your choices so you can get a last chance to change things if you feel you made a mistake. The summary screen appears in Figure 10.48.

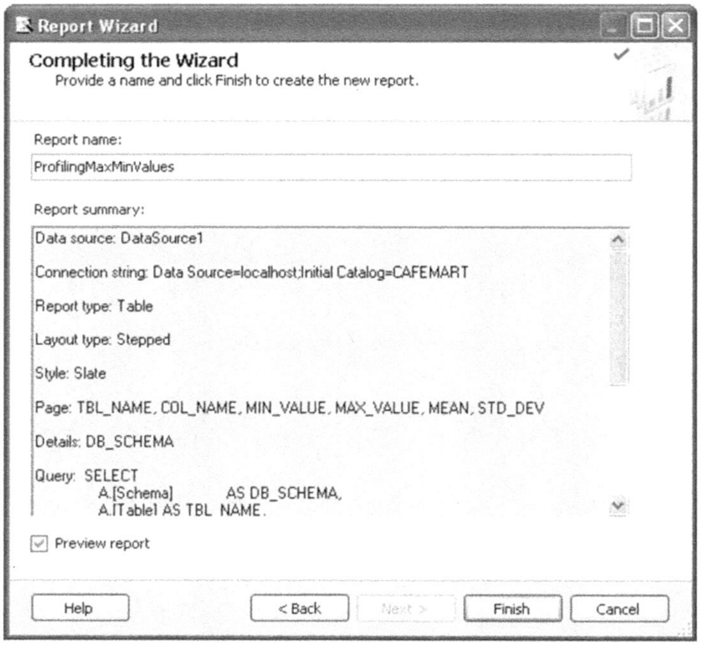

Figure 10.48 - Completing the Report Wizard

That's it! We are finished. Click on the Finish button. You can preview the report to see what it looks like in a web page. Figure 10.49 shows our simple report.

ProfilingMaxMinValues.rdl Report Preview

ProfilingMaxMinValues

DB SCHEMA	TBL NAME	COL NAME	MIN VALUE	MAX VALUE	MEAN	STD DEV
dbo	ORDER_FACT	ORDER_NO	1001	1470	1199.7507418397	188.9796988948
dbo	ORDER_FACT	ORDER_LINE_ITEM_NO	1	16	5.9258160237	4.5910328675
dbo	ORDER_FACT	ORDER_LINE_ITEM_DATE	2011-02-28T 00:00:00.0000000	2011-12-04T 00:00:00.0000000		
dbo	ORDER_FACT	ORDER_LINE_ITEM_QTY	1	100	51.2130563798	47.0548673539
dbo	ORDER_FACT	ORDER_LINE_TOTAL_PRICE	12.50	3100.00	1071.0269673590	1144.3804358297
dbo	ORDER_FACT	CUSTOMER_KEY	1	25	14.4477611940	6.6487201822
dbo	ORDER_FACT	PRODUCT_KEY	1	31	10.6913946587	7.3851051163
dbo	ORDER_FACT	LOCATION_KEY	1	10	6.8620689655	2.5789388842
dbo	ORDER_FACT	SALES_PERSON_KEY	1	10	4.7603448275	2.9591144793
dbo	ORDER_FACT	CALENDAR_KEY	20110301	2011011030	230107659.0724040000	293026455.2633890000
dbo	ORDER_FACT	SYS_LOAD_DATE	2011-09-07T 16:07:43.1800000	2011-09-07T 16:07:43.1800000		

Figure 10.49 - Report Preview

I need to state that the report that was just created is very primitive and simple. The goals was to show you that part of the process is to create data quality profile reports that a data steward can use to make decisions related to the quality of the data.

SQL Server Reporting Services is a powerful tool and many sophisticated reports and scorecards can be created. I urge you to research the many excellent books on this topic so that you can create quality scorecards and reports for your data stewards and other employees responsible for managing data content.

Summary

In this chapter we examined how to:

- Create Data Quality Profiles
- Create ETL that pulled profiling statistics from XML files and load them into relational table
- We also investigated a power tool called fuzzy matching for de-duplicating data

- We created a simple Reporting Services Model based on the three profiling statistics tables
- We created a simple web based report using SQL Server Report Builder.

We have now covered almost all the bases in the design and creation life cycle of an ODS. Next we create a simple data mart that benefits from all of our profiled and cleansed data.

Specifically, we learned:

- What an ODS is.
- What some of the different functions of an ODS are.
- What schema integration is.
- How to apply schema integration techniques.
- How to reverse engineer source databases.
- How to create conflict resolution reports.
- How to create ETL specifications based on the conflict resolution reports.

Additionally, we saw brief examples on:

- How to build ETL processes using Microsoft SQL Server 2008 SSIS.
- How to build data profiling and fuzzy matching processes.
- How to build Microsoft SSRS report server models and reports in order to display data quality statistics.

I hope you enjoyed the book. I did ask you to perform some exercises on your own. Some of the exercises were a bit complex but I suggested that you could come up with your own and try simple exercises first. For example, you might want to start with only two data sources and create a few tables in each. Maybe you want to concentrate on only one subject area such as customer. Create the tables and load them with rows. Make sure you create the tables so that they have common and unique columns and introduce some conflicts as discussed in Chapter 3.

Once you created your databases and tables and loaded them, go through the integration process and generate all the data models, specifications, etc. Once you get the hang of it, try some more complex examples.

Lastly, I used SQL Server 2008 R2 as the vehicle for this book as it is a powerful tool and the evaluation is freely available from the Microsoft site. The techniques described in this book will work for other databases and ETL products such as Oracle and Informatica.

www.ingramcontent.com/pod-product-compliance
Lightning Source LLC
LaVergne TN
LVHW062312060326
832902LV00013B/2181
9781935504221